The teenager standing before him didn't look much like the pretty, well-groomed, bright-eyed girl in the pictures. She was drowsy and shivering, her hair was mussed and she was covered with what appeared to be vomit. She held a small piece of pink paper tied with a gray ribbon. McLean took the cardboard from her, glancing at the writing across the face of it. It read, "Dear God Please forgive me I didn't Mean to hurt her."

Officer Davis and Officer Halligan drove the girl to the station, where she was to be given the gunshot residue test and booked for murder.

"Is my dad all right?" she asked the men in the car.

Davis said yes.

"Is Patti all right?" she said and Davis gave her the same answer.

"How about Linda?" the girl asked. "How's Linda?"

The men said nothing.

A KILLING IN THE FAMILY

A TRUE STORY OF LOVE, LIES AND MURDER

STEPHEN SINGULAR
WITH TIM & DANIELLE HILL

AVON BOOKS ◆ NEW YORK

A KILLING IN THE FAMILY: A TRUE STORY OF LOVE, LIES AND
MURDER is an original publication of Avon Books. This work has never
before appeared in book form.

AVON BOOKS
A division of
The Hearst Corporation
105 Madison Avenue
New York, New York 10016

First Avon Books Printing: February 1991

AVON TRADEMARK REG. U.S. PAT. OFF. AND IN OTHER COUNTRIES, MARCA
REGISTRADA, HECHO EN U.S.A.

Printed in the U.S.A.

RA 10 9 8 7 6 5 4 3 2 1

To Ruth

PART ONE

1

One of those rare Southern California showers had fallen on Garden Grove the previous day and its effects could be felt after midnight. At two-fifteen a.m. the streets were dry, but the air was damp and the temperature was forty-five degrees, a cool early morning in mid-March of 1985. At this time of year in Orange County, the Santa Ana winds come off the desert and blow the smog out to sea, rattling ceramic tiles on rooftops and scaring people who are trying to sleep. David Brown hadn't really slept at all. At two o'clock he'd left his bed and gotten dressed, walked outside, stepped into his Honda Prelude and backed onto the poorly lit pavement of Ocean Breeze Drive. The winds and the rainstorm had washed away the smog, so there were more stars than usual poking through. People in Orange County like to say that the day after a rainfall is special—fresh and clean and wonderful because the sky has been scrubbed and one can see forever.

Brown drove to Brookhurst Street, at this time of night a wide, empty strip of gas stations, laundromats, Chinese restaurants, car dealerships and coin shops, bordered by palms and intersected by freeways. He pulled off and parked in front of an all-night Circle K shopping mart, went inside and bought a Hostess apple pie and a Dr. Pepper. He paid for them and left but turned around and went back into the store, buying four comic books. A comic collector, he stood at the front counter talking with the clerk about his purchases and poking fun at himself, apologizing for the fact that a man in his early thirties, an important and successful man in his chosen field of computer technology, was still reading and enjoying such childish things. Brown seemed almost embarrassed, but that didn't stop him from talking about them with all the eagerness of a youngster with a new treasure.

He drove a few blocks to the Garden Grove Freeway and took it south, moving vaguely in the direction of the ocean. Had he wanted to go straight to the beach, another route would have been faster, but Brown was in no hurry and had no particular destination or goal, other than to get away from home for a while and just drive. At this time of day the maddening and dangerous roads of Southern California were fairly peaceful, more peaceful than some of the recent hours he'd spent at home. Earlier in the evening, he'd argued with his attractive blond, twenty-three-year-old wife, Linda, about their new baby. Eight-month-old Krystal had been crying a lot and that upset Brown, who didn't like it when things around the house were out of control. Linda felt that the baby should be allowed to cry herself to sleep, but he believed that his wife should rock Krystal to sleep. The little girl's tears bothered the man; this wasn't normal behavior for a baby—or was it? A few hours earlier Brown had posed this question to his mother and father, who had come over for pizza, Mexican food, a card game and some television. It was common, they tried to assure him, for babies to cry this much, a natural part of being an infant. Brown apologized to his wife for criticizing her handling of Krystal, but, as was often the case, he still wasn't convinced that everything was all right.

He needed to get away from the house and clear his mind and had chosen an excellent place to go to. Very late at night the highways of Southern California have a particular feel, an air of escape and freedom, a sense of unreality, a sense that one is totally alone in the world and there are no more rules and restraints. Things are so quiet and calm and slow, almost too quiet and slow. It's as if the great freeway wars have finally ended and all of your enemies and all of their cars have been banished and you alone are king of the brutal road. For a few moments anyway, it doesn't feel as if someone is about to drive up your back. Late at night, especially after a rainstorm, you can detect the smell of something other than diesel fuel and exhaust fumes along the road—the scent of eucalyptus is faint, and that of oleander, and the wet earth has its own special odor, and the ocean is nearby, and there is nothing quite like the dark wild tangy California wind, just the sort of thing that can soothe the overheated brain and make one feel better on a slow midnight ride.

Linda and Krystal weren't the only people on Brown's mind. Cinnamon, his fourteen-year-old daughter from another marriage, had also been in a bad mood this evening. In recent weeks the teenager had been moving back and forth between her mother's home and her father's, but she was apparently going to stay at the Brown residence for a while (although recently she'd told her mother, Brenda Sands, that she was ready to leave her father's house, and Sands was making plans to help her do this). Cinnamon, with her blond hair and quick happy smile, could be charming, but she was also at an awkward age and unpredictable. Brown was given to worry and he was going to worry about her. The girl wasn't exactly living with her father full-time, but spending most of her nights in his backyard in a trailer. She'd covered the trailer with stuffed animals and was raising a dachshund puppy in her new home. Over the past few weeks, she'd grown to like it back there—sleeping in the trailer was cool, she told her friends; it gave her a feeling of independence and escape from her complex family situation.

Lately Cinnamon's life had become even more complicated. Two weeks earlier she had transferred from Bolsa Grande High School to Loara High in Anaheim, a move her father believed would make her a safer and more disciplined student. At Bolsa Grande a stranger had exposed himself to the girl and terrified her. Since the move she was trying to adjust to her new classes and teachers, and if all that wasn't enough, she had gone through puberty recently, which made things even more confusing. Her periods were unsettling and she'd been having a particularly difficult one. She'd talked about this with Linda and with Patti Bailey, Linda's seventeen-year-old-sister, who also lived at the Brown residence. The older females had been sympathetic, especially Linda, telling her that it was just something a girl went through on the way to womanhood. It was a stage that passed and she needed to be patient with herself and with the process of growing up. Cinnamon was trying to follow this advice, but it wasn't easy being a teenager or being the child of divorced parents or being moved from school to school or having these new experiences within her body or attempting to get along with everyone in her father's house. Little things upset Cinnamon. Getting older wasn't a simple thing and neither was giving up the position of being the youngest in the family. She liked having a baby in the house but couldn't help noticing that she got less attention since Krystal was born.

The Brown household had only one male and he often found himself surrounded by domestic turbulence, by marital bickering between himself and Linda, by teenage quarreling between Cinnamon and Patti, and by in-laws snarling when his parents came to visit. Petty arguments arose over who should wash the dishes and who got to hold the baby. Brown's own mother, Manuella, considered herself an experienced hand at raising children and she was free with her advice. Sometimes a three-bedroom house wasn't quite big enough for all the family members, all of their relatives and all of their opinions. Right now things were more crowded than usual: Cinnamon was out of school on spring break this week and Patti had not been attending school lately, but staying home and helping Linda take care of the baby. On this night in particular, Brown would later say, everything had become too much for him and he just had to drive to the beach.

He passed Santa Ana and, sometime later, the Crazy Horse Saloon, a well-known country-and-western bar not far from Newport Beach. He passed a series of tall, clean high-tech buildings—Wang, Unisys and Butterfield Savings—which had recently shot up from tomato and strawberry fields. A few vegetable patches were still tucked alongside the road, awaiting the migrant workers who came to them each morning, but most of the old farms had been replaced by new homes, new offices, new people, new parking lots and new shopping centers.

South Coast Plaza, the second-largest shopping mall in the world, was close by and local citizens spoke of it as if it were a landmark or a shrine, a monument to the incredible prosperity of Orange County. Brown had shopped in some of these places, purchased clothes for the women in his life and electronic equipment for himself. He owned several VCRs and had a video library with five hundred movie cassettes. He owned numerous televisions, half a dozen cars, a $9,000 computer, an elaborate security system for his home and most of the latest telephone gadgetry. When something new hit the market—a paging beeper, for example, which let him stay in constant contact with the members of his family when they left the house—he had to have it. He loved electronic devices and he collected jewelry and rare coins, which he kept in a safe that was the size of a refrigerator. He liked guns too, both rifles and pistols, which he had stashed in drawers and closets around the house. Taking target practice out in the desert near Calico was one of his favorite things—he'd made plans for the whole family to go shooting the day before, but it had rained. Brown had not only expensive hobbies but the time and resources to indulge them. He knew a lot about making and spending money. He'd done all right for someone who had dropped out of school after the eighth grade, earning well into the hundreds of thousands of dollars the past few years and with plans to earn much more. He was good at the money game and liked to play it with the computer wizards and the other college graduates with their MBAs and academic pedigrees. He'd played it and won.

Twenty miles from home the freeway ended, and David turned into Newport Boulevard. He drove until reaching a Denny's, where he parked and went into the all-night restaurant, looking around and taking note of a large redheaded waitress and several Hispanic customers. The place was nearly empty and had that strange middle-of-the-night feel of quarter to three, when the world seems to stop for a moment and catch its breath. He went into the rest room, something he did often, as he suffered from colitis. He also suffered from a liver disorder and had difficulty breathing, but he'd kept smoking, the one vice, he told people, that he couldn't shake. Sometimes he complained about a bad heart and he was frequently worried about cancer or other infirmities.

Brown's medicine cabinets were full of prescription drugs for his various ills and he liked to visit his chiropractor. Some people regarded him as a hypochondriac. Some believed he really was ill. He was thirty-two but looked considerably older. As a teenager he'd been much trimmer and lighter on his feet, but the years had added padding around the stomach and more layers on the chest and shoulders. He was a short man who walked with a short stride. His legs were not quite long enough for his torso, which gave his movements a childlike quality. His face had some good features—a strong sharp nose and intelligent dark eyes—but his skin was pockmarked and his jowls were beginning to soften and sag. Everything about him—his build, his gestures, the slope of his broad back—conveyed a sense of heaviness, of wariness, as if he lived in fear that a disaster was about to occur.

Stepping out of the rest room, he looked at the redhead again—she had curly hair and glasses—before walking to his car and leaving Denny's, driving home the same way he'd come, moving as if he were in no great hurry to return to Garden Grove. Pulling into his long driveway, he parked behind the five other vehicles at his ranch-style house, located in a modest but upwardly mobile section of town, several miles from Disneyland.

The neighborhood was quiet, peaceful, well-groomed and

attractively suburban, with touches of kitsch—lawns with wishing wells, pink plastic flamingos and topiary that looked more like teenagers with awkward haircuts than the beasts and buildings they were meant to emulate. A bird of paradise adorned Brown's driveway and shrubs stood by the dark front entry. He walked toward the door, fiddling with his keys and reminding himself not to trigger his elaborate alarm system, something that had happened a few nights earlier. When the system had gone off, he thought it was burglars, but others in the family believed that one of their three dogs was the culprit. Brown speculated aloud that it might even have been someone wanting to kill him and steal the valuables in his safe or take over his lucrative business. He'd called the police but nothing came of it.

He opened the door and went into the living room. Patti was standing in front of him, shaking violently and holding the baby on her hip. She was crying hysterically.

"Call me a coward," Brown said into the receiver, after dialing 911 and reaching a dispatcher at the Garden Grove Police Department, "but I know we need an ambulance."

"What is the problem, sir?" the dispatcher said.

"I'm not sure, okay?" he said, stretching the telephone cord from the kitchen into the living room, near his brown crushed velvet recliner, so he could look out the front window as he talked.

"What do you think is the problem?"

"Either my daughter or my wife or both—I don't know—are dead."

"How did they die?"

"My wife's sister that lives with us—there was a dispute earlier this evening, okay? And my parents were here and after my parents left, I went for a ride."

"Okay."

"And when I got back my wife's sister was holding my baby and trembling at the front door and saying my daughter got a gun and she shot it in her bedroom. We don't know if she was trying to kill her or what. And then, she thinks . . . neither one of us has the nerve to get in there and

9

she heard a couple more shots and my daughter's disappeared. We don't know where she is—we tried looking for her. I just called my dad and asked him to get down here because I'm about to freak out.''

"Okay. You're doing fine. We'll send a policeman and the paramedics out there. You don't—how long did this all—?''

"She said it happened about an hour ago. I can't even stand the thought of being in the house.''

"Okay. Someone will be out there . . . How old is your daughter?''

"Fourteen, fourteen. God, I am getting a headache. My blood pressure must be over two thousand.''

"Okay. I want to keep you on the phone until we get the officer there. Is that all right?''

Brown mumbled something to Patti, who had come into the room with him, and spoke again into the receiver.

Officer Darrow Halligan was cruising near Brookhurst when the dispatcher contacted him on his radio. The officer was only minutes from 12551 Ocean Breeze and drove there quickly, receiving more information to the effect that someone had apparently been shot in a domestic quarrel and the suspect was no longer at the scene. As he approached the Brown residence, the officer was struck by the darkness of Ocean Breeze and the difficulty police would have in locating anyone moving on foot through such a neighborhood. When Halligan arrived at the house, he expected a porch light to be on but it wasn't, so he used a spotlight to locate the exact address near the front door. A man let him in and as he walked into the living room, he saw a young woman in tears and heard the man say that he thought his wife had been shot in the master bedroom.

"I'm afraid to go in there and look, officer.'' Brown's voice was trembling. "Would you?''

Halligan passed through the living room and den before coming to the dark room where Linda slept. The door was half closed so he pushed it open, turning on his flashlight and moving the beam around the room, shining it on the bed and illuminating a woman lying on her back. Guiding the light to her face, he could hear her gurgling, and saw massive amounts of blood covering her T-shirt. Her right arm was extended and her left hand was reaching up and clutching her left ear. He felt for a pulse on her wrist but detected nothing. He looked at her chest—it did not rise or fall. The lower half of her body was under a blue blanket and Halligan observed that the bedspread was smooth—the woman had been shot without a struggle. The beam of his flashlight moved around the floor and fell on a chrome Smith & Wesson .38 caliber snub-nosed revolver lying beside the bed. The officer went into the bathroom that was adjacent to the room to see if the man's daughter was there, but he found no one.

More police officers and medical help had already arrived and were filling up the house, some of them speaking to Patti and David, some maintaining control of the crime scene, some directing the paramedics and some assisting Halligan with his inspection of the bedroom. Officer Dale Farley gave Halligan a Polaroid and he took photographs of Linda before she was removed from the room. After the paramedics had checked her vital signs and watched her draw a very slow and shallow breath, they carried Linda into the den, laid her out flat and began CPR procedures, her blood spilling onto the rug. Halligan continued his inspection, discovering that three drawers of a dresser were open and contained women's garments, numerous bottles of pills, some of them prescription drugs, and an empty holster. The drawers, it appeared to the officer, looked as if they had just been rummaged. The rest of the house was a mess—clothes on the floor, wastebaskets overflowing, things strewn in every corner—and under the bed where they found the woman was a box of twelve-gauge shotgun shells.

Linda was driven by ambulance to the Fountain Valley Community Hospital trauma ward and rushed into the emergency room, where a team of doctors and nurses attempted to treat her. Halligan made the trip to the hospital in his own vehicle before returning to 12551 Ocean Breeze to carry out his assignment of waking the neighbors and asking if they had heard or seen anything.

Alvin Sugarman, who lived directly across the street, had been startled into consciousness around three-thirty by the "sound of a thud," but after getting up and going to the bathroom, he fell back to sleep. No one answered the door at the home just south of the Brown household, and the neighbors to the north hadn't noticed anything at all.

One minute after Halligan had originally arrived at the residence, Officer Scott Davis came to 12551 Ocean Breeze, the second policeman on the scene. While Halligan had examined the master bedroom, Davis interviewed Brown and Patti, who told him that Cinnamon was the suspect and gave him a description of the teenager and what she was wearing. He passed the information on to the Garden Grove Police Department and they dispatched it to other officers who began patrolling the area, driving the dark streets and flashing their lights onto sidewalks and lawns. A helicopter was sent to the address to fly low above the houses and shine a searchlight down into the neighborhood. Davis and Farley went outside to look for Cinnamon, finding nothing in the front yard, but the backyard held a trailer, a garage, a kennel with two doghouses and no sign of the girl. Davis returned to the living room to interview Patti, who was pale and began shaking violently as she watched paramedics carry Linda out the front door.

"Is that my sister?" she said. "Is that my sister?"

"She's dead, isn't she?" Brown asked.

No one answered.

Patti told the officer that Cinnamon had not been getting along with either her father or her stepmother lately, constantly arguing with them about doing her chores and following the household rules. Cinnamon had moved into the house last September, Patti said, and everyone had done fine until the Christmas vacation, when the girl began to withdraw from the family, especially from Linda. Cinnamon had become very moody, Patti went on, and had even threatened suicide with a gun. She was "very rebellious and sarcastic," so rebellious that Linda eventually "kicked her out of the house'' and into the trailer.

At the officer's request, Patti recounted the past several hours in the household, telling how Brown's parents had come over for dinner and a card game but had left the residence around nine-thirty p.m. Linda took a shower and went to bed, while Brown, Patti and Cinnamon stayed up and watched television in the living room. At one point Linda emerged from the bedroom to get a drink of apple juice and to remind Cinnamon to go to bed, but the girl didn't budge. Sometime after eleven Patti and Cinnamon went into Patti's room, where there was a trundle bed, and a few minutes later David told the girls good night and went into the bedroom he shared with his wife. As Patti was getting ready for bed, she felt that something was wrong with Cinnamon, something she couldn't quite identify, and she sensed that the younger girl wanted to talk. When Patti offered to go back into the living room and watch TV with her, Cinnamon accepted the invitation. They watched MTV for a while but Cinnamon wouldn't open up, so Patti said she was exhausted and had to get some sleep. She returned to her own room and a few moments later Cinnamon joined her, asking the older girl to explain something to her before she got into bed. Patti asked what she was talking about, and Cinnamon showed her a small gray handgun which she'd been concealing.

"How do you work this?" she said.

Patti was startled. "Why?"

"Just in case."

"In case what?"

"In case someone breaks in."

Patti explained to Officer Davis that she'd told Cinnamon that no one would break in because their alarm system was so good, but the girl insisted on learning more about using the pistol—"just in case of an emergency."

"I'm not positive," Patti recalled telling her. "I've just seen this on TV. You just cock it back and pull the trigger."

This answer, Patti said, appeared to satisfy Cinnamon, so the girl thanked her and left. Patti went to bed and

Cinnamon went back into the living room to watch television. Patti quickly fell asleep and the next thing she remembered was being awakened by a gunshot, a blast that she believed was fired inside her own bedroom.

When Officer Allen Day arrived at 12551 Ocean Breeze at three-thirty a.m., he was instructed to search the front of the property, which he did, finding no trace of the suspect. At three-fifty he was told to interview David Brown, who was on the living room sofa watching policemen move through his house and give orders, ask questions, snap pictures and tell everyone to remain calm. Brown looked stunned, disoriented. He chain-smoked cigarettes and was very pale. He was sweating heavily, his hands were shaking and he complained of having a terrible headache, but when Day offered him some aspirin, Brown declined. When he talked, his voice was overly loud, a fact that several policemen couldn't help noticing. A couple of officers thought that the man seemed detached from all the activity in his home, but others described Brown's reaction as shock.

He was asked to recount the previous evening and he did, giving Officer Day many of the same details that Patti had. He mentioned the visit by his parents, the card game and that Linda had recently kicked Cinnamon out of the house because of the continual problems between the two of them. His daughter had become increasingly difficult—yesterday afternoon when they'd gone to the chiropractor's office, Cinnamon was abusive to Patti, calling her names. Brown told the policeman that he and his wife had argued about putting the baby to sleep not while his parents were there but after they'd gone home. He said that he and Linda had eventually reached a compromise, Linda rocking Krystal to sleep and carrying the baby to her crib, before going to bed herself. Brown joined his wife in their bedroom, where, as he told Officer Day, he "managed to make up to her." Linda fell asleep between twelve-thirty and one o'clock, and Brown went back into the living room to watch more TV. He dozed for a while and woke up hungry, going into the kitchen and searching for something sweet, then returning to the master bedroom and lying down beside his wife. After scanning several comic books and finding nothing he liked, he got out of bed and dressed, beginning his journey to the Circle K and to Newport Beach.

When he came home and saw Patti in tears, the first thing he remembered her saying was that Cinnamon had tried to shoot her in her room. Patti told him that she did not have the courage to check on Linda, and when Brown started for the master bedroom, Patti grabbed his arm and said, "No; don't go in there." He kept walking toward the bedroom and glanced through the half-open door, seeing his wife lying in an unnatural position. Turning away, he went into the kitchen and found Patti, took the baby from her and told the young woman to go into the backyard and search the trailer for Cinnamon.

This struck Officer Day as an odd piece of information— why would an adult male send a teenage girl into the backyard to look for someone who was armed and potentially dangerous?—and he asked this question. Brown explained that he was "a total coward," afraid to go into his own backyard at night under normal circumstances; it was extremely dark out there and the one huge overhanging maple tree evoked things that he found frightening. When Patti came back inside, Brown telephoned his parents, who lived half an hour to the north in Carson, and told them that Cinnamon had shot Linda. He asked his father to drive down at once and help him decide what to do. After telling his son to call the police, Arthur Brown assured David that he and his wife, Manuella, would be there immediately. David did as he was instructed and stayed on the phone with the 911 dispatcher until Officer Halligan arrived at his front door.

Brown told Officer Day that he owned eight rifles and two handguns, one of which belonged to his wife, and that the pistols were always loaded. Some of them were in Krystal's bedroom on top of the safe. He kept his .38 blue steel revolver in a holster wrapped in a K Mart bag in the bottom drawer of a nightstand in the master bedroom, but he was uncertain where Linda hid her gun. She'd once told him that it was "in with the towels," but she had towels in four different locations around the house, so he wasn't sure just where she meant. Brown speculated that Linda had carried the revolver in her purse when the two of them went to the bank to make large cash deposits from his computer consulting service. When asked to describe the last time he'd handled his guns, Brown said it was eight to ten months earlier, during a target-shooting excursion in the desert. When Officer Day asked if he was absolutely certain that he hadn't touched any guns in the past twenty-four hours, Brown said he hadn't even seen any firearms in his home the previous evening, let alone handled them.

While he was being interviewed, police continued sweeping the neighborhood for Cinnamon, the helicopter darting overhead and flashing its light along Ocean Breeze. Both David and Patti, in separate corners of the room, answered more questions for the police. Patti was also aware that the man was talking very loudly, but she couldn't really hear what he saying and wondered what was wrong with him. She told Officer Davis that after hearing a shot fired in her room, she sat up and looked around, seeing Cinnamon standing next to the bed. The younger girl turned and ran out the door toward the master bedroom. Patti heard the baby cry out in the nursery, which was between Patti's room and the master bedroom. Another shot was fired and then another. After the third shot, Patti lay in bed for a minute paralyzed with fear, while the baby kept crying. Patti ran to the nursery, grabbed the baby and ran back into her room, shut the door and sat down on the floor. When Davis asked her if she'd checked other rooms to see if anyone had been shot, Patti said she had been too scared to do anything but rescue Krystal. She thought Cinnamon was still in the house and might want to shoot her or the baby, who continued to wail.

For fifteen minutes, Patti said, she vainly tried to calm the infant, lying on the bed with Krystal, turning on the radio, looking for soothing music and finally pacing the floor with the baby in her arms. At around three-fifteen, she heard a very light knock at the front door but did not answer

16

it, fearful that it was Cinnamon. The knock came again, gently, and she went into the living room, listening as a key entered the door, certain that it had to be either Linda or David because Cinnamon had no key of her own. When she saw David come through the door, she exploded into tears, telling him about the gunshots in her room and the rest of the house. David checked the entire residence, except for the master bedroom, before returning to her and announcing that everything was all right. Patti told him that Cinnamon must have shot Linda and then shot herself in the master bedroom. She told Brown not to go in there because he "couldn't handle blood."

Officer Davis asked Patti where Cinnamon might have gone—did she have any close friends nearby? Could she be at one of their houses? Cinnamon didn't have many good friends, Patti said, but she did have three "imaginary friends" whom she often spoke to. Patti explained that sometimes she walked into a room and found the girl talking to her make-believe pals, Maynard and Oscar and Aunt Bertha, telling them what she was thinking or feeling or asking them to take her side in a dispute with a family member. The officer wanted to know if Patti had touched the gun when Cinnamon brought it into her room. The answer was no. He asked Patti about the last time she'd handled or fired one of the household guns and she indicated it was more than a year ago.

Arthur and Manuella Brown arrived at the house at around 3:30 A.M. and looked around with horror and bewilderment—what could have happened in the few hours since they'd been in this home? What should they do now for their son and his family? Arthur Brown appeared stricken, pale like his son and apparently stunned at what he was observing. The police quickly informed the parents that there was nothing they could do for anyone at the moment and it would be better if they were not present during the investigation. Within minutes they had prepared Krystal for a journey and were back on the road to Carson. During the trip, they heard about the shooting on the radio. At four-twenty-six a.m., following a quarter hour of open-heart massage at the Fountain Valley Community Hospital, Linda Brown was officially pronounced dead. The Orange County deputy coroner, Joe Luckey, bagged her hands and took custody of her blue socks and the T-shirt in which she'd been sleeping. It was covered with teddy bears and musical notes, and blood. He put her necklace in one plastic bag and her wedding ring in another.

By the time she was dead, Fred McLean had received a call from the Garden Grove Police Department concerning the events at the Brown residence. An ex-Marine and an investigator with the department, McLean did not look much like a cop. He had a reddish face, gentle eyes, graying hair, a small mustache, fragile-looking glasses and he enjoyed listening to opera. He liked cowboy boots, wide belt buckles and had the aura of a middle-aged man who, after eighteen years as a policeman, had seen enough human brutality. Twelve of those years were spent in the detective bureau, working auto thefts, robberies and crimes against persons. It was his job to look closely at a lot of nasty business, but he didn't appear to relish the task.

At five a.m., he came to 12551 Ocean Breeze and began making his official inquiries, as he would be the key investigator on the case for the local police department. He heard Brown and Patti say the same things the other officers had heard. He performed illumination tests on both of them to see if there was evidence of gunshot residue on their hands. This procedure finished, he stepped outside, where daylight was beginning to slip across the eastern sky. He walked into the backyard and saw Officers Farley and Davis checking on the two cocker spaniels and the white Pomeranian that lived with the family. The dachsund puppy had been found in Cinnamon's trailer and the policemen decided to lock it in the kennel with the other pets. McLean and the men went into the pen, which had two doghouses and was bordered by a garage and a three-foot-high chain-link fence. As they were placing the dog in the kennel, McLean noticed movement—a white Van tennis shoe was protruding from the larger doghouse. He walked over to the house and bent down. Inside, a girl was crouching in a fetal position.

"Cinnamon?"

He heard the girl mutter but could make no sense of the sounds.

He extended his hand through the doorway and she took it, crawling out of the doghouse. Since arriving at 12551 Ocean Breeze, McLean had seen photographs of Cinnamon Brown and he knew that the teenager standing before him was the suspect, although at the moment she didn't look very much like the pretty, well-groomed, bright-eyed girl in the pictures. She was drowsy and shivering, her hair was mussed, she smelled of urine and was covered with what appeared to be vomit. She held a small piece of pink cardboard paper, tied with a red ribbon. McLean took the cardboard from her, glancing at the writing across the face of it. He knelt again to look inside the doghouse and saw that its floor was covered with the same reddish substance that was on the girl's sweatshirt. The three men and the girl moved away from the doghouse and Cinnamon was escorted to the front of the residence, placed in a patrol car and transported to the Garden Grove Police Department. McLean was left to consider the dismal prospect that homicide suspects in his town were getting younger and younger, and in this case the word "suspect" probably wasn't strong enough, not strong enough at all. The piece of cardboard he'd taken from Cinnamon's hand had read: "Dear God Please forgive me I didn't mean to hurt her."

Officers Davis and Halligan drove the girl to the station, where she would be booked for murder. On the ride she asked the men, "Is my dad all right?"

Davis said yes.

"Is Patti all right?" she said, and Davis gave her the same answer.

"How about Linda?" the girl asked. "How's Linda?"

The men said nothing.

II

By seven-thirty a.m. Fred McLean was on his way to the police station, where Cinnamon had been photographed, given a gunshot residue test and checked by paramedics. Her speech was slurred, her head was nodding, she looked drugged or intoxicated, her blood pressure was low and she was having trouble maintaining consciousness, but the medical staff indicated that she was not in any apparent danger. She could still talk.

At about eight o'clock McLean turned on a tape recorder and asked Cinnamon if she knew what she was in custody for.

"Because I hurt Linda," the girl said.

"How did you hurt Linda?"

"Shot her."

"All right," McLean said. "Cinnamon, I have got to advise you of your rights."

He told the girl that Linda was dead and read to her the Miranda rights from a card provided by the Garden Grove Police Department, informing her that she had the right to remain silent and that anything she said from now on could and would be used against her in a court of law. She had the right to consult with an attorney, to be represented by an attorney and to have an attorney present before and during any questioning. If she could not afford to hire an attorney but wanted one, a lawyer would be appointed by the court before his questioning began.

"Now, Cinnamon," he said, "do you understand the rights I just explained to you?"

"I think so."

"You think so. What is it you don't understand?"

She told him that she felt sick.

Again he asked if she understood her rights.

"Yeah."

"You understand that Linda is dead?"

"Yes."

"Do you understand that you don't have to talk to me?"

"Yes."

"You understand I want to question you about what happened between you and Linda last night? Do you understand that I want to ask you questions about that? Do you understand that?"

"Yes."

McLean asked her where she lived, when she had moved into the Ocean Breeze residence and where she was attending school. After she'd answered the questions concisely, he said, "Why weren't you living with your mother?"

"Because she yells too much and it made me nervous."

"Why did your mother yell at you?"

"Because I am a brat."

"What do you do to be a brat?"

"I go to the beach every day," she said, her voice growing weaker and smaller. She sounded like countless other California teenagers who might have been tired from staying up all night and were falling into a whiny mood. She told McLean that she went to the beach with her best friend, Krista Taber, and the two of them tanned and "watched the surfers get thrashed."

"What happened between you and Linda yesterday or you and your father?"

"Me and my father get along pretty good, but Linda said

a while back that she didn't want me in the house, so I moved out to the trailer.''

Cinnamon mumbled inaudibly and then stated that Linda had told her that if she didn't move out of the house '' 'by the time I wake up, I am going to kill you.' ''

McLean studied the girl. ''Linda said she was going to kill you?''

''Yes. Me and her had a big fight. I don't know why she started it.''

''You don't know why?''

''Uh-uh.''

''You have no idea why you had the fight between you and Linda, huh, Cinnamon?''

''I'm here. I don't feel good.''

''I understand you don't feel good.''

''It's hard to keep my eyes open.''

''Why did Linda want you to leave?''

''She was tired of me and she didn't want to—she didn't like me.''

''Why?''

The girl spoke several incoherent sentences before telling McLean that Linda was a bad mother who had ignored the baby when she was choking. ''She hits Krystal sometimes,'' Cinnamon said, ''and it makes me so mad . . .''

''You didn't like her treating the baby badly?''

The girl made no response.

''Cinnamon?''

''I'm here. Please, I want to get this over with.''

''Cinnamon, you've got to answer my questions now.''

''Trying to—I'm trying to look at you but I can't keep my eyes open.''

''You don't have to keep your eyes open to talk to me.''

''Okay.''

''I just want you to concentrate on what you are telling me. Now, yesterday, Linda said she was going to kill you if you didn't leave?''

''Yes. That's the first time she ever said that. I thought she loved me.''

''That was the first time?''

"She told me that she hated my guts and I go, 'I guess I hate you too,' instead of arguing."

"Did Linda say why she hated you?"

"No. She wouldn't tell me."

"Did you ask her?"

"Yes."

"You told her that you hated her too, Cinnamon? Cinnamon?"

"I'm here," she said again, before telling McLean that her stepmother yelled at her for the smallest things.

"What did she yell at you about—those little things—what was she yelling at you about? Cinnamon?"

"I'm here."

McLean paused for several moments and then took another direction, asking her whose gun she had fired.

She indicated that it was her father's.

"I found it in the office drawer," she told the detective.

"In the office drawer?"

"In case of emergency."

"Is the office in the house?"

"Yes."

"Is that your father's office?"

"Everybody's office."

"Everybody's office. Okay. Did you ask anybody how to use that gun?"

"No. I did—I shot three shots."

"You shot three shots?"

"Yeah, one of them was in my room with Patti and the other two were with Linda."

The girl began to cough and McLean offered her a paper towel. When the coughing stopped, he asked her why she had gone into Patti's room with the gun.

"Because the thing got stuck and I couldn't turn a light on in her room because she would wake up."

"What thing got stuck?"

Cinnamon made another incoherent remark.

"Okay," McLean said. "Did you ask anybody—Cinnamon? Cinnamon?"

"I'm here."

24

"Did you ask anyone how to use the gun?"

"Uh-uh."

"Nobody showed you how to use the gun?"

"Uh-uh."

"How did you know how to use the gun?"

She slurred again and McLean said, "Have you ever fired a gun before, Cinnamon? Cinnamon?"

"I'm here. Would you quit saying my name?"

"Well, I need to talk to you."

"I know."

"You are not answering me sometimes."

He asked again if she had ever fired guns and she told him that sometimes she went out shooting with her father.

"Have you fired little guns or big guns in the past?"

"Little guns," she said, "because they don't do much harm. Nobody gets hurt."

"Where did you shoot them at?"

"Shoot who?"

"Huh?"

"Shoot who?"

It was obvious that she was becoming more incoherent and drowsier, so he announced, at eight-twenty, that the interview was over. Less than four hours after the murder, the detective realized that he had all he needed for a conviction. Before they left the interview room, Cinnamon told him that there was one other thing that was making it difficult for her to stay awake: early that morning she'd taken more than eighty pills or capsules of some type of drug. In response to this, McLean said that a technician was going to take a sample of her blood.

"Oh, God," she said.

"Have you ever had blood drawn before?"

"No."

"It won't hurt. Just a little pinprick. You won't feel very much at all."

An ambulance took Cinnamon to the Garden Grove Medical Center, where she confessed to Pam French, a policewoman, that she'd shot Linda. The girl was examined by more doctors, placed in bed and fell asleep. At noon an attorney, Alex Forgette, who had been hired by her father, came to the hospital and told the staff that he wanted to speak with her when she regained consciousness. Several hours later she awakened and, following more blood tests, talked with Forgette until six p.m.

That evening Cinnamon was taken to the University of California at Irvine Medical Center for more tests. Her stay was to be for seventy-two hours and she was placed in the jail ward on the fourth floor. Her father planned to visit her soon and offer some advice on what to say—or not to say—to the authorities, but very early the next morning, when Cinnamon was in the care of Kim Hicks, a third-year medical student at UCIMC, she confessed once again to the murder. When Seawright Anderson, a psychiatrist who worked for Forgette, came to the ward to make an initial evaluation of her state of mind, she told him the same thing.

On the morning of the nineteenth, while the police were still working inside their home, David and Patti left the Ocean Breeze residence early, taking along some children's toys and diapers for Krystal. From a pay phone at a doughnut shop, Patti called Ethel Bailey, her mother, and told her what had happened to her daughter. Ethel quickly spread the news to other members of the family. Patti and David drove to their chiropractor to have their muscles massaged and their nerves settled. They drove to Carson to visit Brown's parents and to take a nap, as they were exhausted after a night of chaos. They drove to Anaheim to see Brenda Sands, Brown's ex-wife and Cinnamon's mother. There, David told Brenda that Cinnamon had overdosed on some of his prescription drugs and killed Linda. This seemed as unbelievable to Brenda as it did to many other people who knew Cinnamon and would learn about the murder throughout the day. Brown told his ex-wife that Cinnamon had been especially moody lately and that moodiness was the only explanation he could give the detectives for her sudden violent behavior. He suggested that Brenda tell them the same thing, a suggestion she didn't appreciate. She informed

26

her ex-husband that she would give the police her own view of Cinnamon's personality and nothing else.

Fred McLean also stopped by the Sands home on Tuesday afternoon for a preliminary interview with Brenda. Just two days earlier, she told him, Cinnamon had asked her mother if she could return home to live, which was striking enough but not the thing that now struck Brenda the hardest. The strange part, in her mind, was that Cinnamon got along well with Linda but not with Patti. The teenagers argued a lot, and Cinnamon often complained that she felt like a slave in the Brown home because she had to do more household chores than the older girl. Cinnamon had moved into the trailer, her mother said, not because she'd been thrown out of the house by Linda, but because she wanted to have her own place, away from Patti. And Cinnamon, according to Brenda, not only didn't use drugs but "always put down drug users." There was another curious thing that Brenda passed on to the detective: several months earlier Cinnamon had told her mother about a conversation that had taken place between her stepmother, Linda, and Linda's twin brother, Alan Bailey. The two of them had been talking about "how to get rid of Dave."

One thing was clear to McLean: the more questions he asked about this apparently simple murder and about Cinnamon Brown, the more confusing things became. There were inconsistencies in a couple of the statements that Patti and David and Cinnamon had made since the killing. Patti, for example, claimed that prior to any gunfire the younger girl had come into her room and asked how to use the pistol, but Cinnamon denied doing that. David said that after returning from his drive to Newport Beach he did not knock before entering the house, but Patti said that he did. There was also the business of Cinnamon being kicked out of the house, another story that didn't quite jibe, but none of these things was that extraordinary, considering the circumstances.

When McLean had interviewed the three principal figures left in the Brown home, Patti had been crying hysterically,

27

David appeared to be in shock and Cinnamon was under the severe influence of drugs.

Memory was always a tricky thing; in a situation like this it could be even more slippery than usual. As he left the home of Brenda Sands, McLean found himself in a peculiar position: in a sense the crime had already been solved, but in another sense he wondered if he'd learned anything at all about the murder. His only suspect had confessed repeatedly—the kind of thing that a man in his line of work usually felt good about—but the innocently pretty teenager didn't feel like a killer to the veteran police officer.

Back at his office, McLean would discover several more curious things, this time from Joe Luckey, the Orange County deputy coroner. After tests that involved firing bullets into pork fat, lab technicians concluded that Linda was shot twice in the chest, once from a distance of three to six inches and once from twelve to eighteen inches. She had died with a small amount of cocaine in her blood. They had also discovered that Cinnamon had ingested three bottles of Darvocet. The pills contained more than six times the amount of propoxyphene needed to kill a human being.

On Tuesday morning, while McLean was busy with Cinnamon, Jay Newell came to 12551 Ocean Breeze for the first time, arriving after some of the other officers had left the address. The police had already made diagrams of the house and sawed a chunk out of the wall in Patti's bedroom where a bullet had passed through a tapestry before it came to rest in a stud. Newell was an investigator with the Orange County District Attorney's office, which would be prosecuting Cinnamon, and he wanted to observe the scene for himself while everything was still fresh and unsettled. Newell was a little younger than Fred McLean and looked more like the stereotypical gumshoe, the kind of man who was more concerned with doing a good job than looking good. His pants were a little baggy, the sport coat's lapels a little wide, the shoes unfashionable. Like McLean, he wore glasses, which softened his face, but his shoulders were broader than the other man's and his jaw was squarer. He seemed like a nice guy, very polite and soft-spoken, but there was something about him that suggested determination and action.

He looked like someone who, if provoked, could be tenacious, even dangerous. One got the feeling, watching him lumber through the Orange County District Attorney's office, that he was a little rough around the edges and likely to stay that way.

The son of a school custodian in La Habra, Newell had grown up across the street from a Los Angeles County sheriff's deputy, a man who counseled neighborhood kids and someone the boy admired. After serving in Europe in the Army and working as a telephone lineman, Newell joined the Los Angeles County Sheriff's Department before moving to Orange County in 1977. He believed he could rise faster in a smaller office. He was a dedicated and ambitious cop, earning the 1988 honor of Investigator of the Year from the California District Attorney Investigators Association.

Some police officers don't appear to dislike criminals, despite the fact that they arrest them and put them in jail. Newell came across as someone who often did dislike them, someone who took a personal interest in seeing that justice was rendered. He wasn't one of those cops who want to show up on the six o'clock news. His beliefs were conveyed in the placid stare he wore when he was interviewing a suspect and in the hard line of his chin. He had perfected the sincere expression and the verbal intonation of a man who acts as if he believes what he is hearing and wants you to tell him more. The day he drove to 12551 Ocean Breeze, he could not possibly have known how very long he would be working on this case.

Investigators found a number of interesting things at the Brown home—guns and drugs and expensive coins—but one of the more intriguing discoveries was the writings of Cinnamon and Patti. Some of these were merely letters that had been sent from one girl to the other, chatty letters about clothes and boys and music, but not all of them fell into that category. There were also poems, stories and rambling monologues that had enough emotional clout to transcend their bad grammar and misspellings. Patti had once written at one-thirty-four a.m.:

You are one thing I'll always treasure because you showed me the meaning of life and you made my life worth living. You made me fell [sic] like someone special you got me to see not everyone wants to hurt me. You got me to learn from [sic] past, that was then this is now. You got me calling your name in my sleep but most of all you have my heart calling for you. Can you hear it!

On another occasion she wrote to her "one and only":

I love you more than you will ever know. What do you want from me? I need you to tell me. I want to be there always and forever. Can't you see I am down on my knees begging you please. Show me love and how to love you. I want to know. Show me life's most wonderful things. I'll just die if I cann't [sic] have you forever.

And on another:

I want to sing you a love song like no one else. That would make you cry inside. And hope it would prove how much (I Love You), but it will never due [sic] because it is up to me to prove to you how much I Love You . . . I want to be the one that when you are upset and trouble [sic] you come to me.

Patti also wrote a short story about a boy who believes that he makes his parents miserable, so he kills himself. When his parents find out he is dead, they are happy at last.

If the darkness of Patti's writings was striking, Cinnamon's notes and letters were remarkable for just the opposite reason. There was a calendar for each month of 1985, and her January and February schedules could have served as a model for the typical happy-go-lucky California girl. The days were crowded with going to the movies, visiting friends, going shopping, talking on the phone, cleaning the backyard, taking a long bath, writing love notes, going to Disneyland and hanging out at the mall. When March arrived, the calendar entries stopped, as if her life had suddenly come to a halt.

Cinnamon's letters were also breezy, talking about music and shopping. But one poem in her collection—by an unknown artist—was worth noting. It was significant, not so much because of what it said about Cinnamon the fourteen-year-old but because of how it foreshadowed her future:

> *Forget his name, Forget his face*
> *Forget his kiss and warm embrace*
> *Forget the Love that you once shared*
> *Forget the fact that he once cared*
> *Forget the times we spent together*
> *Remember now he's gone forever*
> *Forget him when he played your song*
> *Forget you cried the whole night long*
> *Forget how close you once were*
> *Remember now it's him and her*
> *Forget you memorized his walk*
> *Forget the way he used to talk*
> *Forget the times he was so mad*
> *Remember now he's happy not sad*
> *Forget his gentle teasing ways*
> *Forget you saw him yesterday*
> *Forget the things you used to do*
> *Remember that she Loves him too*
> *Forget the thrill when he went by*
> *Forget the times he made you cry*
> *Forget the way he said your name*
> *Remember now it's not the same*
> *Forget the time that went so fast*
> *Forget those times they're in the past*
> *Forget he said, "I'll leave you never"*
> *Remember now he's gone forever.*

III

Patti Bailey had a wide, pretty face and a pug nose, the same nose found on almost everyone in her clan. The youngest in a family of eleven children, she closely resembled her dead sister. Even though Linda was blonder, thinner and more athletic-looking, people often said Patti looked just like her sister. In one way Patti was flattered by these comments, but in another way she wasn't: she was her own person, she had to remind herself, and not Linda, although she'd sometimes imitated her big sister's hairstyle or clothing. Patti was a woman/child, a curious mixture of personalities. One moment she appeared to be much older than her seventeen years, almost worldly, and the next moment she was a young, cute girl, barely an adolescent.

One never knew which Patti was about to emerge. The aging child or the near-woman? Her smile revealed both her true age and something buried within her, something that was trying to come out. The smile was explosive and irrepressible. It was defenseless and artless—something she could not fake. It was nothing more than the happy smile of a teenage girl who for the moment appeared to be living a normal life.

* * *

On the morning of the nineteenth, when McLean was leaving the Brown residence to go to the police station to interview Cinnamon, he told David and Patti to come in that afternoon and speak with him at one-thirty. Because of their travels throughout that day, they didn't show up for the appointment. McLean stayed busy with other people: after Patti had told Ethel about the shooting and Ethel had told her daughter Cheri, several of the Baileys drove down from Riverside to Garden Grove and spoke with the detective on the day of the murder. McLean didn't gather much new information about the killing, but he did discover that none of the Baileys cared for David Brown. He'd married Linda not once but twice, and most of her family hadn't liked him any more the second time around than the first. He was moody and distant, they said, and always had to have his way with people, especially with his wife. Cheri, the oldest Bailey sister, said that Linda had called her several hours before the murder and was crying on the phone. Linda told her sister that she was coming to Riverside the next day, and Cheri believed that she was making plans to leave her husband.

"Would you find it more acceptable," Cheri was asked during her police interview, "if you learned that David had done it, rather than Cinnamon?"

"I hate to say it," she replied, "but yes."

Rick Bailey was in the station that afternoon and spoke more directly than his older sister: "David was an asshole from day one . . . He was afraid of his own shadow . . . It sounds like there's pieces missing that just don't make sense."

To Rick's wife, Mary, who was also present, two of those pieces were that Brown had been driving around at three a.m. that morning and that Cinnamon had recently been sleeping out in the trailer. It seemed to Mary, an outspoken woman, that the girl must have been sent to the trailer because her father didn't want her to know about something that was going on in the house, something that was taking place at night. Mary told the detective that Patti had an obvious crush on David and would do anything for the man.

34

She also said that about a year earlier Patti had attempted to commit suicide with some pills, all because of an apparent conflict she'd had with the man.

The next afternoon Patti and David came to the police station and McLean interviewed them separately. David went first and apologized to McLean for smoking in his office, but the detective indicated that he was used to smoking because most cops did it. Brown seemed baffled by the crime, saying that he did not believe that Patti had killed his wife and he could not comprehend how Cinnamon could have done such a thing.

Two weeks ago, he told McLean, his daughter had become upset enough to take an overdose of aspirin, but even then he did not realize how disturbed she was. When McLean changed the subject to life insurance, Brown explained to the officer that he'd once carried more than a million dollars' worth of policies on Linda, but he'd canceled them not long ago and now had just one small policy in her name.

McLean, recalling his conversation with Cinnamon's mother, brought up the name of Alan Bailey, Linda's twin brother, the same brother who had reportedly once discussed killing David with Linda. Brown described Alan as a hothead and an unreliable worker. In recent months Brown had employed him in his computer consulting business but had to let him go because Alan came to work late and blew up when David docked his pay. The young man was volatile and frightening, Brown said, and once had gone so far as to threaten his life outside a local coin shop.

Brown reiterated that on the night of the murder he'd made love to his wife, giving the detective more of the details: "She would hide a jar of Vaseline under the side of the bed and she would tease me for a long time with it . . . We never fought and I always treated her like a queen. I mean I loved her."

Why, McLean wondered, had he sent Patti into the backyard to look for Cinnamon when the situation was obviously treacherous?

"I have never been much for any kind of blood," Brown told him. "I can't even cut up a chicken. And . . . the thought crossed my mind that she might try to kill me."

After sending Patti outside, he went into the living room with Krystal, turned on the TV and collapsed on the couch. "The baby was crying," he said. "I wanted to hold her . . . I called my father because I was shaking and I knew that I was going to fall apart and I wanted my dad there to help me and to check and to see if Linda was okay."

He had little new information to offer McLean and few insights into why his daughter would have been compelled to do such a thing. He sounded like countless other people who have been interviewed about a family member or neighbor after someone close to them has been accused of murder: they knew that the person was occasionally annoyed or depressed, but the depth of the alleged killer's problems was never evident on the surface. Before leaving the detective, Brown pointed out that, regardless of what Cinnamon might have done to his wife, the girl still meant everything to him. Years ago, when he was first divorced from Brenda Sands, he missed his daughter so much that he sued for custody of the girl, a legal battle that he lost.

"I feel about Cinnamon as I do about Krystal now," he said. "I just love her to death."

McLean and a second policeman interviewed Patti, who repeated her story about Cinnamon appearing in her room the night before and asking how to use a pistol. Patti told the detectives that the girl was holding Linda's gun, a firearm Patti recognized from the family's shooting trips out by Calico. McLean again asked Patti if she'd touched the pistol and again she said no. She'd just talked with Cinnamon briefly in her room, said good night to her, fell asleep and was awakened by something loud, which she was "almost positive was a gunshot." With the sound still ringing

36

in her ears, she saw something "like a shadow" at her door and then the door closed.

Was she certain it was Cinnamon?

Well . . . it was a small person, she said, "not small but medium height."

An overweight person?

"Uh-uh."

She described how, after the first shot, she ran into the baby's room, grabbed Krystal and ran back to her own room. "I was panicked, scared."

"Okay," McLean said. "How long were you in there?"

"About half an hour, hour. I mean—just—I was scared. I didn't—"

"You didn't look at the clock?"

"I didn't want to look at the clock. I was scared because if I knew what—"

"Was it—it was still dark?"

"Yeah. It was still dark."

"Outside?"

"Outside."

The baby was crying, she explained to the detectives, and she stayed in her bedroom until she heard a car door shut, then went into the living room with Krystal. The rest of her account was essentially the same as the one she'd laid out the day before and was no more revealing than Brown's. McLean listened as she repeated some of what she'd already told him, preparing to move into more difficult areas of inquiry. He might have already had a confession from Cinnamon, but he'd heard enough from the Baileys to raise at least a few suspicions about other members of the family.

"To wrap it up," he said, "I'm gonna ask you a couple of questions that are—like I told Dave—they're gonna seem cold, cruel."

"I understand."

"I want you to understand that it's not something I'm happy to do, but I will ask the questions."

"Okay."

37

"Do you have any idea when she could have gotten that gun?"

"None. I mean, David always tries to keep most of his guns locked up, except for the ones that he usually kept in his bedroom."

Had David ever before left the house by himself late at night to go for a ride?

Just once, Patti said, "but that's only because he was so upset and couldn't sleep and frustrated. And he just—he goes—he used to go off every once in a while but it wouldn't be so late at night. And just go out and think things out, come back and say, 'You guys, I'm sorry.'"

Did Cinnamon hate Linda enough to want to kill her or Krystal?

"No."

"How about you and Dave? How did you guys get along?"

"At first, I mean, I couldn't talk to Dave at all. I mean I couldn't talk to any one of my brothers. I mean, I always kept to myself, except for me and Linda. We always stayed in contact . . . We were always close. I mean, I have a real hard time talking to any kind of guys. I mean, I just get nervous because I know that my dad left. And I'm afraid that I might get attached and think he's my daddy."

"You don't have a boyfriend, then?"

"No. I don't want one. It sounds funny but . . ."

After several other questions, McLean asked Patti if she'd ever attempted suicide.

"No."

"Didn't [you] take some pills or anything?"

"Well, I tried but I didn't."

McLean paused. "We're friends here," he said. "You can tell us anything."

"I tried but I couldn't."

Did she ever do anything that anyone might have interpreted as making a pass at David?

"No . . . Linda used to have a bad habit of just constantly winking, and I was around Linda so much that I constantly

38

used to wink. Just, I mean—she'd wink at me and I'd wink back and maybe he'd misinterpret or somebody else might have misinterpreted. But there's never—I've never made a pass at David."

"Did you," McLean said, "have any reason to want Linda dead? Anything at all?"

"No. None. I mean—"

"No reason to hurt her?"

"Me and Linda were best friends. There was no reason in the world I'd want to hurt her."

"Did you shoot her?"

"No."

"Okay."

"I mean . . ."

"Those," McLean said, "are the bad questions I was telling you about, I was trying to warn you about. Those are the kind of questions that we ask point-blank. You were the only other person other than the baby that we know who was in the house at the time it happened. So you are the only other logical suspect."

"Okay."

"Other than Cinnamon."

The detective, after showing her the cardboard note that Cinnamon had written and been arrested with, asked Patti the same question for at least the third time: "And you had never touched the gun?"

"No."

"Okay . . . Remember the test that I did on your hands at the house when I sprayed that stuff on there? When I did that test, it was for illumination to determine . . . if somebody were to fire a handgun or rifle or whatever, it leaves debris on hands. There was a fingerprint found on the gun, I believe."

Patti nodded. "Uh-huh."

"I haven't seen it, I haven't checked it out, to determine how good it is or whatever. Though what we'd like to do is roll your fingerprints while you're here because that shows that it's definitely not yours, and do the same with David."

Patti had no objection to being fingerprinted and asked the men if either of them had change for a dollar.

"What do you mean?" McLean said. "Do you want a Coke or something?"

She nodded again.

"I'll get it for you. It's the least we can do if we keep you here all afternoon."

He left to bring her a soft drink. The session was over, the tests were done, and when the results came back from the lab, the detective was even more perplexed than before. David's and Patti's hands had traces of gunshot residue but Cinnamon's were clean. One possible explanation for this was that any residue on Cinnamon's hands would have been obliterated by urine and vomit, but the presence of gunshot residue on David and Patti was puzzling. Another puzzle for the detective was the fact that the coroner's report also indicated that there was no semen anywhere in the dead woman's body, no evidence whatsoever that Brown had made love to his wife the night she was killed.

Three days after the murder, a memorial service, entitled "Turn Again to Life," was held for Linda at the Mettler Chapel in Garden Grove. Before the day of the service, David and Patti had driven to an I. Magnin store near Newport Beach to look for a funeral dress. When they found what they wanted, an old-fashioned blue lace affair, Brown asked Patti to try it on to see if it would fit Linda. She refused, upset by the notion of wearing anything that was going to be on her sister's body. David bought the dress and delivered it to the mortuary where the attendants put it on Linda for the funeral.

Brown rented a limousine for the occasion which he and Patti rode in, and he hired a minister to deliver some remarks over the casket. The pastor, Reverend Gray Valcarcel of the Bethel Christian Center of Riverside, was an acquaintance of David's sister, Susan Salcido, who'd recently become a born-again Christian and recommended the man. Brown was supposed to tell the minister some things about his marriage or about Linda so the reverend would have a general direction in which to aim his remarks, but David was so preoccupied with other arrangements that he forgot to do this. Pastor Valcarcel talked to Susan instead.

Linda's head lay on a wine-colored pillow and each guest was given a red rose to place on the woman as he or she walked by the coffin at the start of the service. While waiting in line to put her rose on Linda, Patti collapsed and nearly fainted. Brown took Patti away from her sister, rode around with her briefly in the limousine and gave her a drug to calm her nerves, while everyone waited for them to return. After all the mourners had filed past the casket, David asked that the room be cleared so that he and Krystal could spend a few last minutes alone with the dead wife and mother before she was gone forever.

For the service itself, Linda's immediate family was placed not at the front of the room but off to the side and behind a screen, so they weren't visible to the other guests. The memorial began well enough and went along smoothly until the preacher said that the road between David and Linda had occasionally been "rocky." The word triggered a hissing sound from behind the screen, and when Reverend Valcarcel turned to look at the dead woman's family, Brown was motioning for him to stop the speech and come over to where he was sitting. The minister paused, deeply embarrassed, looked out at the assembled mourners and did as he was asked. For several moments he and Brown spoke quietly behind the screen, and when the pastor emerged, he told the audience that he was mistaken because David and Linda Brown had a nearly perfect marriage.

Linda was cremated and her ashes were eventually taken to Pacific View Memorial Park, an attractive, expensive, Spanish-style cemetery and mausoleum that sits on a hill above Newport Beach. Here, the air is clean and you can see both the Pacific Ocean and the Fashion Island shopping center, one of the local monuments to prosperity. Linda's ashes were put in a small vault in the Magnolia Court "niche" of the park, which is located next to a number of marble-enclosed coffins. Eucalyptuses hang over the park, their scent mingling gently with the huge sweet magnolia blossoms. A soft breeze comes off the ocean. Light blue water runs in a fountain near Linda's vault, splashing a plaque that reads: "Linda Marie Brown Your love, kindness, caring and beauty will shine forever Love, Krystal and David."

The park's grounds are well-kept and the people who come to visit dead relatives tend to drive Cadillacs and Mercedes. Most of these mourners look like people who expect to die as well as they have lived. Pacific View Memorial Park was an unpredictable resting place for a young woman who had known poverty as a youngster, a young woman who had never finished high school, although she'd had plans to begin studying at home for her diploma the day she was killed; an unexpected last stop for a woman whose family would one day be described by an Orange County lawyer as "white trash."

* * *

Seawright Anderson, the psychiatrist who worked for Cinnamon's attorney, was confounded. The first time he'd spoken with the girl she'd confessed to the murder. Ever since then, she'd told him and everyone else she talked to that she could not recall the events leading up to and including the shooting. According to Cinnamon, something had happened to her mind or her memory, leaving a hole where March 18 and 19 should have been. She didn't know why or how this could have happened—it had never happened to her before. As far as the doctors who examined her could tell, she had fully recovered from the drug overdose, and medical tests revealed nothing wrong with her physically.

Even stranger, according to Dr. Anderson and the other mental health professionals who'd looked at the girl, there wasn't that much wrong with her psychological state, at least wrong in the legal sense of the word. If Alex Forgette, Cinnamon's lawyer, was planning on a defense built around the concept of a deranged mind, he might have to consider

42

an alternative. Cinnamon didn't hear voices or have psychotic episodes. Her penchant for making up imaginary friends like Oscar, Maynard and Aunt Bertha and telling them her secrets fell within the range of normal teenage behavior. The girl was lonely at times, she had experienced depression, she came from a difficult domestic arrangement and on occasion she might appear selfish or preoccupied, but those were hardly enough to drive her to murder someone within her own household. She apparently hadn't suffered from physical abuse. Linda hadn't beaten her; neither had her own mother. And David Brown wasn't that kind of man, most people said; that just wasn't his way. Cinnamon didn't appear to have been pushed into this by parental violence.

Jay Newell had been studying the murder and he felt, from having worked on similar crimes, that killings within families don't just happen. The buildup occurs over a long period of time, step by step, until an explosion comes. That's what was missing from this case: the idea of shooting someone appeared to have surfaced in the girl's mind one night and before morning came, a twenty-three-year-old wife and mother, a woman whom everyone professed to love, was dead.

There had to be something more, Newell believed, more background, more buildup within the family itself, and whatever that information might be, it was going to have to come from the suspect. Patti and David had told their stories and they were plausible. Linda was dead and Krystal couldn't talk. If anyone was obviously concealing something, it was Cinnamon: reasonably healthy fourteen-year-old girls—and Cinnamon was, by some measures, reasonably healthy—do not simply lose their memory. They also don't usually confess to first-degree murder or allow themselves to be caught without even trying to run away. What did the girl not want to remember?

The authorities kept posing this question to her and Cinnamon kept saying nothing. Weeks went by while she sat in jail and her attorney attempted to put together a defense. Her father had paid Forgette $25,000 in cash, so the lawyer wanted to make a good effort, but unless something dramatic changed before the August court date, the attorney's chances of winning were nonexistent. As he looked for a legal strategy, Cinnamon wrote innocuous letters from her cell to Krista Taber. Fred McLean and other police officers spoke to more of Brown's neighbors and to Cinnamon's teachers, who told them that the girl had been "acting out" in recent weeks, her grades had been falling and her behavior deteriorating since roughly the previous holiday season. The officers also spoke to more of the Baileys and Browns (David's own family had seven offspring to go along with the eleven Bailey children). Although Alan Bailey admitted that he had quarreled with Brown over money, his harshest words were not for his former employer but for his baby sister. He told the detectives that Patti was spoiled, needed psychiatric help and had been very jealous of Linda because she had money, jewelry and a husband.

"Patti," he said, "hated my mom. Still does and that hurts my mom bad."

If there was general agreement that the Baileys disliked Brown, the one thing about him that they, and especially Alan, did like was his money. He had more of it than anyone in their family and he occasionally threw some their way. He'd given Alan a job in his business and paid Ethel for her bookkeeping chores. He'd bought lots of things for Linda and Patti: all-terrain vehicles, dirt bikes and automobiles in general. He'd even invited the Baileys to go into the desert with him and raise hell in the dust. That was fun and made some of his bad moods and grumpier traits more acceptable.

The police also interviewed Susan Salcido, David's sister, who echoed some of the Baileys' sentiments: her brother was often sour, had a dominant personality and became angry if you crossed him. Like others who knew Cinnamon Brown, Susan was mystified to learn that the girl had killed someone. "I've known Cinnamon her whole life," she told the detectives. "She's just a delight. She's never bad. She's never angry. She has an invisible friend, Maynard, a frog. She always told her grandma not to sit on Maynard and they made a big play out of it, just to annoy you, as kids do. Patti played this game too. Patti was like a little fink who was always looking for an opportunity to get Cinnamon in trouble.''

When she was a teenager, Susan mentioned to the police, her brother, who was seventeen at the time, tried to molest her but she successfully resisted him. ''He told me that he was afraid to be in the house with me, that he was going to rape me, and it scared me,'' she said. ''For years I wouldn't really have anything to do with him until I got into my adult life and I had my own boyfriends.'' She'd never spoken of any of this to her parents. ''If you'd told me that David had been shot and murdered, I mean I could halfway understand. I mean, he doesn't have any friends. But Linda, my God. That woman never said a bad word to anybody except David because she was always on the defense—'cause David was always yelling at her.''

While the family members were telling the detectives what they thought might have led to murder (and it was surprisingly little), David decided they had to leave 12551 Ocean Breeze. He wanted a different environment in which to raise Krystal. They felt that the house was now grim, at times it even felt haunted. One night Patti was convinced that Linda's empty old chair was rocking back and forth in the living room. She could often feel Linda's spirit in the room, she told Brown, and it was not a good feeling. David had made her scrub Linda's blood off the master bedroom walls, which was a chilling enough experience, but there were bloodstains on the carpet from when the paramedics had tried vainly to save Linda's life and a bloody handprint on the floor next to the nightstand. These things wouldn't wash out and you couldn't avoid seeing them and remembering. They left Patti feeling ill.

One night an anonymous caller phoned the residence and told Brown that he knew who had really killed Linda—it was David himself, wasn't it? Brown soon had an unlisted number. Another night Larry Bailey, the brother in the clan

45

who was considered the most volatile, phoned David and told him that he was going to kill him and everyone else in the house. Brown was terrified—he thought Larry was capable of anything. So did Patti, who was starting to have nightmares, horrible visions that came to her whenever she closed her eyes. Brown's stomach was in turmoil and his nerves were troubling him. He took everything that had belonged to his dead wife out of the house, and when he thought that Patti looked too much like Linda, he made her dye her hair. Even that wasn't always enough to erase Linda's image from the residence. Sometimes he and Patti went to visit his parents in Carson just so they could get away from Ocean Breeze, or Arthur and Manuella came to their house just so David and Patti wouldn't have to be alone with the memories. The two of them believed that moving to another address would help put the night of the murder behind them.

Cinnamon's trial began in early August in Orange County's West Court, before Robert Fitzgerald under juvenile jurisdiction. During the proceedings, Alex Forgette made one final attempt to get her to talk, explaining to the girl that if there was anything that she had failed to tell him—anything at all—this was her last chance to divulge it before facing an almost certain conviction. Cinnamon was unmoved. She still couldn't remember a thing, she said, and she continued to plead not guilty by reason of insanity.

Seawright Anderson testified on Cinnamon's behalf, saying that she had a depressed personality and was suffering from amnesia. Patti testified that on the night of the crime she had seen only a "silhouette" at her bedroom door and not Cinnamon, a contradiction of what she had previously told the police. Before Patti's court appearance, Brown had told her to portray his daughter as unstable and even crazy, as this might lend her defense some credibility. Patti went on at some length about the imaginary friends, Oscar and Maynard and Aunt Bertha, whom Cinnamon was always speaking to.

Brown himself did not come to the trial. He had been

subpoenaed by Mike Maguire, the prosecuting attorney, but he had a liver ailment and claimed to be too sick to leave the house. David might have missed the proceedings simply because he wanted to avoid some of the courtroom revelations. Dr. Thomas Howell, a clinical psychologist employed by the Orange County Department of Mental Health, interviewed him before the trial and told the court that "Mr. Brown provided me with an extensive history of patterns of physical abuse, sexual abuse and violence and drug abuse contained within his own family and within himself . . . One area that was specifically important was that he had three psychiatric hospital admissions, by his own account. He indicated that he had threatened to kill himself and to also kill Cinnamon's mother with a gun at one time during this period after their divorce. And that he had a propensity for using guns, and that on the request of friends and, it seems like, his therapist, that he decided to place those in the custody of the Orange County Police Department . . .

"Additionally, in terms of his history, he was raised in a very physically abusive home and, it seems like, a home that's provided very poorly for his needs and forced him to leave his home at the age of fourteen, a very young age for someone to be out on his own . . . Here he is a fourteen-year-old, off on his own, trying to live within the world."

"What influence," Forgette asked Dr. Howell, "can you as a psychologist draw from those facts as it applies to Cinnamon?"

"Parents learn how to deal with their children, to discipline them, primarily from their experiences, from their own parents, or additionally learn through their own exposure to the child. He was probably a poor disciplinarian and was, in fact, probably physically abusive himself. I had to file a child-abuse report on his statements to me that he had . . . struck his daughter when she was twelve years old, pulling her pants down and spanking her with a belt so forcefully that he was trying to get her to cry and she steadfastly refused to do that."

Dr. Howell testified that Brown believed that his daughter

47

was incapable of committing a murder: "His quote was, 'Cinnamon is about as capable of hurting others as much as I am.' And in my opinion, he is capable. His past history documents that. So it was kind of a strange statement for him to make . . ."

Did Mr. Brown's mental history have any bearing on Cinnamon's problems? Forgette asked.

"Yes, I think it would."

"How so?"

"We're talking about a person who's had three psychiatric hospitalizations, both suicidal and homicidal, and from what I can determine, he was sometimes excessively anxious. The stress that was occurring within him was because of the child's arrest for murder and it was causing him to have strenuous psychological signs and even physiological signs to the extent of high blood pressure, ulcerated colon, allergies and, although not recorded in the report, vague angina pains. So we're talking about a person who is not entirely psychologically intact, and when a parent is this disturbed, that would have an effect on his ability to care for or be a parent to an adolescent."

Dr. Kaushal Sharma, an M.D. who interviewed Cinnamon prior to the trial, testified that the girl's reaction to the murder was one of "massive denial."

"A few times," he told the court, "she got up from the chair, wanted to leave the chair, wanted to leave the interview room. She told me that I was boring her. She told me that I had no business suggesting that her stepmother might be dead, told me that she did not really wish to discuss anything because there was nothing to discuss. So overall her attitude was very uncooperative, hostile and angry."

Dr. Sharma said there was no evidence to support the notion that Cinnamon was "unable to distinguish the difference between right and wrong." She had, he told the judge, no delusions, no hallucinations and no signs of being mentally ill.

After five days of testimony, a number of witnesses and few courtroom surprises, Cinnamon was found guilty of first-degree murder and sentenced to twenty-seven-years-to-life in the California Youth Authority near Ventura, up the coast from Malibu. If she served the first eleven years of her sentence without creating more trouble for the state, she would be released from CYA at twenty-five and her criminal record would be expunged. The case was closed.

PART TWO

IV

Ethel Bailey was born in 1931 in a sod house in Curtis, Nebraska, one of five children and the daughter of a farmer. In time she became a waitress in nearby North Platte and eventually married Richard Jurgens, who worked on the railroad. Jurgens fathered a number of children with Ethel, then abandoned his family. A while later Ethel met a man named Ralph Dalrymple, a cross-country trucker who parked his rig in North Platte and changed careers, finding a job as a cook in the restaurant Ethel was working in. Dalrymple called himself Ralph Bailey because of a previous run-in with the law. Ralph told Ethel that he was sterile, and she believed him until she got pregnant with twins. He fathered a number of children with the woman, including Alan, Linda and the baby of the family, Patti. In 1962 the Bailey family packed up their camper and headed west and south, moving back to Dalrymple's native California, stopping at Santa Ana in Orange County, one of the richest, fastest-growing and most changeable places on earth.

In the 1870s Santa Ana was the terminus for the Southern

Pacific Railroad. Fares were designed to move people west: one could travel from Kansas City to Los Angeles for a dollar. By 1875 the first citrus ranches had been planted in the area, known as the "Valley of the Smoke" because of its constant fires. In 1889 Orange County was created as a separate entity from Los Angeles County, and the orange groves were followed by fields of sugar beets, lima beans, celery, olives, walnuts, peanuts, grains and canneries. Santa Ana became the county seat in 1901. Twenty years later oil was discovered in Huntington Beach, during Prohibition illegal rum was run into Laguna Beach in big black ships and in World War II the farms began to give way to military installations and factories. Anaheim was a prisoner-of-war camp for Italians and Germans, while Japanese citizens were processed at the Santa Anita Race Track.

The great Orange County boom, which would include both the Bailey and the Brown families, did not really start until after the Second World War. One-tenth of all World War II veterans settled in California. Optimism and unlimited growth were articles of faith in California. And the faithful were right. From 1950 to 1963, Anaheim grew to nine times its original size. In 1956 Garden Grove was an unincorporated citrus center. In 1963 it had 104,727 residents. The civic motto for Irvine was "Another Day in Paradise," although paradise was getting crowded. Disneyland opened in 1955, the same year Orange County unveiled its first drive-in church. All of this development brought mega-freeways, mega-traffic jams and mega-dollars: Orange County has the thirtieth largest economy in the world. In 1990 it had 12,000 yachts and the median price for a home was $246,000. It has been called a millionaires' ghetto even though in some neighborhoods one can now see nearly as many homeless people on the streets as Mercedes. For decades Orange County has been the butt of jokes about the nouveaux riches—the county's real cultural center, the line goes, is the John Wayne Airport. A Ku Klux Klan outpost in the 1920s, Orange County's reputation for racial tolerance could be better yet it has absorbed wave after wave of new immigrants, the most recent being from Southeast Asia.

Like most people, the Baileys came west in search of more financial opportunities and a better life. Southern California is as much an idea as it is a piece of geography, and the core of that idea is that things move faster here, change is the only constant in the landscape and everyone can get rich. The towns have no boundaries, no centers, no separate and distinct identities, and everything flows into everything else. Fantasy, reality, competition, Disneyland, business, entertainment, murder, shopping centers, drive-by mortuaries, movement and commerce, psychological torture and amusement parks.

The region has been compared to the largest and wealthiest high school ever created, a high school from which no one ever graduates. New communities have jumped out of what recently were strawberry fields ("History," people say in Los Angeles, "is what you ate for breakfast"). Towns like Garden Grove seem almost finished and almost real, but not quite, the kind of place that is so undefined that one could do just about anything and get away with it.

People think about money rather differently in this environment, and that was especially true in the 1980s when everything got bigger, faster, more expensive, more crowded, and more uncontrolled. People's financial expectations rose higher and higher. Statistics will tell one that things got better—and worse. In those years the local economy grew by 90 percent while California's prison population doubled. In Southern California, as in many other places during the 1980s, one's notion of being rich or poor was set by where you lived: a family in Orange County earning $40,000 a year could qualify for low-income housing.

In such an atmosphere money not only talks, it dominates thought and planning and many conversations. Everybody has more money than he ever thought he would, but nobody has enough. How do you get more? How do you get it now? How do you get it without too much effort? How do you avoid paying taxes on it?

It's difficult to live in such a place and not be preoccupied with money, and doubly difficult to live amidst such wealth in grinding poverty.

In California, Ralph Dalrymple went back to driving a truck. One day his tractor trailer flipped over and caught on fire. The wreck left him with a tingling sensation in his spine and nightmares in which he saw himself stuck in the cab, slowly burning to death. He refused any physical or mental therapy and began to drink heavily. After he lost his job, his children say he became violent and irrationally demanding. If a dish wasn't properly washed, he dragged the culprit out of bed and made him redo not just the smudged glass but everything else in the rack. He yelled at the girls and he hit the boys. He once hit his step-son Rick so hard that thirty years later the man can hear only a fraction of what is said to him. After spending the money he had collected as a result of his trucking disaster, he vanished.

He left Ethel with eleven children, the youngest, Patti, age one, having arrived in 1968. Ethel went on welfare and found clothes for her family at church charities. There never were enough beds. Patti slept with her mother, sisters or brothers until she was ten. They ate cold cereal for breakfast, for lunch and sometimes for dinner. They supplemented the cereal with potatoes, a food that Patti still despises. Soda pop and Kool-Aid were fantasies to the children, luxuries their mother did not buy. There wasn't enough bread or milk in the house. "Her cigarettes and beer always came first," Patti says. A hamburger at McDonald's was a great culinary treat for the Baileys and a fishing trip to Bullhead City, Arizona, was a foreign vacation. Ethel smoked all day long and started drinking in the morning. Her hands shook, her head shook and at times all of her appeared to be shaking. She smoked hard and spoke in a husky voice. Despite all the years of alcohol and tobacco, she was an attractive woman who stood up straight and frequently squared her shoulders, looking out at the world as if she were mustering all of her courage and resolve to give life one more try. Most of the time, she looked overwhelmed.

When Patti was five, her family left Santa Ana and Orange County for Riverside, a community to the east of Los Angeles that has been nicknamed "The Devil's Anvil." Riverside is hot, flat and dusty, with a more working-class feel than Garden Grove. The air smells of rubber and fertilizer. Only the peaks of surrounding mountains are visible through the smog. The air has an aftertaste—metallic and chemical. The town has all the generic stucco houses, low-slung malls and quick-stop food marts found in the rest of Southern California, but lacks the Orange County aura of being upwardly mobile. "When you can't afford to live someplace else," one hears in Los Angeles, "you live in Riverside."

Arthur Brown came out of the Midwest and met his wife, Manuella, while he was in the Army. She was a cotton picker in Texas, he was a mechanic, and the two of them began a migration from the Panhandle to the Pacific. In 1952, in Phoenix, they had a son David, who spent a nomadic youth with them, wandering from Phoenix to Needles, California, to Bakersfield and then to Wilmington, California. As soon as David was old enough to drive he left them.

On his own he moved to Salt Lake City, back to Wilmington, to Long Beach, to Santa Fe Springs, California, to Anaheim, to Orange and finally, in the mid–1970s, to Riverside. Because of back troubles and high blood pressure, he never served in the military, and his career was as transient as he was. He claims to have labored in a pillow factory and for any number of high-tech computer businesses, but as he got older and filled out more employment applications, he changed his educational background and past work record to suit his current mood. One thing is indisputable: he changed jobs, cars, addresses, dogs and wives with great regularity.

His addresses tended to be on dead-end streets, streets with women's names, such as Lenora, June and Edith. He was a man without a past, or with a past that he'd fictionalized so many times that it had little bearing on reality.

Regardless of what he'd claimed he'd done, he knew that some people would believe and some wouldn't. He could work with those who did. He believed that he had something for everyone—it was usually money for men and some form of affection for women—the things that people thought they wanted the most.

At seventeen he married Brenda Sands, a teenager who was anxious to get away from her mother. At the time of the wedding, she was pregnant with Cinnamon. The marriage rattled along for several months until David told his wife that, because they had wed so young, he wasn't ready to settle down. He wanted to go hunting—"dear hunting," he joked—as in pursuing the other sex. Despite this, he wanted his wife to be absolutely faithful to him.

David was fanatically jealous: whenever Brenda went to the bathroom in a restaurant, he would wait outside the door for her, afraid that she might do something in the ladies' room. One night, after he told her that he was working late at the office, she found him in a restaurant talking with a young woman. When he returned home, she screamed and threw plates at him, but he did not fight back. He was, according to Brenda, terrified of any violence directed toward him. When the china had shattered and the angry words were spent, she decided to leave him. She was the last woman for many years to come who would say no to Brown. During the divorce proceedings and while fighting for custody of Cinnamon, Brenda thought that her husband was strange, but not really that strange.

"He didn't have money back then," she says. "When he got it, he also got some power and that changed him. He thought he could do anything."

In the early '70s Brown was living in Riverside with his second wife, Laurie Carpenter. Their house was on Randolph Street, two doors away from Ethel Bailey and her brood. Ethel's house was modest and stucco with an aging asphalt roof and a weathered split-rail fence. The only landscaping was a lone mulberry tree that grew in the front yard and bore no fruit. Brown's home was larger and his yard had a mulberry, a palm tree and a few rose bushes. The neighborhood is in a particularly flat part of town and in summertime heat waves bounce off the pavement and the asphalt roofs, making the wind even drier. Riverside feels more like a Midwestern industrial city than a part of Southern California—too far away from Los Angeles to be glamorous and too parched to be lush.

When Brown met the Bailey girls—Pam was thirteen, Linda was eleven and Patti was five—he began inviting them to his home. He told them that he was suffering from cancer of the colon and did not have long to live; his wife was gone at work all day and he could use some help around the house. One reason Ethel let her girls make the visit was that Brown was a dying man. Another reason was that her neighbor was very generous, taking the girls shopping and buying them clothes, bringing the family a turkey at Thanksgiving or a ham at Christmas, giving the children gifts that Ethel herself could not possibly afford.

Ethel had only known men who took from her and left, hurtful men. Brown could be gentle. He could be funny. Some people found him charming. There was something about him that certain women found seductive. It was not his looks, they said, and it was not really his personality. It was that he took an interest in them and bought them things, and when he wanted to make someone feel special, he could do that. He could pay attention.

Rick Bailey's wife, Mary, was a close observer of both the Brown and the Bailey households. She fits well into the Bailey clan, but because she is not a blood relative, she is something of an outsider and willing to take a hard look at things. When Mary was seven she wanted to know if her pajamas were fireproof, so she lit them: they were. Mary wears a broad scar below her throat.

She has a childlike happy smile, leads with her emotions and is the first to admit that she likes to talk. She has a good eye and a sharp tongue, and her favorite description of herself is that she is a "poor white woman who has to work."

"It was amazing to me," she says, "that Ethel couldn't see what was going on from the start. First David dated

Pam and then Linda. I guess Ethel thought he was going to croak. Ethel just went for the money. Money and alcohol are the things in her life.

"When Linda's dad was around he yelled at her a lot. Every time he yelled, she just shook, so when David came along I guess he looked pretty good to her. He wrote her mushy cards. He sent her flowers and I thought, How neat, he can't be all bad. He was always soft-spoken and he could work you into a situation. Linda fell madly in love with David. It was like your first love. She was fourteen."

Linda was headstrong and, according to Mary, had a "drop-dead body" even as a teenager. It wasn't long before Brown, who was in his mid-twenties, divorced his second wife and began discussing marriage with the girl. At sixteen Linda moved out of her home and into Rick and Mary Bailey's, where she had the freedom to sneak off and see her lover. Her brother and his outspoken wife didn't approve of the liaison, but like the rest of the family, they were still waiting for Brown to die. Mary encouraged Linda to use birth control and told her to slow down, but when she was seventeen, Linda went to Las Vegas for a quick wedding in the desert.

"That," Mary says, "was a shock."

The marriage lasted one month and twenty-four days before Brown announced that he no longer wanted Linda, and she returned home to her mother's.

"After the divorce," Mary says, "she dropped from one hundred and twenty pounds to ninety-eight pounds."

Brown left Riverside and was married again in Las Vegas in May of 1980. That didn't last long either. His emotional life might have been shaky, but his career was starting to move forward. In the '70s he'd earned a degree from Control Data Institute, where he was trained as a computer technician, and by 1978 he was working at Sperry Univac in Irvine. The following year he went to ConRac Airport Systems in Monrovia and after that to Memorex in Fullerton, where he stayed until 1981. While at these various jobs, he tested computer disk drives to see if they worked, he repaired them if they didn't, and in the meantime he came up with an ingenious plan for earning money, lots of money, a plan that would also allow him to emerge as a very unlikely hero in this high-tech field.

As computer technology spread throughout the United States in the late '70s and early '80s, people who used the sophisticated equipment lived in terror of the crashing disk: if a computer suddenly "went down" and suffered a total and mysterious inability to function, all of the data stored on its disks could be lost. Brown either discovered or borrowed an idea that was ripe for exploitation. If one were simply to take these disks, wash them with a certain kind of liquid and remove from the surface the dust or dirt that was causing the problem, it might then be possible to retrieve the data. Brown kept the liquid a secret and enjoyed building up the complexity and mystique of his service. The night his wife was murdered he told Fred McLean that "only two people in the world know the secret formula for Coca-Cola syrup" and only two people knew the secret of his business—Linda and himself.

In 1979, after Brown was instrumental in recovering the data that everyone feared was lost in the MGM Grand Hotel fire in Las Vegas, he was suddenly in demand. As the news of his operation spread throughout the relatively small high-tech community, he earned a reputation, garnered a mention in *Computerworld* magazine and received letters of commendation from Northorp, Rockwell International and the Air Force. He also began to make good money.

The most intriguing part of his business was that he often could not do anything helpful with the disks. He told customers up front that the odds were long and his prices were high but they had nothing to lose. If they employed him and were able to recover their data, everyone would benefit and his service would be worth the cost. If he tried but failed to succeed, they could pass the expense along to their insurance company, which would take the loss. Brown was one of the first people, if not the first person, in the country to come up with this strategy, and he was a busy man. His service was called DataRecovery, and it was associated with a larger computer outfit in Long Beach named Randomex. He worked out of an office at the rear of the Randomex building on a lot surrounded by pumping oil wells.

"I met David in the mid-seventies," says Bill Hersey, an electronics engineer for Randomex. "I thought he told a lot of good stories. When you're a technical person like myself, you know when a guy is telling the truth or not telling the truth. It was easy to figure out where he was coming from, but he did what he did and he made a lot of money at it, so I guess that makes him a success.

" 'Computer' is the most overused word I've ever heard. You can tell people a little bit about computers and they think you're a whiz. If you went out and charged someone fifteen thousand dollars a day to clean something, you could make a lot of money, right? And at that time there was no one else who could provide the service. And if he failed to recover it, he still got paid. David was at the right place at the right time. The computer business was so competitive then, and if you didn't offer the customer a warranty, they had to get repair service elsewhere. And Dave was there."

Brown liked to tell people that he worked closely with the Pentagon and had a high-security clearance with the defense industry, that the American government had called him in to recover lost data from the 1986 Challenger shuttle disaster and that world leaders telephoned him when their computers were on the fritz. He was given to exaggeration, but without question his income did begin to rise. In 1981 his reported earnings from the business were $11,255. In 1982 they were $98,143. In 1983 he made $124,905 from DataRecovery. In 1984 the figure jumped to $171,141. In 1985 he earned $114,081 and in 1986 he reported $134,083. He didn't like to pay taxes and the federal government filed liens against him with some regularity. The amount of money that he might have made and not reported is unknown, although Brown would later tell people that he had invested heavily in rare coins and jewelry and had $500,000 or one million dollars or two million dollars or three million dollars buried in the California desert.

In 1982 he married Linda Bailey again, his fifth wedding in just over a decade. In the years since her first marriage,

Linda had had another suitor, and when she decided to remarry Brown, her sisters wondered why she would leave another man and return to David, who had dumped her so quickly and unceremoniously after their nuptials. She explained to them that Brown was going somewhere and the other contender wasn't.

After David and Linda were wed for the second time, Brown suggested that Patti, who was now fourteen, come live with the couple. It would be good for everybody.

There were unpleasant rumors that Patti was having a difficult time at home, where she was constantly squabbling with her mother and fending off the advances of one of her brothers. She needed a father figure, a male presence with authority, someone to help her. Brown offered to play that role and he had the financial resources. Ethel, for her part, was ready to listen. She'd lately been thinking about opening a gardening business, a longtime dream of hers, and if Brown was willing to part with $5,000, she was willing to part with her youngest child.

Patti was soon living with her sister and brother-in-law. The threesome—and occasionally Cinnamon—began another series of moves that scattered them all over Southern California: Anaheim, Yorba Linda, Brea, Yucca Valley and eventually the Ocean Breeze address.

Ethel's gardening business never took off.

In 1983 Linda, David and Patti were living in Yucca Valley, a small desert community about an hour from Palm Springs. Yucca Valley borders the Joshua Tree National Monument, and the surrounding landscape is spare, dry, eerie and oddly powerful. The Joshua tree got its name because its extended branches evoked the outstretched arms of the prophet Joshua. Its leaves are shaped like swords and its trunk, curling up from the desert floor, conjures up the Old Testament and the harsh wages of sin. At night the sky over Yucca Valley is spectacularly clear and full of stars, and countless pilgrims to this part of California have reportedly had spiritual or otherworldly experiences. The area has been the site of many New Age retreats. When it's dark outside and the wind howls off the desert, becoming louder and more insistent with each blast, when the night blows dust into the sides of buildings, shaking the walls and squeaking the rafters, it is possible to believe that many strange forces are alive in the air.

Not everyone comes to the desert for spiritual growth. Some people come to kick up a little dust on dirt bikes, cutting trails in the earth and dodging rocks. The Brown family liked to ride all-terrain vehicles through the heat, racing one another and occasionally smashing up. It was around Yucca Valley that Brown also hid some of his alleged earnings. This is not to suggest that the man was totally ignorant of the metaphysical happenings taking place in his new environment.

David was quick to pick up New Age lingo as it filtered into the language in the mid-'80s and, on occasion, he liked to tell women that he had known them in past lives and they were now soulmates. He told Patti that he was in communication with a being from another planet who was helping him write a science fiction novel and giving him instructions on how to save the earth.

Linda herself was drawn to psychics. Two of them told her that she would die young. This information frightened her and made her more agreeable when her husband wanted to take out several life insurance policies on her.

Brown was closest to Linda, Patti, Cinnamon and his parents—the people who paid attention to him when he felt sick. He wasn't close to his brothers or sisters or to the Baileys, and he didn't really trust his in-laws. The Baileys were like most families, only more so. They were an unpredictable bunch and a little scary. The females tended to be critical of him and the males were excitable. The men were thin, wiry and well-muscled. They weren't big but appeared to be wound awfully tight. They had the facial markings of men who had been in a number of fights and won their share. If you crossed one of them, several of the brothers might jump in a truck, drive out to Yucca Valley and lose their collective temper.

Larry, the family members agreed, was probably the most

volatile. Not only did he threaten Brown's life after the murder, but there was speculation all along that he might have had something to do with Linda's death. He was in jail the day she was killed but had been released a few hours before the shooting. He'd asked his sister to bail him out and when she refused, he was hot.

David had been afraid of Larry for a long time. As he'd readily admitted to the police, he was a coward, afraid of his own backyard at night. In his own way, he was a sensitive man. One could see that in his short pale soft hands, which appeared to have never known manual labor. One could see it in his sad, frightened eyes. One could see it in the way he turned his head, looking uncomfortably over his shoulder, and in his short determined stride, as if something were chasing him. He wanted protection. He preferred the company of women.

Brown didn't really have any adult friends, although he'd enjoyed playing video games with Alan Bailey. He wasn't the kind of man who went to a bar and chatted over a drink. He didn't care much for alcohol or drugs and had an oddly puritanical streak when it came to such things. His one vice, he told people, was the Marlboros or Camels he smoked all day long. His first choice was to stay at home with his family; family, he always said, was most important to him. He'd buy $400 worth of Perrier at once (and $200 worth of lottery tickets), then sit at home and sip the elegant mineral water, surrounding himself with his comic books, his video library and his closest relatives.

At home he could turn up the heat to where he wanted it, sometimes near eighty, thinking that heat might improve his health. "A sick man," was often how he described himself. He was comfortable at home, telling the girls to fetch his meals—he was partial to Spam and double-fudge cookies—or help him slip on his socks and shoes or directing them in their household chores. He could do what he wanted around the house. If he didn't feel like bathing for several days, he didn't bathe, and if his hair got dirty, he put baby powder in it. He was afraid to bathe because he was afraid of catching a cold, and he was serious about having clean white washcloths. After using a cloth once, he expected it to be washed immediately so he could use it again. If he wanted to spend the whole day in his pajamas watching television or talking on the phone or watching one of the many violent movies that were part of his library, that's what he did. The girls didn't seem to mind any of this, or didn't say anything if they did. Teenagers were much easier to talk to than adults and were thrilled when you spent money on them. He liked driving Cinnamon and Patti to the beach, the mall, the chiropractor's office, or to pick up another fast-food meal at Round Table Pizza or Del Taco.

At home Brown was known as something of a joker. When he was in a good mood and his health wasn't falling apart, he enjoyed making people laugh. He liked telling funny stories and making biting remarks about Hispanics, remarks that were supposed to be humorous. He couldn't stand Hispanics—they were the ethnic group that bothered him the most. There were too many of them—they were everywhere in Southern California. Whenever someone pointed out to Brown that his mother was Hispanic and that he himself bore some resemblance to her, he angrily denied it. She wasn't Hispanic and neither was he. They were of Spanish blood, and that was a completely different thing. People of Spanish descent were more refined than the Hispanics who were overrunning California. Sometimes, when Brown was alone with the girls and they were riding on the freeway or stuck in a traffic jam, he said that his wife was no longer the woman he'd married—she'd changed for the worse—and made jokes about killing her.

"Linda's got PMS," he would say. "Let's run over her."

V

Following Linda's funeral, Brown and Patti had to get away from the murder home, and their next stop was at a modest house on Breckenridge in the town of Orange, a neighborhood that lies in the shadow of Summitridge. Brown quickly made plans to move to Summitridge, by far the poshest address he'd ever had. A winding road carries one up to Summitridge, located in the Anaheim Hills and rising above most of the urban sprawl in this part of Orange County. With its manicured hedges, spotless streets and traditional-looking homes, with its attempt to appear much older than it is and with the quiet removed atmosphere that such a place strives for, Summitridge is distinctly upper middle class. The home Brown purchased in August of 1985 was nouveau-Tudor, with shakes on the roof, a triple garage and leaded stained glass in the windows. The mailbox sat on a stone column. In the backyard were a swimming pool, a hot tub, fragrant eucalyptuses and two large decks. Atop the house stood a tower, as if the new residence were indeed one man's castle.

David and Patti sent no photographs of their new home to the prisoner near Ventura. After Cinnamon was taken to the California Youth Authority in September of 1985, her father visited her with some regularity, usually telling her that Patti was going to move out soon, but as time passed these trips began to taper off. Cinnamon knew about their house on Breckenridge, but Brown told her almost nothing about the Summitridge address, except to say that it was in a shoddy neighborhood, a step down from Ocean Breeze. He told his daughter that he didn't want her calling his new home, so he only gave her the number of his answering service. When she asked why, he said that he was involved in top-secret government work and had to maintain the highest standards of security. He also let it be known that he didn't want Patti's relatives casually dropping in, so for months Ethel and the rest of the Baileys stayed away from Breckenridge and then Summitridge. The clan tried to put Linda's death behind them and go on with their lives, but it was impossible to forget or understand the crime fully. The wound was too raw and no one in the family was really satisfied with what had come out at the trial.

"We had a lot of arguments back then," Rick Bailey recalled a few years later. "This family fought a lot about what went on in that house the night Linda died. It pretty much tore us apart."

The detectives who had been assigned the case still had a few questions in their minds about the killing, especially Jay Newell. Although the murder was legally resolved, Newell had quietly and persistently stayed with it, tracking the activities of the transient Mr. Brown, paying attention to his move to Breckenridge and his purchase of the Summitridge home. How much did the house cost? How was it paid for? Where did the money come from? The detective did some research into the life insurance that Brown claimed to have had on his wife at the time of the shooting and discovered that there hadn't been one small policy on Linda, as David had once stated to Fred McLean, but four separate policies, and they weren't that small either, not after they were added together. Especially since a couple of them paid off double for an "accidental death." These benefits were also untaxable, which gave them another boost. Newell checked Brown's bank account and learned that it had contained $100,000 before the murder and $300,000 several months later. There was a pattern to these events, but Newell could do nothing with this information unless someone was willing to help him. And so far, no one was.

At the coed CYA compound on the outskirts of Ventura, Cinnamon was doing well in every area of rehabilitation but one. She was a far better student in the facility's school than she'd ever been when living with her mother or father and was on a pace to graduate ahead of schedule. She had a part-time job and was saving a little money. David had given her free rein with his Visa card and she'd tested the limits of his credit, ordering all kinds of things to be sent to her in care of CYA. She sang in the prison's church choir and had a boyfriend.

Cinnamon got along well with teenagers and adults; people liked her soft smiling pretty face, her long cherry-blond hair, her good manners and her sharp wit, which can be particularly useful in jail. Humor lets other inmates know that you're hip and bright, but it can also keep people at a distance. Certain areas were off limits with Cinnamon and she had a way of letting folks know that. The only person she spoke to about her past was Ronnie Song, her boyfriend, and she once told him that she was thinking of going to the authorities and telling them what she knew about the murder of her stepmother.

Life at CYA was not unbearable. The compound, located next to lemon groves and artichoke farms, has the feel of a rural retreat. No massive brick walls surround it, the grounds are spacious and sunny, there are softball diamonds, basketball courts and a weight-lifting pad; the outdoor visiting area is a pleasant side lawn with picnic tables and a little shade. CYA guards are unarmed and escape attempts are common but usually fail (on top of the perimeter fence are large coils of barbed wire). Fistfights break out all the time—the boys tend to punch each other, while the girls swing at the authorities. When the inmates aren't tussling, attending school or working, they are locked in private rooms within low-slung red brick "cottages." The sexes are segregated but manage to connect at the slightest opportunity. Birth control is not provided and girls have been known to get pregnant in the CYA rest rooms. The prophylactic of choice is often bubble gum.

No one at CYA had any problems with Cinnamon, except the parole board. A key part of rehabilitation, in the eyes of the board, was confronting one's crime, talking about what had happened and why. They wanted the inmates to recognize their responsibility for committing an offense and to show some sense of guilt. Cinnamon had already expressed remorse but refused to discuss the murder. The board tried cajoling her, tried offering her the hope of an earlier release date, tried provoking her into talking—tried everything before finally telling her that she had no chance of leaving CYA before age twenty-five unless she was willing to open up about her case. A year went by and she said nothing. Then another. Then part of another. Every time she came before the board members for a review she thought about their request, and every time she refused, still believing, in a remote corner of herself, that something or someone within her family might help her out.

Nothing had made her talk—not the psychiatric treatment she'd received since her arrest or the demands of the parole board or the probings of the detectives or her lawyer—but there were other forces working on Cinnamon, forces that were more powerful and subtle than the attorney, the cops, the shrinks and the board. Only one predictable thing goes on inside a prison: people get older. The young girl was growing up, and with each month at the compound she moved further away from the people she'd been raised by and the daily life inside the Brown household. Some observers might have said that she was changing or maturing, coming of age on her own. Others might have said that she was starting to crack.

Occasionally when David visited the CYA, Arthur Brown went along with him and had a few moments to speak with Cinnamon alone. Arthur was a short round man who had been a laborer for most of his life, not the kind of person who immediately comes to mind when people think of the money and glamour associated with Southern California. He was quiet, unassuming and small. He didn't socialize much outside of his family, and like his son David, he was most comfortable smoking his cigarettes, watching TV and joking with his family. In recent years he'd done some work for David in his computer business and was impressed with his son's ability to make money so effortlessly. It was far better than sweating eight hours a day for low wages for a stranger. Arthur had never been this close to financial success before and he knew just how hard it could be to earn a dollar. He admired David's business acumen. At the same time, he was an emotional man. He was a family man with family feelings, and those feelings had grown more complicated since Linda's death. He'd cried at her funeral, more than his son had done. It disturbed Arthur that his granddaughter was spending her adolescence in prison, cut off from her friends, her freedom and the normal experience of being a teenager. It bothered him even more than one might have expected. He told Cinnamon that she didn't belong in prison and someone else did. After thinking about that, she went to her parole officer, O. J. Harkey, and told him that she was ready to talk.

On the fifth of January, 1987, nearly two years after the murder, the Orange County District Attorney's office received a letter from Harkey. The letter stated that because of some inconsistencies the parole board had uncovered on December 18, 1986, in their last review of Cinnamon's case, they wanted the D.A's office to interview Arthur Brown. The board had discovered that Cinnamon's grandfather had, during a telephone conversation, told her that he knew who killed Linda. "The Youthful Offender Parole Board of the State of California," the letter concluded, "will review this case again in approximately ninety days. They would greatly appreciate any information from the District Attorney's Office that could be utilized in the decision-making process in this case. The Board has stated that 'Much evidence suggests that Cinnamon might not be responsible for this crime.' "

On January 28, 1987, Jay Newell, posing as real estate

agent Jerry Walker, went to the Brown residence on Summitridge. He waited until Arthur came outside and approached him, quickly dropping the pretense of being a salesman and asking about the murder. The grandfather wanted to talk but was nervous, looking around and noticing that, at least for the moment, his son was inside the house and out of earshot. Arthur said that he'd spoken to Cinnamon and told her that he was certain "who planned the whole thing." He mentioned to Newell a conflict between Linda and Patti and another quarrel between Linda, Alan Bailey and David over docking Alan's pay because he came to work late. Arthur told the detective that he would "bet his life" that Cinnamon wasn't in on the killing alone. Arthur went on to say that he had heard Patti say she had listened to Linda telling someone how she was going to do away with David, so that she could take over his business. He added that Patti had sworn she'd get rid of Linda before she'd let that happen.

"If I push my neck out too far," he said, "I'll lose my son and my granddaughter, plus another granddaughter."

Newell wanted to know exactly what he meant by those words, but before he could answer, David came outside and interrupted them. He asked Newell what he was doing at the house and asked a few more questions to determine if the man was in fact in real estate. Evidently, Newell's answers were good enough and he left quickly.

Three weeks later, on February 20, Newell, Fred McLean and Dick Fredrickson, a deputy district attorney for Orange County, went to the CYA facility to visit O. J. Harkey, but they did not speak to Cinnamon. On March 4 Fredrickson wrote to Harkey and stated that, based upon Newell's interview with Arthur Brown, the detectives had concluded that the grandfather "believes that Cinnamon's stepsister was somehow involved in the killing of Linda Brown. It is that belief that Mr. Brown says he relayed to Cinnamon. Mr. Brown told us that he has no evidence to support that belief.

"It is no surprise that the grandfather has suspicions of other involvement in the killing of Linda Brown. Every person who has more than a passing knowledge of the case is struck by the inconsistencies and implausibilities in the stories of the father and the stepsister which suggest that either one or both were involved. However, in none of those theories is Cinnamon Brown innocent. The physical evidence and her relatively detailed account of the killing and her activities [statements] after the killing to two separate persons (the investigating detective, Sgt. Fred McLean, and, later, to an examining doctor, Kim Hicks) preclude her not being involved.

"Cinnamon's consistent denial of memory of the significant facts is as implausible as other parts of this case. It is significant that Cinnamon lost her memory of the events surrounding the killing only after talking to her attorney for the first time, which was only one day after her statements to the aforementioned doctor. The next day the doctor in discussing the matter again with Cinnamon was given the 'I don't remember' position from which Cinnamon since steadfastly refused to deviate.

"It is clear that Cinnamon either was the sole actor in the killing or was acting as part of a conspiracy. Under the current state of the evidence, however, Cinnamon's recollection is the key to any ultimate resolution of the possible involvement of others. We do not, however, regard the case as closed, but are continuing with our investigation as time and manpower permit."

Months passed and little changed. Cinnamon went before the board again and revealed nothing, the investigators turned their attention to other matters, David and Patti stayed on in the house on Summitridge and Arthur Brown talked to his granddaughter on the phone, letting things slip in his conversations with Cinnamon, things he had concealed from her in the past, things she had no other way of learning. Her grandfather said that Patti had not moved away from the new house, as Cinnamon had frequently been told she would, but still lived with David. Arthur mentioned that the Summitridge home was large, impressive and expensive, much nicer than the Ocean Breeze residence and not at all the kind of place Cinnamon had been led to believe it was.

David and Patti sometimes neglected Krystal, Arthur said, and this piece of information landed especially hard. Although she rarely saw the baby anymore, Cinnamon still felt close to Krystal and protective of her.

In addition to what Cinnamon learned from her grandfather, several other things began to erode her silence. In January of 1988 she was assigned a new parole officer, Carlos Rodriguez, who developed a good rapport with the teenager and told her that it was time to speak out. Cinnamon's boyfriend at CYA, Ronnie Song, was also nearing the end of his sentence. He was about to walk out of the place and she now had a stronger reason than ever to attempt to free herself: she wanted to be with him. The third thing was connected to a piece of news Cinnamon had known about for some time, but it took months for her to feel its full impact. Early in 1987 Patti had become pregnant, and the word that filtered up to CYA was that the father was someone named Doug who had run off before Heather was born on September 29.

Cinnamon was no longer fourteen, no longer a naive child isolated within the Brown family. On her own, sitting in prison and waiting for her best friend to leave her behind, she couldn't help wondering who Heather's father really was and how that was going to affect her chances of anyone ever coming forward on her behalf. More than anyone else, it was her father who had been promising, ever since her arrest and conviction, to help get her out of this mess. It was finally sinking in that that was not going to happen. Cinnamon was finally realizing that she was all alone.

There was another piece of information that would have interested Cinnamon, but no one in her family bothered to pass it along because no one but David and Patti knew about it: on July 1, 1986, they'd flown to Las Vegas, stayed at Caesar's Palace and gotten married at the "We've Only Just Begun" chapel to the strains of "Only You." The small chapel features a heart-shaped backdrop, in front of which people are joined in matrimony, and a lobby where happy couples can buy instant wedding kits with two champagne glasses, a cake knife and garters.

Two years after the wedding, on July 3, 1988, Cinnamon turned eighteen and, in a legal sense, became an adult. She no longer had to consult with anyone before speaking to the authorities. She asked for a meeting with Carlos Rodriguez and on July 19 he contacted Jay Newell. Three years after her conviction, Cinnamon was finally ready to open up. She had a lot to say.

VI

It was a three-way call between the D.A.'s investigator, Jay Newell, Deputy District Attorney Fredrickson and Cinnamon. At first Cinnamon thought that Fredrickson might be under the control of her father, but after the men assured her that he was not, she agreed to speak with him. The phone connection was not perfect and at times it seemed that everyone was having difficulty hearing and responding to what had been said, but Cinnamon began to tell her story.

"Will I be protected or will my father be listening to this?" Cinnamon asked.

"Will who be listening?" Newell said.

"My father."

"Oh, definitely not."

"Okay. I realized that he was in the wrong for what he did and I was too young to realize it. And I know now it is time for him to take the responsibility for the crime that takes place. That's basically what I am trying to come about here, and I was a little bit involved because I knew what was going to happen, but I didn't actually do the murder."

"Well," Newell said, "why don't you just, in your own words, tell me what you are talking about. Tell me what took place that you are saying [about] his involvement."

She indicated to the men that she would prefer to do this in person, but Newell was reluctant to do that unless Cinnamon was willing to tell the whole story. The girl spoke hestitantly.

My father . . . said that Linda was going to be killing him—something for insurance or something of the sort— her and her twin brother. And he said, 'We have to do something about it unless you want daddy dead.' And I said, 'Well, what is it that you want me to do?' And he said, 'Well, we are going to have to think of a way to get rid of her, or I am going to have to leave town.' And I said, 'Well, I don't want you to leave town.' And he said, 'Well, then, you have to help me then . . .'

"So we went for several drives with Patricia to discuss the ways they could dispose of Linda. One day we went shopping with Linda. Linda had a small child. She had taken her out of the car to change her. I was walking around the store, and I had seen Patricia and my father kissing."

"Uh-huh." It was what Newell usually said when he wanted someone to keep talking.

"And I was scared. I turned—I didn't know how to react and I took off in the store. My father had chased me and he said pretend like I didn't see that . . ."

"Uh-huh."

"So I agreed with him because I thought he was in the right, and I accepted it, and I didn't tell Linda what had happened. Well, later, things started getting worse. They would take off together, him and Patricia, and sometimes I'd go with them like to banks and stuff to cash checks . . . We would be gone for hours."

"Uh-huh."

"Well, I hear them discussing about ways they wanted to get rid of Linda. And Patricia suggested that we would throw her out of the van when we are driving down the freeway to make it look like an accident—the door wasn't shut all the way. She suggested hitting her over the head to knock her out, just different ways that they could get her out of the way. And I was listening, but I wasn't really participating at the time. I was just listening for what they had to say. I had told my mother about part of it. What I knew, my father told me not to tell anybody, but I told my mother anyway . . . Also my grandfather was in the van at the time, too, so he heard what we were talking about. He could probably verify that with you."

"Uh-huh."

As Cinnamon described it to the men, during one of these discussions her father had said that the killing needed to take place soon, and on the actual night of the murder he told her to go get the note he had made her write a few days earlier.

"I wrote it," she said, "and I kept it inside of my trailer. And I was staying inside because I wasn't feeling too good on that night. Well, that night my father came and woke me up and Patricia, and told me it had to be done tonight. And he told me to get out of bed and go outside after he had given me some pills. He had went into Linda's room and he had brought out some pills to me in the kitchen . . .

"And he said to take these to make it look like I tried to kill myself and be sorry for what was going to be done. So I took them and he told me to go outside. So I went outside and he says go back there. So I went back toward the doghouse and I stayed there. And I heard a gunshot. At first I wasn't sure it was a gunshot. I was kind of scared. And then I heard two more and almost immediately after each other. And then I knew it was a gunshot and I stayed back there. And I was scared and I was shaking. And there was, I think, there was about three dogs back there with me. Then I guess it was early morning. I heard the police come out there. My father said make sure that I made them think that I did it so that he wouldn't get in trouble, because he would get more time than I would. But I know he wasn't in the house, because when I went outside I heard him leave the house and take off in the car. I know Patricia was in the house along with the baby and I wasn't really thinking about the baby at that time because I was too nervous, but the baby stayed in the house."

"Uh-huh . . ."

"And when I was going to court and when I was in the hospital, my father told me not to say anything, just to keep my mouth shut. And if they don't think I did it, say yes. Then later he told me not to say anything at all. And I did what he told me because I trusted him and I thought he was right at the time."

"Now," the detective said, "what about the gun that was used? Where did—where did that come from?"

"I know that belonged to Linda because they told me afterwards. My father had got it from his room and Patti had wiped it off with a towel in her room. And I asked her what she was going to do with it. And she said, 'Be quiet.' And then my father came back into the room and after he went and got the pills. And I took them. He told me to go outside and I did and he told—"

"Did they ever have you take the gun somewhere?"

"They had me carry the gun out—this was a day or a couple of days before that. I remember, because they were going up to the mountains with my grandpa."

"Yeah."

"I carried them to the van. I can't remember if it was that particular gun I carried or not because there was a couple of them. There was rifles as well as handguns."

"Uh-huh."

"I'm not sure if that particular one was the one I took with me."

"Okay. Have you had any communication with your dad lately?"

"I believe I talked to him about four weeks ago. I asked him to send me a few things that I needed. That's the only reason I really talk with my father."

"Have you ever talked to your dad specifically about what he asked you to do that night and you going to jail for it?"

"Well, yes. I tried to talk to him about it but he—I don't know—he says, 'You will be out soon.' But that's basically all he said. He doesn't talk about what has happened."

"Do you call him on the phone at all or does he call you on the phone?"

"Well, he can't call me, so I call him sometimes and I check on my little sister and my grandparents and, like, I ask them to send me little things that I need."

"On the phone do you ever talk about the shooting of Linda at all?"

"No, he doesn't discuss it with me over the phone at all or up at visiting for some reason. He does not talk about it at all, and when I bring it up he pretends I didn't even say anything."

"How about Patti? Do you talk to her about it?"

"No. Patti does not come to visit me at all."

"What about on the phone? Do you ever talk to her on the phone?"

"She picked up the phone [and said], 'I love you and I miss you.' And I just say, 'Get my father on the phone.' I don't communicate with her at all."

"Okay. And are you willing to give us a formal statement about this and discuss what can or can't be done to open up the investigation?"

"I can probably help you if you think it would, if you think this is maybe going to help me, because I don't want to endanger myself."

"Yeah."

"I don't want to endanger myself with my father."

"Are you afraid of him, or what do you mean?"

"Yeah, I'm afraid of him. To me he is very powerful and he frightens me."

"But there is going to have to be maybe some other things done to—in opening up the investigation. I want to know if you are going to cooperate with us in that. If so, we will come up and sit down and discuss it . . ."

"Will I get any benefit out of doing this, or will I just be in the same place I am but in more danger?"

"I can't say that. I can't. I can't make you any promises like that because I don't know what it is that you are going to lead us into."

"Okay."

"And I can't—our office doesn't make those type of promises."

"Okay. I understand if I give a formal statement . . . will I be able to go back to court with this?"

"We wouldn't go back to court unless it was good enough. We will put it that way. We wouldn't create a wall of movement that wasn't going to do anything."

"Meanwhile, this is going to be kept confidential from my father, right?"

"Pardon me?" Newell said.

"This will be kept confidential from my father, right?"

"It will be as long as it is under investigation. It definitely will be, yes."

"Okay. And will I be under protection if it does end up back in court?"

"If it does go to a point where you are in jeopardy, yes, your safety will be one of our main concerns, same as any other witness or any other person that is testifying in a case for the prosecution."

Fredrickson interjected and told Cinnamon that he wanted to ask her two questions: "Did you mean to say that your father had already left the house before Linda was shot?"

"My father, when he had told me to go outside, I heard him leave the house and he took off in the car."

"And it was after that that you heard the shot?"

"It was after that that I had heard the shot."

"At any time that night had you handled that gun at all?"

"Not that I can recall, unless I picked it up to hand it to somebody, but I can't really remember. I can't remember whether I picked it up or not, especially that particular gun because my father had many in the house . . ."

"So what you are saying is that your—you did see your father get in a car and leave, or did you just hear him?"

"I heard him. I didn't see him."

"How do you know who it was? What I'm trying to figure out is how do you know it was he that got in the car and left? There were other adults there. I guess Patti was there too."

"Patti doesn't know how to drive, or she didn't know."

"Oh, she didn't?"

"No. Only Linda and my father knew."

"Oh, I see."

"And the car that he was driving—Linda didn't drive that car. It was—he had the Ranchero and it made a lot of noise."

"So that was the car that left?"

"Right."

"Okay."

Cinnamon asked Fredrickson, "Did you know that Patricia had a baby?"

"Oh, I know that, yes."

"Do you know that it belongs to my father?"

"Yes, I know that. I know . . . most things about them, where they are living and what they are doing and—"

"Well, my father doesn't let me know where he lives."

"Okay. Well, we all know that."

"Well, I hope you guys can help me because I feel that it is about time they take the responsibility for what was done."

"Okay. Well, we need to come up there and do this in person and get some real detail . . . and in the meantime, this is what I want you to do. As you think back about what happened, jot down some notes to yourself as to, you know, how you remember these things."

"Okay."

"All right?"

"Okay."

"And then we will make arrangements to come up and talk to you in person."

"Okay. Will you tell me in advance when you are coming up?"

"Definitely."

"Because I have a job now and I work a lot."

"Okay. But nothing—just treat your father and everyone else as you did before. If you call them periodically, then do the same thing."

"Carry on the same?"

"Yeah."

"What about my mother? Is is okay if I discuss with her what we talked about?"

"No. Don't talk to her about any of this."

"Don't talk to anybody about this?"

"No, not your mother either."

"Okay."

"She has been calling me, as a matter of fact," the attorney said. "I think she has probably told you that."

"Yes, she told me she has been trying to get ahold of you."

"Okay. I wouldn't even confirm with her that you have talked to us so far, okay?"

"All right. I'll keep it to myself."

"Okay," Fredrickson said. "Put Mr. Rodriguez back on."

Before Cinnamon gave the phone to her parole officer, Newell got back on the line.

"Thank you very much for your time," Cinnamon told the detective. "Bye-bye."

"Bye," Newell said.

VII

In the summer of 1988, while Cinnamon was talking with the two men from the district attorney's office, Newell and Fredrickson, Patti was considering leaving her husband. For years she'd thought about getting away from Brown, but only once, when she was fifteen and her sister was still alive, had she briefly returned to Victorville to live with her mother. She'd gone because Linda, who suspected many things but never directly confronted Patti with any of them, insisted that she move out. Brown let her leave, but after a few days he called and said that if she did not come back immediately, he would divorce his wife and break up the family. Patti returned and Linda never again demanded that she go.

Now Patti was his spouse and could not easily run away. She'd had mixed feelings about marrying Brown until he informed her that his health was failing again, he didn't have long to live and he didn't want to die without knowing that someone would always be there for Krystal. She couldn't let Krystal down, could she? . . . The little girl needed Patti . . . Everyone needed a mother . . . Patti had responsibilities to other people, especially to someone who had given her a home and a new life away from her mother

. . . If he died and Krystal had no family, she would be put in a foster home . . . What would happen to her then? . . . Brown also explained to the young woman that spouses were legally protected from having to testify against each other. If things got sticky in the future, marriage would ensure that they would never turn on one another. He made a persuasive argument, probably more persuasive than was necessary. After Linda's funeral, Patti felt that the very least she owed her dead sister was to take good care of Krystal.

And even if Patti could break away, where would she go? Not long before the murder, Brown had insisted that she drop out of high school so she and Linda could be tutored at home. He didn't like the idea of Patti associating with boys her age. When she had attended school, he'd made her wear the most ungainly clothes he could find—no blue jeans or tank tops, everything baggy and nothing tight. He dictated her hairstyles—no perms and nothing fashionable—and did not allow her to use makeup. When he pulled her out of school, he assured her that the home-study idea was much better and she could earn her diploma while helping Linda raise the baby. The murder derailed that plan and Patti had never returned to school.

She was twenty now, with a husband and a child but virtually without an education. Years before, her mother had even kept her from watching sex-education films at school because Ethel believed they were dirty. Patti had no work experience, no income and no visible resources. If she moved out, how would she find a job? Where would she live? She'd been so isolated for so long that she barely knew how to make friends. How could she give up the lifestyle that Brown had provided for her, which included a swimming pool, a hot tub, a variety of cars and a better home than she'd ever imagined living in? She had no strategy whatsoever for making her way in the world. A few years earlier, the only clear alternative she'd seen to marrying Brown was moving back in with her mother in Victorville, but that sounded worse than staying put, so she'd gone along with his plan for a quick and secret wedding in Las Vegas.

She saw no real alternative now to staying married and was afraid to look for one.

There was another reason she did not want to leave the man, one that was intangible and went beyond the fact that she was broke and scared. Patti was emotionally attached to Brown—the only such attachment she'd ever had—and still believed that he loved her. She wanted to please him and had tried everything to do just that, not just physically and sexually, but going so far as to sign a pre-nuptial agreement which stated that everything the two of them owned was the sole property of her husband. If she left, not only would he stop loving her—she would go without a dime.

After their marriage, Brown had wanted Patti to become pregnant with his child, but by the time it happened, early in 1987, he was growing more and more paranoid. He told Patti to abort the fetus: what if someone found out who the real father was? Wouldn't that look suspicious? Wouldn't it tip off the police? Patti said no to an abortion. She believed that having a baby would give her more of a life of her own and, for the first time ever, provide her with something that was truly hers.

During her pregnancy she became so lonesome, depressed and frustrated, because she could tell no one the truth about the child's father or her marriage, that she tried to escape everything by taking two boxes of tranquilizers.

When Heather was born on September 29, 1987, Brown refused to come to the hospital, saying that childbirth made him squeamish and his being at her side would look even more suspicious. Both Patti and David continued telling Brown's parents and everyone else they knew elaborate stories about the mysterious "Doug," who had begun dating Patti months earlier, often sending flowers and other presents to the house. He'd gotten her pregnant and fled. Patti thought this story was amusing, absurd. The idea of her actually having a date with someone else, even before she was married, was unimaginable.

When Linda was still alive, Patti had gone out one evening with Tom Brown, David's brother, and David was convinced that the two of them had become intimate. She denied this again and again, but Brown was unshakable in his conviction. In order for her to prove that she was "pure and untouched by another man," he wanted her to take an overdose of sleeping pills and kill herself. She would, Brown explained to her, soon be reincarnated in the neighborhood and become Krystal's best friend. Patti took the pills and survived, but was sick and groggy for several days. In the future when Tom Brown came to visit, David made the girl hide in the bathroom until his brother had gone.

If Patti now looked at another man while she and her husband rode along the freeway, Brown went into a jealous rage, asking her if she would like him better if he lost weight and had a smoother complexion. Should he go to a gym and work out? Should he build up his muscles? Should he have plastic surgery? Should he sandpaper his face?

No, she always told him. Those weren't the things she wanted at all.

What was it, then? What did she want?

Just a normal life, Patti said, and the chance to tell others that they were married and he was Heather's father.

That was something they could never do, Brown replied. If people knew they were married, it would raise questions everywhere and the detectives would be knocking at the front door. He was worried enough without that, convinced that unmarked police cars had been driving past their address lately and photographing their home. His phone was probably tapped and somebody had been tampering with the mail. He heard the voices of policemen speaking just beyond the front door. In his sleep he imagined young women crying or laughing at him. Awake, he was subject to panic attacks—perspiring and trembling and turning pale. The man had never bathed that frequently, and the way he was sweating, Patti wished it were more often now.

The Summitridge house was starting to feel haunted too. Patti could sense her sister's presence in some of the rooms, and one day Manuella saw Linda standing in a pool of light. Those kinds of stories were more than Brown could tolerate; it was about time to move again. The people in this upper-class neighborhood were snooty, he began telling his wife, snooty and suspicious and cold—and he was soon in the process of buying another house in a less fashionable suburb.

While still at Summitridge, David insisted that Patti wear a beeper every place she went so he could keep track of her. If he sent her to the store for cigarettes, she had to wear the thing, and if she went into the next room, she had to have it on her hip. She wore it in the car and sitting beside the pool. She wore it in the kitchen and when going to the bank or into the backyard. She wore it if people came to visit, (and few did) and whenever it beeped, she moved. It beeped whenever he wanted something from her and it beeped every few minutes. She hated the thing but was afraid to turn it off. It was as infuriating as Brown's habit of making her channel all of her calls through a speaker phone in the house so he could listen to everything that was said. Or as infuriating as his habit of occasionally unplugging all the phones so no one could receive a call. Or as infuriating as the fact that he sometimes locked his wife inside the house when he left and didn't give her the combination for shutting down the alarm system. If she tried to break out, the thing went off. Patti was developing chronic headaches. Her favorite times now came when she was vacuuming the house, because she could put on earphones, listen to Pat Benatar or the Miami Sound Machine and momentarily escape the beeper and his voice.

Since Linda had died and Cinnamon had gone to prison and the Bailey family was not welcome at the Summitridge address, Patti had few female acquaintances. Her closest teenage friend was a young woman named Annie Blanks, whose father, Robert Blanks, had sold Brown some of his insurance policies. Before the murder, Annie had spent time at the Brown residence, and in subsequent years she continued to visit, doing chores for the family and taking care of the baby. After Patti was secretly married to Brown, her friend offered to let her move in with the Blanks family. Annie, who had no knowledge of the relationship between

Patti and David, believed that Patti needed a break from the man, from waiting on him all day long, from getting his meals, cleaning up after him, fetching his slippers, cutting his toenails and being told to flush his toilet. Getting away from Brown would have been next to impossible, but something else influenced her decision, something complicated and entangled.

On one of the few occasions when Brown let his wife out of the house alone, Patti and Annie had driven to Victorville to visit Ethel. On the trip, Patti asked her friend a question that had been troubling her for some time: did Annie have a boyfriend? No, the young woman replied, she didn't. Why not? Patti prodded her. She just didn't. Patti kept pushing, asking some other questions and not accepting the answers, until Annie finally confessed that she was having an affair with someone.

Who was it?

Annie couldn't say.

Why not?

Well . . . it was just too intimate a secret and the man had made her swear that she would reveal the truth to no one.

Patti pressed harder, until Annie gave in and said she was in love with David. Patti recoiled, said nothing and much later described the sensation of that moment as a combination of being relieved that someone else was sleeping with the man—and being punched in the stomach.

Before the shooting, Linda had asked her husband to pay for therapy for Patti, but he'd refused. After the killing, Patti had briefly seen a psychiatrist and found it useful, although Brown insisted on being present at the sessions to make sure she didn't bring up the murder. During the summer of 1988 Patti asked him if she or both of them could go into therapy again, but he said no, he would not waste his money on such a thing. In July of that year, when she could no longer stand the beeper or her confinement, she finally rebelled and planned a trip to Oregon. She had an acquaintance there, an older female friend of one of her sisters, and Patti intended to take Heather and spend some time in the Northwest. Surprisingly, Brown agreed to let her go and drove her to the Orange County airport for her first-ever flight and first adventure away from her husband. Secretly, she was thinking of moving to Oregon and starting her life over.

Before she boarded the airplane, he beeped her at the Orange County airport and demanded that she phone him during her layover in San Francisco, which she did. When Patti arrived in Oregon, she had several messages from Brown, insisting that she call home (the woman whom she was visiting was impressed by these messages: any man who paid this much attention to Patti must have been unusually sensitive and loving). Throughout her stay in Oregon, Brown kept phoning and asking what she was doing up there and what she was talking about with those people. She hadn't told them anything, had she? Wasn't it time for her to return? He missed them. Krystal needed her and so did he. He wasn't feeling that well. When was she coming back? After four days of fielding such questions at long distance, she caved in and flew home.

VIII

Cinnamon's next step was a conversation with Jay Newell and Fred McLean on August 10, 1988, when the men drove to CYA to interview her in person. Their talk covered some ground that was already familiar to the detectives, but this time more details were forthcoming. After a few preliminary remarks, Newell told Cinnamon to "start anywhere that you want to start and tell us what you remember about the incident."

"Well . . . I believe that it started one day when I was in the living room with my father and Patricia. Patti had left to go in the kitchen and . . . before she would reach the kitchen, she had stopped there by the door and I looked at her and I said, 'What are you doing?' She goes, 'Shush!' so I was quiet. I thought she was acting up. When I looked over again, she was just standing there. I go, 'I'm thirsty, I'm thirsty.' She goes, 'Wait a minute, wait a minute.' And so I said okay. My father goes, 'Tell her to hurry up,' and I said I did. She was standing there for a while, like seven minutes. And she went inside after a while, and she came out with our sodas. My dad goes, 'What took you so long?' She goes, 'I heard the strangest thing by the door in the kitchen.' "

Newell interrupted: "Heard the strangest thing?"

"Right," Cinnamon said.

"Oh, okay."

"I said, 'You are strange.' She goes, 'No, I'm serious.' And she goes, 'Linda was talking to Alan.' And Alan is Linda's twin brother. And she goes, 'I heard Linda talking to Alan about killing David.' And my dad goes, 'What have you been smoking in the kitchen?' She says, 'I wasn't smoking anything. I was serious.' And he goes, 'Okay, what did you hear?' And she goes, 'I don't want to talk about it here.' So he goes, 'Well, when do you want to discuss it?' And she goes, 'Not around here, because what if she hears me tell you?' And I was saying, 'She is pulling your leg, she is pulling your leg.' "

"You are saying that to who?" Newell asked.

"I was saying that to my father. I said, 'She is pulling your leg. She wants attention.' So after a while Linda came out. Everything was okay. She told me to go get ready for dinner."

"Were Linda and Alan in the kitchen to your knowledge?"

"No, Linda was on the phone."

"I mean at the time that you—that Patti was standing by the door?"

"Linda was on the phone talking to Alan. I assume it was Alan."

"So she is hearing one side of the conversation?"

"Right, I know."

"You have the time frame when this was, how long before Linda was killed?"

"I don't know. That was at least seven months [before] because I went around talking to my mother about it and my father told me not to, but I did anyways. That was a mistake."

"You talked to your mother about that?"

"Right. Well, anyways, next day we were going to the chiropractor because we all had back problems from a previous accident we were in. And my father brung up the subject of what she heard on the phone. And she said that she heard Linda talking to Alan. My father asked, 'How do you know it was Alan?' She heard her saying Alan's name, so Linda was going to kill my father to get him out of the way . . .''

"Who was going to the chiropractor?"

"All three of us were."

"Okay."

"Linda was going to go later. And Patti was up there talking. I can't remember exactly everything she said about it. She was up there panting and explaining what she was hearing. And I was, 'Oh, no.' I was just laughing in the back. So we went there. We came back home . . . Linda went to the chiropractor . . . and I went with her this time. Sometimes I went with her, sometimes I didn't. I felt like being obnoxious, so I went out of the house again. I got hyper every once in a while, so I took off with her. We went—she goes, 'How are you?' And I go, 'Fine.' And we had a convertible. She put down the convertible and we were laughing and stuff and having a good time. And I was thinking about what Patti was saying. And I was looking at her and thinking, Linda wouldn't say something like that. I was looking at her because she was so pretty. And I go, 'No, Patti is the—' I go, 'Uh-uh.' So I went to the chiropractor, came back, called my mother and she took me for the weekend. My father told me in the car not to tell anybody what Patti said because he wasn't sure how true it was.

"So I went over to my mother's house and I told her anyways. And somehow the word got back to my father that I had told my mother and I was sorry I ever did that. I told her what Patti had heard on the phone. And my mother goes, 'What could she want, his insurance?' And I don't know. I don't pay any attention to the insurance money. Their money doesn't concern me really . . . So somehow [that] got back to my father and my father said, 'I thought I told you not to tell anybody.' And I was playing stupid. I said, 'What are you talking about?' He said, 'Telling your mother.' I said, 'I didn't think it was really that important.'

He said, 'You don't decide what is important.' And I said, 'Okay.'

"And I backed off and I got in trouble some there, after my father started coming up to me frequently and saying, 'Linda is going to try to kill me, she is going to try to kill me.' It was almost like a paranoia statement . . . I said, 'What makes you think that?' I started asking him questions—'Why do you think she is going to kill you?' And he said, 'Just don't worry about it. I just know she is.' And I said, 'Okay.' I didn't know how to respond to this. And he goes, 'Just believe me. I am your father. I know she is. Okay?' At first I thought that they are pulling my leg, because our family is a bunch of practical jokers, okay, and I went along with it for a while. And I continued going to my mother's house and my mother would ask me what was happening and I said, 'I didn't hear anything,' because I didn't want the word to get back to my father that I was telling her."

"Yeah."

"And so I was quiet. I had to go back home. There would be a lot of tension in the family in the house because I want to go tell Linda or something, but my father is always there and my father—I am afraid of my father a lot."

"Did you tell him you wanted to go tell Linda?"

"No. Uh-uh."

Cinnamon again described to the detectives how she'd seen her father and Patti kissing in the shopping center, giving the men more of her reaction: "I stood there and stared, you know. I couldn't breathe that well. I was in shock . . . 'Oh, no, something is wrong here.' "

"Do you remember what kind of—an embrace kiss or just—?"

"It was an embrace kiss and they were holding each other. And I was looking around the store. I thought I was crazy or something. It was the kind of store—I looked back and they were still there. And I go, 'Whoa!' and I was looking out into the parking lot to see where the van was [and] if Linda was still here. The van was still there. The back door was open and Linda was still changing the diaper. I was

96

standing there staring at them. I couldn't move. I was think-ing, What's going on here? Then my father turned around quickly and he looked at me. And I go, 'Oh, no.' I ran across the store and he had chased me. He goes, 'Cinny, Cinny, what's wrong, what's wrong, what's wrong?' And I said, 'Should I seen you?' He said, 'What did you see? What did you see?'

"And I told him, 'I seen you kissing Patti.' And he said, 'I'm sorry you had to see that, I'm sorry you had to see that.' I said, 'What are you talking about? Are you trying to make me crazy? What are you talking about?' And I was crying at that time. I was already crying. I said, 'I don't understand.' He goes, 'I didn't expect you to understand. But we wanted to tell you, but we didn't.' I said, 'You want to tell me what?' And he goes, 'About me and Patti.' And he was just saying, 'Will you forgive me? Will you forgive me?' And I was saying, 'I just don't understand. I don't even want to talk to you.' And I took off in the store again.

"And by that time Linda was already—she already came into the store. And she goes, 'What's wrong with you?' And I was looking at her crazy, and she goes, 'What's wrong with you?' And I said, 'Nothing, I'll be all right. Are we done shopping?' She said, 'We just got to go to the register.' And I was being really quiet. I was scared of my father . . . So we were on our way home. Linda had went to the back [of the van] where I was. Usually she sits with my father. She came back where I was and she goes, 'Are you okay?' And I said, 'I told you, I'm going to be fine.' She goes, 'I don't believe you.' I said, 'I'm going to be okay. I want be be left alone.' She goes, 'Did you want something in the store and you didn't get it?' And I said, 'No, that isn't it, because you know I have money.' She goes, 'Oh, you mean your allowance money?' I said, 'Yeah.' She said, 'I didn't know you still had it.' And I said I still had it. She said, 'Fine, I'll leave you alone.' She went up to the front of the van.

"Got home, we left—we went inside the house. Linda went home with the baby, Patti went into her room where she always stayed. She is like a hermit in her room. And my father had stopped me by the front door. And he goes, 'Don't tell anybody what you seen in the store. It's very important to me.' I said, 'I won't and I told you already I don't want to talk about it.' And he said, 'Okay, fine, I'll respect that.' And he left me alone. So I went out to the trailer and I cried for a while because I was confused. I didn't know how to deal with them, too.''

''Were you living out in the trailer at the time?'' Newell asked.

''Yeah, they had already put me out there into the trailer . . . because me and Patti didn't get along that well. We were always arguing . . . So I went out to the trailer and my little dog was out there and I cried for a long time. Then my father came out there later and he said, 'It's going to be okay, it's going to be okay. I'll explain to you more later.' And I said, 'Fine, fine. I told you I want to be left alone. Can't you respect that?' And he goes, 'I can respect it, I can respect it. I just want you to understand.' And I told him to get away and I closed the door. And I heard him go back inside. I heard the door slam and so I stayed out there the rest of the night. I heard Linda tap the window, the back window, the sliding glass door, and she said, 'Are you going to come in and eat?' And I said, 'No.' She goes and I stayed out in the van. I had stuff to eat out there anyway, so I wasn't really worried about it.''

The next thing Cinnamon remembered was another family excursion on the freeway, traveling from Long Beach to Los Angeles. The radio was on, her father and Patti were in the front seat of the van talking and she was in the back.

''Whenever I hear something,'' she told Newell and McLean, ''I start cuing into the conversation. I go, 'Turn the radio off.' And he goes, 'Huh?' I go, 'Turn the radio off.' And he goes, 'Okay,' because the van was long. It was kind of hard to hear that well. And they were saying, 'We have to get rid of her. I don't know how we are going to do it.' And they were up there talking. They started getting quieter.

''So I started to move into the next seat behind them,

and I was sitting there. My father goes—he looked back at me and he goes, 'What are you doing?' And I said, 'I am just sitting up here.' And he goes, he goes, 'What did you hear?' And I said, 'Does it matter?' He goes, 'Don't get sarcastic.' I said, 'Well, what does it matter?' And he goes, 'She probably heard it already, so just sit up here.' So I sat between the two front seats and he goes, 'What did you hear?' And I said, 'Nothing.' And he goes, 'Tell me what you heard. It's important.' I said, 'I didn't hear anything.' And Patti goes, 'I don't care if she knows. She will probably end up knowing anyways.' My father said, 'That's true.' I said, 'What are you guys talking about?'

"Patti said, 'Remember before, I told you about Linda on the phone. Well, I heard them again on the phone and they said they were going to kill Linda'—I mean kill my father. And I said . . . 'What did they say this time?' And they said, 'This time they are serious.' I go, 'How do you know they are serious? Linda could be talking to herself on the phone for all you know. You don't know what's happening on the other line.' She goes, 'I just know we have to get rid of her before she kills your father.' I said, 'She is not going to kill my dad.' She goes, 'You don't know Linda. I know Linda. She is my sister.' I said, 'Fine, you know her, fine.' My father was talking about either we can get rid of Linda or [he] could leave . . . And I said, 'Why would you leave us? What are you talking about? Why don't you get a divorce?' My father is familiar with divorces. He has a lot of divorces. So I thought it was the easy way out for him. Get a divorce, it's always worked before.

"He said, 'No, I don't want a divorce. I don't want another divorce because we have to get rid of her. She will still kill me if I divorce her.' I said, 'If you go away, where are you going to go to?' And he goes, 'I'll just leave you guys. I'll leave you guys with everything and take off and start over again.' And I said, 'I don't want you to leave me, daddy.' I said, 'I don't want you to leave me.' And he goes, 'I have to, I have to. Either that or we have to get rid of Linda.' And I was thinking, Oh, no, daddy is going to leave . . . So I said, 'How can I help, how can I help? Can I talk to her for you?' And he said, 'No, don't. Don't ever talk to her about what we talk to you about.' I said, 'Okay.' And then that's when I started listening to my father and he started telling me things. And I was thinking it was right because I believed my father . . .

"We stopped at the beach and my father said he wanted to talk to Patti alone . . . He told me to go play in the sand, so I took off in the sand. And I kept looking back and they were still talking. They weren't having anything intimate. My father was yelling at her. And she was saying—I heard her yell, 'David, these—a bunch of—!' and she started cussing. And I . . . start going the other way again. And then my father goes, 'Cinny,' so I came over and I go, 'What?' He goes, 'Are you mad because I was talking to her alone?' I said, 'I'd like to know what you discussed.' He said, 'I'll tell you later.' I said, 'Why can't you tell me now?' He said, 'Because it doesn't concern you right now.' I said, 'Oh, okay.' He said, 'Get in the van, we are going.'

"So I got in the van. My father talked about maybe we could get rid of her by either sending her away somewhere, giving her a lot of money and sending her away. And Patti said, 'No, that won't work.' And I was looking at Patti and I said, 'Well, what will work?' And she said, 'We'll have to get rid of her.' And I said, 'What do you mean by get rid of her?' And she said, 'We'll have to kill her.' And at that time to me that didn't seem like a reality. It just seemed like Patti was talking. I said, 'How do you plan on killing her?' She goes, 'I have been thinking that maybe hitting her over the head.' I go, 'With what?' She goes, 'With something hard.' And I said, 'Would that kill her?' She goes, 'I think so.' And my father butted in, 'If she hits her hard enough in the right place, that would kill her.' And I go, 'Oh.' And I was looking out the window.''

"You did what?'' Newell said.

"I was looking out the window and I felt Patti looking at me. And she said, 'Do you have any suggestions?' And I was looking out the window and I said, 'To kill somebody?' And I go, 'In the movies I have seen in the bathtub and they throw an electrical appliance and I'm not sure how good that works.' She goes, 'No, no, no. We would have a hard time getting Linda in the tub.' I said, 'What are you trying to say?' And she said, 'Well, you know she is always showering.' And I said, 'Okay.' And we were laughing about that for a while. And we went home. They were just— I can't even remember what they were talking about from then on. I had went into the back. My father had turned on the radio.''

How long before the murder, Newell asked, had this trip taken place?

"It's hard to say," she said.

"Okay . . ."

"So next time we mentioned it—it was—we go to the chiropractor again . . .''

"Who was there then?"

"It was me, Patti, my father. Sometimes they wouldn't let me go with them, but this time I was with them. And I heard what they were saying. This time they were in the smaller car, the Maxima . . . He said, 'We have to get rid of Linda as soon as possible. I just know she is going to kill me soon. I can't delay it anymore.' At this time the baby was already born. I remember that, because on my way out to the car Linda was telling me to get stuff out of the car, put it in the house for the baby. He goes, 'It has to happen soon. Like right away.' Patti is all—'Yeah, it has to happen.' I'm all, 'Well, how do you guys plan on doing it?'

"And he goes, 'We need your help, we need your help.' He goes, 'Do you love me, Cinnamon?' And I said, 'I love you, don't be stupid.' And I hit him on the back of the head. He said, 'Don't do that when I am driving.' I said, 'I'm sorry.' He said, 'Do you love me?' And I go, 'Of course, I love you.' He goes, 'How much do you love me?' And I said, 'I love you a lot.' I said, 'I love you more than anything.' And he goes, 'Would you do anything for me?' I said, 'Yeah, I'd do anything for you. I love you.' He goes, 'I want to make sure that you love me enough that you will do anything for me.' I said, 'Of course, don't be ridiculous.' And he goes, 'I'm being serious with you.' I said, 'I'm being serious with you, too.'

"Then I started getting emotional. I was going, 'Oh, no, he is going to leave me and I know he is going to leave me.' And he goes, 'I'm thinking about leaving.' I said, 'No, please don't leave.' And immediately right after that, he goes, 'Well, then, how are you going to help me?' And I was thinking, Did I just put myself in something? I said no, father knows what he is doing.

"I was sitting back down. There was a long pause because I was thinking to myself. He then said, 'I need your help, I need your help. We have to get rid of Linda.' I said, 'How do you want me to help you?' He goes, 'I need you to help me. I need you to help me get rid of her.' I said, 'Do you want me to kill her?' He said, 'I want you to help, yes.' And he goes, 'If you feel you have the stomach for it, I want you to do it.' I said, 'I like horror movies but I don't have the stomach for that.' He said, 'You know me.' And I said, 'I didn't think you would.' And he goes, 'I don't either.' And I looked at Patti and I said, 'Does she?' And he said, 'Me and Patti have been discussing it.' I said, 'Oh, great, you guys have been discussing. I don't even know what you guys are talking about. I don't know what's going through your guys' head.' He goes, 'If you love me, you will trust me. Just believe what I say. I'm your father. I know what's best.' ''

The next time the family discussed killing Linda was during a February 1985 evening trip to a hospital in Riverside. David, Patti, Cinnamon, Arthur, Manuella and the baby were present. Linda was also there, but when the subject came up she was inside a hospital room visiting a sister-in-law and Manuella was in the lobby watching Krystal. The other four walked out to the van and Arthur asked what was going on. Patti said they were thinking of "taking care of it tonight . . . on the freeway."

"Patti was explaining," Cinnamon told the detectives. "She goes, 'We are going to be driving down the freeway. Father is going to go fast. David is going to go fast.' She calls him David. 'He is going to go fast, not real real fast to exceed the limit, but he is going to go pretty fast. And when Linda gets in the car, we are not going to shut it [her door] all the way.' She goes, 'We are going to take off the light.' But I don't remember her taking off the light in the van so you can't see in the van with the door open . . .

"Linda had come out. We were on the freeway and I was waiting for Patti to open the door and push her out like she said she was, and I hadn't seen anything. I said, 'Good, good.' I wasn't ready for this. I wasn't ready to deal with this. So I need to spend more time with her [Linda]. So Patti had came back to the back and said, 'You go do it.' And I said, 'Are you crazy?' She said, 'You go do it.' I said, 'No.' She goes, 'Why not?' I said, 'For one thing, I'm not strong enough and no, I'm not going to do it. No.' My father looked back at me and . . . I leaned back and I was shaking my head no."

"Was your grandfather doing anything at the time?" Newell asked.

"No. My grandfather was sitting next to my grandmother in the seats. Patti was in between the seats."

"Was he able to hear this?"

"My grandfather?"

"Uh-huh."

"I'm not sure, but he heard them talking about pushing Linda out of the van."

"He did?"

"Yeah, and he was telling my father, 'I don't think that's a good idea, David. You better not do it.' My grandfather is trying to knock some sense into him: 'You are doing the wrong thing, David.' My father wouldn't listen: 'You don't know what's right. You are getting old.' He said all this stuff. And my grandfather came back with me after a while because we had stopped to get something to eat, and this is, like, halfway between the trip. Patti came back to change. She goes, 'You need to do that.' I said, 'You don't know what I need to do. I am not ready for that.' She said, 'If you love your father, you will do it.' I said, 'I love my father, but I am not ready to do something like that.' She goes, 'You don't love your father, otherwise you wouldn't have any hesitation. You would go do it.' And I started feeling bad. I was thinking, Maybe she is right . . .

"My grandpa had went to the back seat with me and sat down and he said, 'I think I'll keep you company.' And he goes, 'What's all this nonsense he was talking with Linda?' And I couldn't hear him that well because they had the radio on and they were talking up there and [it] sounded like a circus in there. I was listening to my grandpa saying something about, 'Your father is wrong. Whatever you do, you know it's wrong. He is a sick man. I'm telling you he is a sick man.' And I was, 'What do you mean he is a sick man?' And he is, 'Just believe me, he is a sick man.' And I can't remember exactly what me and my grandfather talked about that night, but it wasn't directed toward what was going to happen to Linda."

Cinnamon told the men about the aborted target-practice trip into the desert two days prior to the murder and was ready to begin her account of the night Linda was killed. Before starting, she informed the detectives that if she kept talking she was going to be late for work at the prison and that worried her.

"We get yelled at here," she said.

"I imagine you do," Newell replied, explaining to her that she had permission to speak to them for as long as she wanted—he would write a note to her supervisor.

"All right," she said, relieved. "So on that night my father called my grandparents around six o'clock or so, told them to come down, we can have dinner and stuff and play Uno. We used to play Uno, liked to play Uno a lot. It is a card game. So they came down and we were in the living room. Linda was cooking dinner. I can't remember what we had, but it was one of the bigger meals that took a long time to make. And I was in and out of there grating the cheese and stuff, coming out, going in and out, helping her here and there. And my grandmother was sort of helping her. They didn't like grandma in the kitchen too much because she would, like, take over."

"Yeah," Newell said.

"So she [Linda] sort of pushed her out a little bit: 'Oh, go take care of Krystal or something.' We started up a game in the dining room at the pool table and we were playing Uno cards. My grandpa was cussing me out. I was laughing because I kept on zapping him on the game, giving him a bunch of cards which he didn't need. So he was yelling at me, saying, 'You son of a—' and I was laughing. My grandpa goes, 'I don't want to sit by her anymore.' And he was yelling and he was serious. He started getting stressed out: 'Get her away from me, get her away from me. I don't want to sit by her anymore.' And I started to take it to heart because usually he's just cussing me out and I enjoy that, you know. So I—we started going a little down . . . My father started getting mad because I started giving him a lot of cards, too, and then he started fighting back and I ended up getting kicked out of the game, right?"

"Literally?"

"Literally kicked out of the game. I mean I lost, okay? I had all the cards. They were in the deck, okay? They really got me good."

When dinner was over, Linda told Cinnamon to wash the dishes. She protested—"Why doesn't Patti do them?"— and Linda asked her not to "make a scene" in front of her grandparents. Cinnamon went into the kitchen and did what her stepmother had requested. When Manuella tried to tell Linda how to put the baby to sleep, there was more bickering until the grandmother turned on the television and watched MTV, a favorite channel of hers, while the others kept playing Uno. Arthur was the next one to be kicked out of the card game. Linda decided to take a shower and the older couple said it was time to go home.

"So they had left," Cinnamon told the men. "It was just me, Patti, my father left in the living room . . . My father was in his recliner saying, 'It has to be done.' I'm all, 'Well, who do you expect to do it?' He says, 'You. If you love me, you will do it. If you love me, you will do it.' I said, 'How bad is it?' He said, 'It is really bad. Any day she can kill me.' I said, 'Is it really urgent?' And he goes,

'Yes, Cinny, she is going to kill me. Do you want her to kill me?' And I said, 'No, I don't want her to kill you.' And he said, 'Would you kill her?' And I said, 'Yes, but I don't think I have enough strength to.' And he said, 'Not even for me?' And I said, 'I don't know, I don't know.' And I started crying on the floor.

"Patti looked at me and she goes, 'You are always crying.' I said, 'Don't worry about it.' She got mad and she yelled at me. She was sitting on the couch. She is all, 'Well, we will discuss it later. I have a few things in mind.'"

"Where was Linda at this time?"

"Linda was in the shower or in the master bedroom. As far as I know, she was back there somewhere in the master bedroom . . . Then about ten minutes later I heard Linda come out of her room, went to the kitchen, got some apple juice. She was standing in the hallway and she goes, 'Cinnamon, go to bed. It's late.' And I said, 'I'm going to go to bed right now.' She goes, 'Okay, I trust you. Go to bed.'

"So she had went back into the room. My father had followed her, went back in there with her. Patti and me were left there. Well, by this time I was on the couch, Patti was on the floor. She fell asleep on the floor and I was on the couch and I was dozing off and stuff, dozing off. I woke up and so I watched one video and that sort of woke me up a little bit because I was interested in that group. And I woke Patti up and I said let's go to the room that was her room, because my father had already set the alarm and there was no way for me to get out of the house to go to the trailer. I didn't have the code . . .

"So I had went to the room with them—with her. She had pulled out the little bed that she had in there. It was like a little cot thing. So I went to sleep on that. She went to sleep on her bed. My father had woke me up—he opens the door and he goes, 'Girls, girls, wake up.' So I woke up and I go, 'What time is it?' And I was looking around all crazy. And he goes, 'Get up, get up, we have to do it now. We have to do it now. She is asleep.'

"I'm all, 'What?' . . . I didn't know what was going on at that time. I wasn't sure."

"Uh-huh . . ."

"Let me tell you a few days before that . . . he had told me that after I finish up my homework in the trailer to write a note that said something to the effect like I didn't mean to do what I did. So I ending up writing, 'Dear God, please forgive me, I didn't mean to hurt her.' I put that in as my own personal touch. But he told me to write the note and I put a little ribbon around it and I put it in there because he told me to . . . hide it inside of my—inside the trailer. So I had hid it.

"So anyways, back to the other night, the night it happened. I was in the room with Patti. Patti was telling me, 'Just do as you are told.' I said, 'Don't tell me to do as I'm told. You are not any older than me. You better shut up.' And I was being obnoxious because I didn't care for Patti too much. I don't care for her at all. My father told me, 'Come with me,' so I went with them. And I was standing at his master bedroom door. Linda was asleep and I can hear her."

Cinnamon described how Linda, before falling asleep, had turned the baby monitor that she kept next to her bed up to full volume. The monitor amplified the sounds from the nursery and was there to warn Linda if anything was wrong with Krystal.

"I could hear the baby breathing—that's how high she had it up," Cinnamon told the detectives. "And . . . I go, 'Why does she have that up so loud?' "

Patti told her that Krystal had a cold and her mother wanted to make sure she didn't choke in the night.

"My father," Cinnamon went on, "had brought out bottles of pills. They were either two or three. I go, 'What are these for?' "

"Two or three pills or two or three bottles?" Newell said.

"Two or three bottles. I'm sorry. And he said, 'Come with me,' so I followed him into the kitchen . . . He goes, 'Get a glass of water.' I got a glass of water. And he goes, 'Take these.' And I go, 'Why?' And he goes, 'Because I wanted to make it look like you tried to kill yourself in case it does go through tonight.' And I said, 'If it doesn't go through tonight, it is going to look like I tried to commit suicide.' And he said, and he goes, 'It will go through, it will go through. Don't worry about it. I have a feeling Patti is going to do it tonight.'

"And I said—well, I was concerned—'Is this going to kill me—the pills?' Because there was a lot of pills there and they looked like horse pills. And I . . . took them. And I set the glass on top of the washer or the dryer, because that's where we were. And he had turned the alarm off. And he said, 'I want you to go outside . . . I just want you to go out there for a while. And then I want you to go inside the doghouse.'

"I go, 'The doghouse? I won't be able to fit in there.' He said, 'In the big one, you will too be able to fit in there.' And he was talking about the bigger dog [house]. And he said, 'You can fit in there, you can fit in there.' And I said, 'Thanks.' So I had went out to the back and I was standing around. And my father . . . opened up the door again and he goes, 'Get that note I told you about before.' And he goes, 'Do you know where it's at? Did you forget?' I said, 'I know where it's at. Don't be stupid.' "

"Had he seen the note?" Newell asked.

"No, he didn't . . . but he told me to do it and he knew that I would do it."

"Okay."

Cinnamon said that she went inside the trailer and, at her father's request, got the note she would later have when the police found her. Her father had also told her to burn the other notes she had written and decided not to use.

"So I went and I had burned them," she said to the detectives.

"Where at?"

"In the trash can that I had and—"

"In your trailer?"

"In my trailer . . . in this little trash can. It didn't make much of a mess because there was only a few pieces of paper. And I—it started—the flames—it was like a lot for

108

a little piece of paper because it sparked up. And I turned the trash can over onto the ground out in the driveway area, went outside the gate and I wait for it to cool down. And I tried to put it inside of the plastic bag in the trash-can area. Then he comes back out again. He goes, 'Did you do that?' And I said, 'Yes, I did that.' He goes, 'Where did you put them?' And I said, 'In the trash can where you told me to.' And he goes, 'Don't get crazy with me.' And I said, 'All right.' He goes, 'Go where I told you to and take that note with you.' So I went back in there and I—''

''Did he look at the note at that time?''

''No, he didn't look at it at all . . . He just told me what to put on there basically. So I went out to the place and I was laying down there. I wasn't feeling too good. I started feeling nauseous and the dogs were running around making me dizzy in there. And—before I did that, he told me to go out to the trailer. He told me to take the note with me. So I was standing there for a minute. I was looking around thinking, What are they doing in there? Thinking, Should I go back in there? No, he told me to stay out here. You know, I didn't want to get involved with what exactly they were doing inside the house because I was afraid. I didn't know what was going to happen because I loved Linda a lot.

''I heard a car door open and close. Me, I'm the nosy one. I opened up the red fence that was there, and I had went out. And I had looked and it was my father's car and it was driving out, pulling out of the driveway. And I was scratching my head. I'm all, 'Did they do something and leave me here?' And I am thinking, Oh, no, what happened? And I had heard something like, I wasn't sure if it was a gunshot at first. I just heard a shot and I was all—I wasn't sure if it was from the house or from around the neighborhood. And I was all, 'Oh, no, I'm getting out of here.'

''So I went inside the doghouse where he told me to and I curled up and I was in there shaking. And I heard two more and—two more of the same sounds. They were, like, right after each other, two of them. And I was shaking. Then I started getting sick and I was throwing up and vomiting really bad. And then I didn't hear anything after that . . . except for I can barely remember my father had came back there and . . . it was dark out, it was really dark out and I couldn't see no other. I recognized his voice and I recognized it was my father. And he said, 'It's done, it's over with.'

"Previous to that, he told me if anything was to happen that I would say that I did it, for one because I was younger and I would get less time. And for the other that he said that I probably wouldn't get any time at all. They would probably just send me to a psychiatrist about twice a week or something because they would think I was crazy. That's what my father told me that I would do if I ever did the murder."

"Uh-huh," Newell said.

"Well, he had came out there [and] he is saying, 'If they ask you, say you did it, okay? Remember what I told you before. You are not going to get in trouble. If they ask you, you did it, you did it.' And . . . I asked him what happened. And he was telling me that Patti had shot Linda and . . . everything was going to be okay now. And I was all, 'Everything is going to be okay now?' And I was feeling really bad. I didn't really want to talk to him. He said, 'Just say that you did it, Cinny,' if anybody was to ask me, so that they don't get in trouble because they would really get a long time."

"Uh-huh."

"He says, 'If you love me, you will do this.' I said, 'I love you, I love you. I will do it.' "

Newell asked if her father specifically told her that Patti had killed Linda.

"He didn't say that Patti did it. But he said, 'She did it,' so I assume that was Patti. I can't remember him saying Patti's name, no."

"What's the next thing you remember after being in the doghouse and being sick?"

"Next I remember is some men coming to get me, but I can't remember what they looked like, who they were.

Can't remember the questions they asked me either, because I was gone."

"Okay."

"I remember being at the police station and them asking me."

"At one point in time you went to UCI Medical Center?"

"Uh-huh."

"And you talked to some people there about you doing it. Do you remember that . . . ?"

"First my mother came to visit me and then my father . . . And he goes, 'Try to keep—try to keep it simple and try not to make it too complex because you'll confuse yourself . . .' I was going to tell them that I had did it. I had already planned that out in my head."

"For what reason?"

"For the protection of whoever did it—my father and Patti."

"What were you going to tell the police as to why you did it, or had you thought about that?"

"I hadn't really thought about that . . . My father was confusing me. He was telling me in the hospital—he was telling me when he first went there, 'Tell them that you did it, tell them that you did it.' And then I believe it was Mr. Anderson—he was a black psychiatrist, I think."

"Uh-huh."

"A Mr. Forgette had asked him to come help. I had told him that I did it, and I guess my father talked to the lawyers that that's not a good idea. And my father came in and said, 'Never mind. Tell them that you don't remember anything, tell them that you don't remember anything at all . . . That will work because of the medication.' I said, 'Are you sure?' And he's all, 'Just tell them you don't remember anything, anything at all, because you'll end up saying something that will get all of us in trouble.' And I said, 'Okay.' And he told me this in juvenile hall too."

Cinnamon explained to the men how Forgette had come to her during the trial and said that if her father or Patti was involved in the murder, now was the time for her to reveal what she knew.

"And I was thinking," she went on, "what my father said, 'Don't ever tell anybody.' I was afraid of my father . . . He [Forgette] said, 'If you are afraid of your father, we will protect you.' And I was thinking, No, I can't do this, I can't do this. And I said, 'No, no, not that I know of. They don't have anything to do with it.' And he says, 'You don't remember anything?' And I said, 'No.' And he goes, 'Okay.' ''

Newell asked if she had talked about the murder at any of the psychiatric workshops at CYA.

"I went to workshops but I still continued telling them, 'No, nothing happened, I can't remember what happened,' or 'I don't want to talk about it.' ''

"Okay. At some point in time obviously, you changed your mind or we wouldn't be here."

"Right."

"What—where was that transition? What made you change your mind?"

"Well, within the past year my grandparents had been telling me what had been going on at the house. There has been a lot of neglect going on with the baby, Linda's child. There hasn't been a bunch of attention being paid to her, and that my father didn't tell me that Patti was pregnant."

"When did you find that out?"

"I don't know. I don't even know how old her kid is. I don't have anything to do with Patti. I don't talk to her. All I know is that the child's name is Heather . . ."

"How did you find out the name?"

"My father told me, but he told me that she got pregnant by a boy down the street. My father is very possessive and there is no way he would have let her out of the house to go down the street—okay?—even to talk to the boy."

"Are you just surmising then that Heather is Patti and your father's child, or did you—did somebody tell you?"

"I asked my father if it was his baby and he said, 'Why do you ask that?' He started getting defensive . . . And he goes, 'No, no, she is not my baby.' I said, 'Okay.' And then I asked my grandfather. I said, 'Do you know whose baby it is?' And he said, 'It is your father's. Don't let him tell you anything different. You know he doesn't let that girl out of his sight.' I said, 'Wonderful, wonderful.' And he said, 'Don't listen to anything your father says. He lies to you all the time.' . . . And he [David] was asking me, thinking that I knew something when I didn't. He says, 'Do you think they are watching us?' And I said, 'I don't know. If I were you, I would be careful.' And he started getting scared and he said, 'Do you know anything?' And I go, 'No, I don't know anything.' And he—I don't know—he's, like, been acting really weird. I started getting less and less visits from him. So now I hardly ever see him.''

"So you are saying that the reason that you are now telling that you remember is why? Because . . . he and Patti had a baby?"

"I feel I have been manipulated when I was younger, and I started dealing with it within myself. I kept a journal here when I have been at Ventura School of how I felt about the incident, about what had happened. And I feel like I was manipulated by my father, by the whole thing, because, like, he would say, 'If you love me, you would do this.' And I knew it was wrong. Now I know it is wrong. I know it is wrong, and I don't think I should take all the responsibility for what had happened.''

"You had, like, a diary, you mean?"

"No, it's just a log. I just put in there about things that had happened that night, but some of it that I wrote in the log wasn't even true, because I didn't want my counselor to know. I was hiding it within myself. I just wrote down what I think wouldn't get me in trouble . . .''

"Okay. How long have you been keeping that?"

"Well, I haven't wrote in it for a long time. I had tore it up because I took it up to board [the parole board at CYA]. Some of it is still together, but I took it up to board and I showed it to them but they don't care about my program. I had wrote down things that I have learned since I have been here, and they don't want to know anything about it. And I feel like all the programs I have been [in] here since I have been here are a complete loss. They don't care about that. They just want to hear about the crime. So I

113

took that up there, even with this stuff written in it about the crimes, and they didn't want to see it. And I had talked to them and they didn't want to see it."

"You still have that book?"

"No."

"Partial portions of it even?"

"Very little portions of it. I have pictures in there of like—it really does not concern what we are talking about today."

"It doesn't implicate your father or Patti in any way or—?"

"No."

"Or you talk about them or your feelings about them?"

"Not really. I have destroyed that, I remember, because I was mad."

"What were you mad about?"

"I was mad at board because they just want me here to do time. They don't care about who I am, what I am about or anything. They just want me to do all the time. They have no concern about my values . . . and I was upset with that. Like, I went through all this work for a complete loss."

"You were doing it—writing it for their benefit to show them your accomplishments?"

"Right."

"How were you dealing with it?"

"I had wrote down my goals since I have been here. I graduated two years before I was supposed to since I have been here . . . I have accomplished a lot here. I am in the work program. I wasn't even eighteen when I started working. I did a lot of stuff and they didn't appreciate my efforts. I have been putting out, trying to better myself . . ."

"So you feel at this point that no matter what happens in your life, the next so-many months or years you are going to be spending here because board is not going to give you any time off?"

"Right, because of what I am in here for. Somebody is in here for heavy time, like I am, they want to keep them away from society because they feel like we are a threat. But I don't think I am a threat to society. I was just young and I got manipulated. I was talked into participating in something with a family member and now I'm older and I know better. I know that was wrong, but at the time I know I seen that as being the right thing to do . . ."

"Have you told them [the board members] that you are not the only one that was involved in that murder?"

"Yes, I did. And they said, 'You are going to have to take that back to the court. We don't deal with that here.'

"I see. Do you feel that you have benefited from being here?"

"Yeah . . . I have been to college. I am in the TWA program. It's a good job. I stay there. I work four hours and I stay an extra four hours because I work with the supervisors because I know a lot about the program there. I have been involved for a while and I help them a lot . . . I am not in here basically just for myself. I am in here for the people that might be in danger because of them, too. Do you understand what I am saying? I am not doing it all for my own benefit. I am doing it for, I guess, as you guys call it, society. In case, you know, they plan on hurting somebody else in the future."

"When you say 'they,' you mean who?"

"My father and Patricia."

"Okay."

"That's basically why I am doing it and for Krystal, the baby . . . She is in danger because my grandparents say they have been neglecting her quite a bit. And I feel like if Patti wanted them that much out of the way, what if they want the baby out of the way because now they have a new baby?"

Newell asked Cinnamon if she knew "anything about any money?"

"Board had told me when I went to board that there was a million-dollar life insurance policy involved in my case. And I said, 'What are you talking about?'

"What board—how long?"

"Board here. The first time I went to board, I said, 'I am not aware of that. I don't remember hearing that in court. If they did, I would have paid attention or I was crying too hard or I wasn't listening.' And they said, 'There is a million-dollar life insurance policy involved.' I said, 'He didn't get the money, right?' They are all, 'I don't know.' So I asked my father next time he came in to visit, 'Did you get that million-dollar life insurance policy?' And he said, 'How did you know?' And I said, 'Board told me.' And . . . he said, 'No, I didn't get it because somebody in the family was murdered.' I said, 'Oh, you mean somebody killed somebody within the family.' He goes, 'Yeah, that's what I mean.' I said, 'Oh, so you didn't get the money, right?' And he says, 'No, I don't get the money.' I said, 'Oh, well.'

"Grandfather came up about a month ago and he said, 'Your father is out there living it up.' And . . . he tells me he's out there just going out having a blast. And for some reason we got into the subject of the insurance money. I go, 'He didn't get that money.' He said, 'Don't let him lie to [you], he got that money.' I said, 'He did? He got the million dollars for Linda being killed?' And he goes, 'Yeah, he sure did. Don't let him lie to you like that.' And my grandfather [is] telling me that he is always lying to me, and he sits there and listens to it."

"So you didn't find out about the million-dollar policy regarding Linda's life until after you were here?"

"Until . . . just a month ago."

Cinnamon told the detectives that she was afraid to confront her father with this information: "I don't want to get my grandfather in trouble . . . so I am not going to say anything about that to my father. I am careful of that."

The men posed several more questions and then McLean told her, "You shouldn't discuss what we have gone over tonight—today—with anyone, not with your mother, your grandfather, nobody . . ."

"That sounds familiar," Cinnamon said. "It sounds like what I went through back in '85—'Don't tell anybody.' "

"Yeah, this is for two reasons," McLean said. "One is to protect you and the other is to protect any possibility of our investigation being compromised before we can do any good with what you told us today."

"What do you mean by 'compromised'?" the young woman said.

"We don't want Dave and Patti to find out at this point that you have told us this."

IX

At the suggestion of the detectives, Cinnamon called her father and asked him to visit CYA. For a long time, he'd held off her requests by telling her that he was making elaborate escape plans for her, but by August of 1988 his promises had lost their power. Brown was reluctant to visit CYA, but when Cinnamon said that she needed to talk with him—*now*—he could hear the urgency in her voice and it alarmed him enough to make him plan an outing.

On Sunday, August 13, three days after Cinnamon had finished telling her story to the detectives, Brown's family and parents drove to Ventura in his motor home. While they made the drive, Newell and McLean helped Cinnamon prepare for the visit: they strapped a miniature tape recorder and microphone underneath her blouse. They would be watching and photographing the visit from inside. What they wanted Cinnamon to do was get some evidence of David's involvement in the murder on tape. David, Arthur, Manuella and Krystal went into the facility, while Patti and Heather stayed in the vehicle. In the small yard next to the administration building, David and Cinnamon chatted by themselves in the shade of a pine tree. The air was warm and the yard was crowded with other inmates and visitors eating at picnic tables, drinking sodas and playing cards. Guards strolled between the tables, making certain that none of the prisoners spoke with each other, a violation of the Sunday rules. Another guard stood in a tower overlooking the scene, and if an inmate walking across the grounds strayed from one of the sidewalks, he was quickly reprimanded by a bullhorn from the tower.

Brown and his daughter made small talk, trading family jokes and old observations about CYA, until Cinnamon steered the conversation toward the murder. The first thing Cinnamon told David was that she wanted to tell the authorities the truth.

"You can tell 'em the truth," Brown said, "if you don't tell 'em the whole truth. Because if me, grandma, grandpa and Patti had knowledge of what was going to happen, then we'd all go to jail . . . That doesn't make any sense because we didn't do anything wrong . . . Patti knows that I wouldn't stay here [in prison] a week. She knows I'd kill myself."

"I feel stupid," Cinnamon said, "because I was so young and I loved you so much that I was gullible enough to do it."

"There's no gullible. Grandpa was going to do it, if you didn't."

"You know grandpa couldn't have done it."

"You don't know grandpa like you think you do."

Cinnamon was fighting back tears. "I don't know anybody," she said, "like I think I do."

Brown told his daughter that if she really wanted Patti to take her place at CYA, Patti would confess to the crime. Cinnamon ignored this statement and asked if Heather was his child. He tried to deny it humorously, saying that he hadn't had a woman for so long that he didn't know if he now preferred men.

Cinnamon guided him back to the crime and told her father that she did not commit the murder.

"I honestly do not know to this day if Patti did it," he replied.

"Well, I didn't do it," Cinnamon said. "I didn't see her do it. I know I didn't do it."

"Now I understand your confusion. I wish you'd told me a long time ago."

"But you said . . ."

"I told you, 'Don't do it.' "

"I didn't do it."

"You said, 'I'm not going to let Linda and Alan hurt you.' "

"You said if I loved you, I wouldn't get very much time. They wouldn't even send me to jail . . ."

"That's what I understood."

"I still want to make sure that I remember exactly what you told me because I feel like I'm about ready to lose it in here."

"Don't lose it."

"Patti did it."

"It's no wonder I've been afraid every night she's stayed in the house . . . I have been so confused because Patti has said she hasn't been able to sleep since it happened."

"I'm confused, daddy, because I have to deal with this shit every day."

"If I would have known, I would have made her confess to it a long time ago, but you didn't tell me."

"You told me what to say. You didn't ask me."

"The last thing I remember when I left the house was I said, 'Don't do anything. I'm going to the beach and I'll figure something out.' I don't think it's fair that you should have to suffer anymore or that me or grandpa or Krystal or anyone else should have to suffer. Let Patti take the blame for it. You don't know anything, okay?"

"They're not going to let me go. I've already been convicted."

"You don't understand. They convicted you on evidence that was not real. All this time I really thought you did it because you loved me."

"Isn't me being up here—in here—enough?"

"Yes, Cinny. This isn't what I wanted."

"Well, it's happened."

"No, I would much rather have had you at home all this time."

"I would have liked being at home."

"I didn't know. This is the first time you've told me what really happened. Don't be angry at me for something I didn't know. There. I'm sorry I didn't know."

"Does it matter if it was me or her? I'm still in here."

"Now it does, yes. Because you've proven yourself more than you should have to. I didn't want you guys to do it at all."

"Wait a minute. What do you mean you wouldn't have had it done at all?"

"I wouldn't have let it happen at all. I would've let Linda and Alan take their best shot and just hoped that they'd miss and they would have been locked up forever. That's what I wanted to happen."

"So should I tell the people the truth?"

"No, let Patti tell 'em the truth."

"Why don't you want me to? That might help me."

"Cinny, if Patti confesses, they have to let you go."

"No, they don't, because I've already been convicted of the crime."

"Yes, they would, because they'd have to rescind the decision. That I guarantee. They have no proof other than the statement you made to the nurse. That is the only proof they have, and the fact that you were in the doghouse and you took the pills and a note. But the note didn't say you did it."

"What kinds of pills were those things? Those things really had me knocked out."

"I have no idea."

"Yeah, remember what you handed me?"

"Patti said you didn't take that. She said you took something else."

"What are you talking about?"

"Patti said you didn't take what I mixed because it was too gross."

"Yes, I did."

"You did? She said it was too gross."

"Great. I don't know anything anymore."

"Cinny, try to understand something, okay? Please?"

"Do you have a tissue?"

"I have a handkerchief."

"No, thank you."

"Do you see any reason for five people's lives to be ruined, for me to die now and for grandma and grandpa and everyone else . . . ?"

"But I'm not responsible for this."

"No, I know. Do you see any reason for all of us to go to jail because we knew it was going to happen beforehand?"

"I don't know. I really don't know anymore. I'm tired of the lies."

It was Patti, Brown said, who came up with the notion that Linda and Alan Bailey were going to kill him. It was Patti who was behind the entire scheme. Cinnamon listened to her father for a while before resuming her argument with him about who was responsible for the murder.

"Patti's the one," he said. "You and I didn't plan anything. Patti's the one who heard it. Patti's the one who did it. Isn't it only logical that you're not going to get out of here if they find out that you knew about it, okay?"

"I was young, daddy. I didn't understand."

"I know."

"I was very immature then and very passive."

"I know, but isn't it logical that if Patti did it, then Patti should be punished for it? I didn't want it to happen. You should remember that. I told you guys, 'I don't want any part of this.' I told you guys, 'I don't want you guys to do this. It is too . . .'"

Cinnamon began to cry. "But before that you wanted it."

"No, I didn't. I wanted to live. I wanted to be with you guys. Can't you understand I'm as confused as you?"

"No. I don't understand that. I can't understand why you didn't tell me until now."

"Because I'm afraid. I've been afraid at home every night wondering if she's going to do it to me."

"I'm afraid here. The people here—they want to know the truth."

123

"Then your truth is, you don't remember anything. You don't know anything. Because if they come to me, that's what I'm going to tell 'em. If I go to jail—I can't survive in jail, especially with my heart and my liver, my kidneys. I can't. I will kill myself before I'll let myself die a slow and painful death in a cell. It's a lot worse on grown-ups in prison."

"It's a lot worse on me because I don't fit in here."

"I know you don't fit in here. All I'm telling you is that Patti is going to confess. Okay?"

"Right." She sighed.

"Now I guarantee it. Okay? But you have to stick to you don't know anything."

"Stop lying to me."

"I'm not lying to you."

"You wait a minute," Cinnamon said, as one of the guards approached her and told her to come with him. During the conversation, she'd spilled soda on her identification pass and the man made her go inside the administration building and get a new one. While in the building, the guard informed her that Newell wanted her to tell David to bring Patti into the prison to talk. When Cinnamon returned to her father, he questioned where she'd been but she dodged his suspicions.

Brown told his daughter that once Patti had come forward and confessed, Cinnamon would not only be released, she would also be reimbursed by the state of California for being unfairly imprisoned.

"I don't want you lying to me," Cinnamon said.

"I'm not lying to you."

"You're always lying to me. Ever since I was small, you lied to me."

"I'm not lying to you. I told you exactly what I thought is the truth."

"You've never lied to me before in my whole life?"

"Well, maybe, about if I ate your M and Ms or something, but . . ."

Before Cinnamon could tell her father to bring Patti with him next time, the other members of the Brown family came

124

over to where they were sitting. When Cinnamon saw them approaching, the discussion about the murder was finished.

Two weeks later, Cinnamon called her father and asked him and Patti to drive up for a visit that day. He explained to her how terrible he had been feeling:

"To tell you the truth, Cinny, this thing's tore my heart out so bad. Not bein' able to see you and go to Disneyland and everything else with you—I think that's why I'm always so damn sick all the time . . . Now I know what a real broken heart feels like."

"What do you mean?" she said. "This is not hardly Disneyland . . . I'm sure you'll find other things to do."

"No, I haven't in almost four years, Cinny. I love you too much."

"Oh." She laughed into the receiver.

"I'm serious. I'm being very serious . . . You just don't realize how much I love you."

She laughed again.

"It's true. Patti and everyone knows nobody'll ever take your place in my heart. Nobody could."

"I love you too, daddy."

"Cinny, why do you think I never ran away from you like a lot of other fathers did?"

"What fathers?"

"You know, other fathers who divorce their wives."

"Don't stereotype fathers."

"You know what I mean."

Cinnamon mimicked his voice: "You know what I mean."

"They hate their wives so much that they don't go visit their kids, and I always said, 'I always loved you.'"

"That's great."

"It's true. You're my number one. I always will—"

"Daddy, I can't talk very long. I'm at work . . . You better come up here, 'cause I'm lonely."

"I know, I'm tryin' . . . I'm gonna try and unless I stop

125

breathin' or something on the way up there, I'm gonna make it."

A few hours later, on Sunday, August 27, Brown drove to Ventura again, this time with Patti, Annie Blanks, Krystal and Heather in the motor home. The man was tense, smoking hard, outlining to his wife what they should say to Cinnamon when they arrived. They parked on the large asphalt lot outside the CYA, Brown and Patti left the vehicle and went inside. They passed through the security guards at the front door and met Cinnamon in the meeting room of the administration building before stepping out onto the lawn. As the trio sat at a picnic table in the late summer sunshine, Brown asked his daughter if she wanted some coffee. She laughed, indicating that she couldn't handle any more caffeine right now because, as she put it, "I'm wired for sound." He thought the remark was funny. For the rest of the afternoon their dialogue took on the quality of ultra-modern theater, a play in which everything is disjointed or absurd.

Cinnamon asked her father why, if he didn't want her and Patti to go through with the murder, he instructed her to write the note.

"I don't remember that," Brown told her.

"Are you trying to make me crazy?" Cinnamon said to Patti.

"No."

"Were you guys there with me?"

No one answered her.

"What do you know about the note?" she said.

"Just from the stuff I read in the newspaper," Patti said.

"I'm trying to make sure I'm not crazy," Cinnamon said. "I'm trying to find myself."

"Truth is," Brown told her, "I don't remember a lot of stuff. I remember you said you were sorry."

Cinnamon stared at him, becoming more exasperated. "Are you related to me?"

Her father made no response.

"I've been in here and it's fucked up my life."

"I'm fighting the best I can," Brown told her.

"They were both after him," Patti said, "and we didn't want him to be gone."

"Why are you saying this now?" Cinnamon asked them. She received no answer.

"You guys just left me there hanging. I mean—why did you do it?" Cinnamon told them.

Larry Bailey must have broken into the house, Patti said, and killed Linda.

Cinnamon brought up seeing Patti kiss her father in the shopping center. Patti acknowledged that that might have hurt Cinnamon but said that she loved David and would never leave him. Had Linda been killed, the prisoner wanted to know, so that the two of them could be together or just because they wanted a lot of money?

"It was [done] to save his life," Patti said.

When Cinnamon asked her father about collecting a million dollars' worth of life insurance, he denied receiving any money.

Brown said that Linda had been sleeping on his side of the bed that night and whoever came into the room and fired the gun must have believed that he was killing the man of the house.

"Patti says she doesn't know who did it," Brown told his daughter. "She doesn't think that you are capable of it either. You're always too lovable. You're always too funny and cute. Like me."

"Don't push it," Cinnamon said.

"You were. You were always funny. You like crackin' jokes and doing things like I like to do. You don't have a bone in your body that would allow you to hurt anyone."

"Why are you so sure it wasn't Patti?"

"I'm not sure," he said.

The three of them continued to dance, Brown and his wife trying to move the subject away from the killing and Cinnamon constantly trying to bring them back.

"If you didn't do it," Patti told her, "and they've stuck you in here for what you didn't do, the least I can do is the same thing for you. If you're in here for nothin', I'll go back in for nothin' because I love you to death.''

"I'm near death," Cinnamon said.

"Well, I love you," Patti replied.

"You'll get the chair," Brown told his wife.

"I don't care."

"I'm scared," he said.

They danced some more.

"Cinnamon says she knows she didn't do it," Patti said. "I know I didn't do it. If I end up going to the chair, then at least the one who did it might come forward out of guilt, you know."

"I don't think Larry has a guilty bone in his body," Brown said.

"I can just say I don't remember anything but I know I did it," Patti said.

"Why are you coming forth now?" Brown asked her.

"I don't know."

"Well, that's what you're going to have to think of," he said.

"Why are you coming forth now?" Cinnamon asked her.

"I didn't do it. Why I am coming forth now is to make you both happy."

"That's what they're going to ask you," Brown said.

"A guilty conscience, okay? I don't know. I'll think about it. I can say I heard you got engaged and I felt bad and . . . I don't know. Help me."

"Patti," Cinnamon said, "just tell the truth."

"I don't know the truth," she said.

PART THREE

X

On September 21, less than four weeks after David and Patti's second trip to CYA, Jay Newell and Jeoffrey Robinson, a deputy district attorney for Orange County, filed first-degree murder charges against Brown and his wife. As those proceedings were quietly unfolding in the courthouse in Santa Ana, Brown was settling into his new Chantilly address, a two-story stucco affair with a bare front yard, a guest house and his motor home parked to one side. He had plans to install the latest high-tech security system, which featured cameras that could videotape three hundred and sixty degrees around the house. Brown intended to stay in the house for a while and had put considerable time into designing the master bedroom—which had a king-sized bed, a love seat and a skylight—as well as his own bathroom, which was done in black with golden faucets and glitter in the sink. Ethel Bailey, who was allowed to visit her daughter at this residence, had lately been staying in the motor home, and just after dawn on September 22, she looked out the window and saw men rummaging in the garbage, men moving in the field behind the house. She thought they were hunters.

When Patti went to answer the front door, the intercom

wouldn't work, so she asked Brown for his help. He assumed that Annie Blanks was paying them an early morning visit and, as Patti returned to her bedroom, he opened the door and faced Newell and a band of police officers. He was immediately arrested without offering resistance. Four cops found Patti in bed and moved toward her. Panic shot through the young woman and a sense that what she was seeing and hearing was not real—or too real. In the recent past, she'd been having nightmares and premonitions of disaster, going so far as to contact a travel agency, getting brochures and making plans for the family to take a long trip and get away from California, perhaps for good.

Patti wasn't the only one with premonitions. Before the police arrived, Brown's moods had been steadily growing worse, his paranoia intensifying and his whims becoming more outlandish. Some days he'd insisted that Patti dress and wear her hair exactly as Linda had done; other days he'd insisted that she not look anything like her dead sister. To calm his nerves, Brown had drunk more Perrier and munched Tylenol. Months earlier, he'd burned his and Patti's prenuptial agreement and destroyed a videotape that had been made of their marriage in Las Vegas, ridding the house of all evidence that she was his wife. He'd lately begun playing a game with Patti: he would act like a detective who'd just arrested her and was grilling her about the murder. How would she handle it? What would she say? How would she protect them? Patti went along with this game but believed there was still time to escape, still time to plan a long vacation . . . but now real cops were standing in front of her and asking if she was Patricia Ann Bailey. When she said yes, they said that she was under arrest for the murder of Linda Brown.

David had begun sweating and shaking, telling the officers in his home that his health was delicate, that he suffered from colitis, anxiety attacks and a ''bleeding problem''— so they should treat him accordingly. He and Patti were handcuffed and taken to a patrol car, where they were briefly locked in by themselves, the police hoping that they would admit something incriminating while in the vehicle. Brown told Patti to say nothing and he would have them released within seventy-two hours. He believed that the car was wired, and to prove his theory, he began yelling, "Help me! Help me!" Within moments the police had come running out to see what was wrong. As Brown and Patti were leaving the Chantilly address, he gave the driver detailed instructions for the fastest route to the Garden Grove Police Department, adding that his health was miserable and he needed his medication. He asked Newell, who had brought along a bottle of Perrier for David, if he could drink it in the car. The answer was no.

In a small room at the district attorney's office, Newell and McLean interviewed Brown first. The men had waited nearly three and a half years for the opportunity to ask him some hard questions, and the strain of that much waiting showed on Newell. He maintained his politeness, but there was an underlying urgency to his manner, some aggressive shifting in his chair, a kind of relish in his questions, a subtle delight at finally having the man across from him under arrest. McLean said almost nothing. The interview began at seven a.m. with Newell reading Brown his Miranda rights. When that formality was completed, Brown opened by telling the men that "a lot of my health problems now are a result of my having lost Linda. I never have and never will love anyone like her."

Newell gave one of his patented stares and asked Brown what he remembered about March 18, 1985.

"That day, I was fielding calls from the Pentagon and others for my computer business," he said. "I don't think this is a loss anyone can ever get over. I can't seem to deal with her death. I am suicidal prone. I can't remember . . . Linda and I made love. Linda and I—I don't remember specifically what we did—she could control me and get me screaming—you know what I'm talking about? If she's having her monthly problem, she still loved to touch me and kiss. Sometimes, she didn't mind having intercourse during her period, although I wasn't particularly interested in it. That night she drove me crazy. I got a climax that night and every night. She knew what I liked and took care of me and I took care of her. We tried very often not to do the same thing night after night and kept the fire going. I treated her like a queen.''

Brown spoke in a soft voice, smoking one cigarette after another or lighting a new one off the last butt (he kept the pack stuffed inside his shirt). He sipped Perrier not from the bottle but from a cup the police had provided, and as he talked he was virtually motionless, his thick torso filling up the chair, his manner flat, his tone emotionless. He looked immobilized by his own weight, as if he did not have the energy to stand. He seemed slightly annoyed by the arrest, as if he couldn't understand why anyone would question him in this way. When he denied having any direct involvement in the murder, nothing about him suggested remorse or guilt.

As he talked he shared little asides to Newell and McLean about being a family man and wondered if they too had families. He talked about feeding the baby, about loving his wife, about his triumphs in the computer business and about his sexual prowess, as if he wanted to befriend the detectives and be one of the boys at the station. The whole thing had a surreal air, the same air that had surrounded his talks with Cinnamon and Patti at the prison. He acted not so much like a deceptive criminal or like an innocent man but like someone who did not understand that rules existed outside his own household and like someone who could not imagine being told no. If this was a staged performance, it did not come across that way. It came across as the behavior of someone who winked in and out of reality.

''That night Linda was deeply troubled about something,'' he said.

What was it? Newell asked.

''I honestly don't remember what it was. After making love . . . I went for a ride. Took off. I took off to the beach, one of the most peaceful places in the world to me. I stopped at Circle K for something to drink. I drove up Pacific Coast Highway where the derricks are . . . I got the balls up to make a decision about what was best for our relationship . . .

told Patti to say nothing and he would have them released within seventy-two hours. He believed that the car was wired, and to prove his theory, he began yelling, "Help me! Help me!" Within moments the police had come running out to see what was wrong. As Brown and Patti were leaving the Chantilly address, he gave the driver detailed instructions for the fastest route to the Garden Grove Police Department, adding that his health was miserable and he needed his medication. He asked Newell, who had brought along a bottle of Perrier for David, if he could drink it in the car. The answer was no.

In a small room at the district attorney's office, Newell and McLean interviewed Brown first. The men had waited nearly three and a half years for the opportunity to ask him some hard questions, and the strain of that much waiting showed on Newell. He maintained his politeness, but there was an underlying urgency to his manner, some aggressive shifting in his chair, a kind of relish in his questions, a subtle delight at finally having the man across from him under arrest. McLean said almost nothing. The interview began at seven a.m. with Newell reading Brown his Miranda rights. When that formality was completed, Brown opened by telling the men that "a lot of my health problems now are a result of my having lost Linda. I never have and never will love anyone like her."

Newell gave one of his patented stares and asked Brown what he remembered about March 18, 1985.

"That day, I was fielding calls from the Pentagon and others for my computer business," he said. "I don't think this is a loss anyone can ever get over. I can't seem to deal with her death. I am suicidal prone. I can't remember . . . Linda and I made love. Linda and I—I don't remember specifically what we did—she could control me and get me screaming—you know what I'm talking about? If she's having her monthly problem, she still loved to touch me and kiss. Sometimes, she didn't mind having intercourse during her period, although I wasn't particularly interested in it. That night she drove me crazy. I got a climax that had applied for the policies jointly but he was always turned down because of his health and she was always accepted. When were the life insurance policies taken out? Newell asked.

"Honest to God," Brown said, "I don't know."

And then he told the men, "If I were going to stage something, I would stage something much more sophisticated than this."

Newell told Brown that he didn't think he was the killer.

"Until today," the detective said, his voice growing more impatient, "I didn't know if you pulled the trigger or not."

Brown nodded and announced that it was time for him to confess the whole truth: there was no doubt in his mind that Patti had killed her sister. Lately he'd been hearing Patti talk to Linda in her dreams, as if she were actually reliving the murder.

"I fixed up the medication for Cinnamon," he told the men. "It was Tylenol, Bayer aspirin and baking soda . . . We had tons of pills in the house. Tons."

"Why did you prepare this concoction for her to drink?"

"For months she'd been saying that she had to protect me. She was headstrong, just like Brenda. Cinnamon was dead set that she had to do something to protect me from being killed by Linda and Alan."

After grilling Brown for several hours and listening to his contradictions—why, for example, if he had nothing to do with the murder, had he given his daughter something to drink right before the shooting?—the detectives changed gears. They brought out the photographs taken of David and Cinnamon when he'd visited CYA and played fragments of the recorded conversations between the two of them.

Throughout the morning Brown had been drinking his Perrier from a cup, but when he saw the photos he grabbed the bottle and took a gulp, the first sign, in Newell's mind, that the man was not completely in control of himself. Brown lit another cigarette and told them that until this moment he hadn't fully realized what was happening and that he was under arrest. He wondered if they would mind dismissing everything he'd said up until now, reading him his Miranda rights again and starting the interview over, as he was ready to give them some facts. Until now, he thought they'd been joking. "You guys do this every day," he said, "but I've never been arrested."

The detectives, who had seen a lot in their careers, had never seen this. They stared at the man.

Brown said that Patti had once wanted to push Linda out of a moving car and mentioned several other ways the young woman had come up with for killing her sister.

"If you're going to talk to me," Newell said, his patience finally slipping, "tell the truth. Have some pride, okay?"

Once again Brown denied having any personal involvement in his wife's death and acted as if his feelings were hurt.

"I think this is bullshit," Newell said, preparing to leave the room. "We're just going over old ground and this is a waste of time."

As Brown was being handcuffed and led away, he glanced at his cigarette burning in an ashtray on the table.

"There's no way I can take that with me, is there?" he asked.

"No," McLean said.

Newell interviewed Arthur Brown in the same room. David's father also smoked intently, talking in low, gruff spurts and squirming like a befuddled and uncomfortable animal with one leg in a trap. He didn't have much to say to the detective, but like his son, he did blame Patti for many things, saying that she "is so goddamned stinking jealous that it's a shame. That's why she keeps grandma away from Krystal . . . Bein' separated from Patti is the best thing that could ever happen to David. He would never believe me that Patti was no good . . . The problem with David and Patti is that they tell one goddamned lie and then they have to tell you another one to cover it up. That doesn't benefit everyone. David didn't used to be like that. You used to be able to take him at his word . . . When all this happened, I was havin' heart trouble and my head was screwed on all wrong and I had trouble rememberin' my own name . . . I don't wish Patti dead or nothin', I just wish her out of the house.''

On September 22, Newell also spoke with Patti in the same cubicle, while the prosecuting attorney, Jeff Robinson, secretly listened to the conversation in another room. Patti drank a soda and at the start she was unemotional, flat and distant, much as her husband had been. At times she looked like a bored teenager, slouching in her chair in front of a peeved teacher, anxious to get up and leave the room. Newell himself was no longer as patient as he'd been earlier in the day, his voice a little tenser, his movements sharper, as though he sensed that after years of waiting he had arrived at the moment when he could at last confront Linda Brown's killer.

"I don't want to remember a whole lot about that night," Patti told him. "Sometimes people have hard times dealing with the dead. I saw it as Linda was on vacation. The psychiatrist I saw got me to realize that she wasn't on vacation and that she wasn't coming back. My mother tried to discuss all this with me. She'd jar and jar and jar . . . but I guess I didn't want it to come out. The whole past years are blocked out. I can barely remember what I did last week.''

Was it true, as David had indicated, that Linda was murdered because of a conversation Patti had heard between her sister and Alan Bailey about killing Brown?

"I probably blocked it out . . . It's like you're sleeping and you wake up and you go, 'Wait a minute,' and you just go back to sleep.''

"Do you ever dream about Linda's death?'' Newell asked.

"No. I dream about picking Linda up at the airport, but I don't dream about her death . . . This really hurts, you know. I told my mom the other day that I finally understood that Linda wasn't coming back. I just understood what death meant. So I'm not saying you shouldn't ask these questions. I'm just saying, 'Go slow,' because this really hurts.''

Patti began to cry. "I mean I find myself driving down the street trying to find her. I mean something's wrong. I

138

went out driving, hoping that maybe it was just someone's idea of a practical joke and it took me three years to get it and I don't want to have to take another three years to have to forget it.''

"Okay," Newell said. "Let me—"

"Go slow but deep if you have to."

Newell gave her some Kleenex.

When she had composed herself, she said that she did not think that Cinnamon committed the murder. Newell asked about her relationship with Brown.

"I don't get along with David, but I stay in his house because I take care of Krystal and that's the only key I have left to Linda and I don't want to lose it. I cook and clean for David and I wouldn't leave unless he told me to get the hell out. I wouldn't leave until I feel better about myself . . . Linda was more my mother than my mom. I wouldn't hurt her for anything. I do know that David was getting threats from my brothers . . . Ever since Linda was thirteen and started going out with David, everyone always made threats at David.''

Newell played for her segments of the CYA recording in which both Cinnamon and David point to Patti as the killer. Snapping off the tape recorder, Newell told her that David had already said that she was the one responsible for the murder.

Patti looked stunned by the remark and didn't immediately respond.

"I couldn't live with myself knowing that I hurt someone," she said. "I get upset when I have to spank Krystal."

Newell suddenly dropped his gentle paternal manner and said that it was time for Patti to start remembering what happened and talking about it. He suggested that it was Patti herself who'd given Cinnamon the medication to drink.

"I wouldn't give her the medication," she said. "I wouldn't even give her Tylenol without her dad's permission."

"Oh, bullshit," Newell said, nearly leaping from his chair. "You tried to kill her that night."

"I did not."

"You did."

"I did not."

"And we're gonna prove that besides—"

"I didn't and I want to leave this room if you're gonna be an asshole."

"David is the one that said you are the one who gave her the medication. Not him. What do you think about that?"

"I don't have anything to say."

Newell picked up some papers, stood and walked toward the hall. "I'll be right back," he said, shutting the door behind him.

"Okay," Patti said, glancing at the table and then at McLean, who maintained his silence.

Out in the hallway laughter exploded and echoed, Jeff Robinson's voice carrying into the small interview room, where Patti heard herself referred to as "a murderer" and "nothing but white trash."

XI

Cons frown upon grown men doing anything criminal involving children or even teenagers. Because of what Brown was charged with, his lawyer requested that he be placed in protective custody at the Orange County Jail in Santa Ana. Had he not been separated from the other inmates, his welcome at the prison might have included a beating or worse. Patti was not given similar protection and her routine was grim. She was awakened every morning at four a.m. and served breakfast at four-thirty. Prison food, she said, tasted like "lizard's toes," but she ate it out of boredom and gained weight. Other women inmates taunted her for being a killer, and one threatened her life. The guards greeted her with "How's the murderer today?" Patti stopped menstruating, developed a cyst on her uterus and cried a lot. She learned to sit, read, wait, do nothing, then sit and wait some more. Her bed was a hard, two-inch-thick layer of mattress on top of a slab of concrete. She had no pillow and at night the cell was so cold that she wore socks on her hands. The dark walls spun around her and talked. She dreamed that Brown was calling her name, dreamed that she was dead and lying on top of Heather. In her sleep she screamed until other inmates became so angry that she had to be moved, but no matter how much she yelled or cried, she could not push her dead sister out of her mind. Linda was everywhere in the cell, and when Patti looked in the mirror, she was there too.

During the first weeks of Patti's incarceration, David used the prison mails to send her biblical passages that said a woman should always be loyal to her husband. He told her to "do the right thing," told her that she was "trusting the wrong people," told her to "watch her back," told her that unless she did something to help him, he was going to kill himself. Patti read the material he sent and failed in her attempt to hang herself with a sweatshirt. The guards put her in a room with a cement floor and padded rubber walls, dressing her in a bright red jumpsuit so their camera wouldn't lose sight of her. Patti relieved herself in a hole in the cement. When she got out of the rubber room, she passed the time by speaking to her absent daughter and longing for Heather, who was being cared for by Rick and Mary Bailey. Patti imagined that television sets inside the prison were winking at her—blinking off and on, on and off. During her first weeks at the jail, one person befriended her, a 250-pound woman who had murdered a seventy-two-year-old man, a huge creature who terrified Patti. The Orange County authorities let Patti sit in her cell and absorb the prison experience for a while, indicating to her lawyer, Don Rubright, that there were ways for the young woman to help herself. If she wanted to be in protective custody, she would have to cooperate with them and agree to testify against Brown. Wasn't that much better than going to trial for first-degree murder with a man who had already accused her of pulling the trigger? Patti wasn't ready to listen.

The day after the two of them were arrested, Annie Blanks went to see Newell and McLean. She was barefoot. The twenty-year-old blonde, who had a defiant mouth and a face that did not conjure up innocence, described herself as having been "like a nanny" to Krystal in the Brown household. She told the men that she'd come to them because she was worried that Krystal was being mistreated by David's parents, who were now in charge of the little girl. When asked about the murder, she said that Patti and David had told her that someone broke into the house and killed Linda, thinking it was Brown lying in the bed, someone who wanted to take over his business. The plain-speaking young woman characterized David as "like a hypochondriac guy. It's kinda like he's sick all the time, but I don't think he always is. He's faking . . . Three or four times I had sex with him. I didn't go upstairs and fuck him. He always wants me to. He treats me like shit. No, there's no loyalty. He always makes me cry. All I want to do is spend some time with him, but he hurts me . . . I think I just want to hear from him that he loves me."

"That David loves you?" Newell said.

"Yeah," Annie said. "It's a bunch of bull. He doesn't."

Five days later Newell interviewed Ethel and Larry Bailey by phone. She said that, like Cinnamon, she had not been allowed to call the Summitridge home for the past several years but had to leave messages for Patti at the Randomex business number. She and her children, Ethel said, had still not recovered from Linda's death: "I mean it just tore this family to holy hell . . . Patti has called me many times wanting to commit suicide because of Linda. I want to kill myself so I can go be with Linda."

In her opinion, David Brown was a master salesman who "could sell you out of your own teeth." In 1981, he'd asked Larry to run over one of the sheds on his property so he could collect the insurance money. If he would simply destroy the shed with a car, he would receive $50,000, give him $3,000 and use the rest to build the "dream house" that Linda had always wanted.

On another occasion Larry inadvertently wrecked one of Brown's ATVs, but when David learned that the insurance wouldn't pay for repair damages, he pushed the the machine off a cliff and collected the full purchase price. "He always wanted me to do things that were against the law," Ethel said, "and I didn't want to do it."

She recalled the time she was visiting the Ocean Breeze address and Brown's elderly next-door neighbor lost control of her car, running into a wall of Krystal's bedroom. Damage to the house was minor, but David went into his study, picked up his Commodore home computer and threw it to the floor, smashing the machine and later collecting enough insurance money to replace it with a $9,000 IBM. If memory served Ethel well, the man had staged seventeen car accidents, the reason that the family was always visiting the chiropractor. Patti herself had collected $35,000 from three of these wrecks but immediately turned all of the money over to Brown. Ethel didn't mention that Brown had told her family about burying half a million dollars or so near Yucca Valley; she didn't talk about her plans to go into the desert with her sons and some shovels.

A number of Patti's relatives visited her in jail, including the outspoken Mary Bailey, who believed that the young woman should get her own lawyer rather than use the same one David had hired. For $300,000, Brown had enlisted the services of Joel Baruch, a successful Orange County attorney and volatile ex-Vietnam veteran, a former gunner in the infantry. A grenade had left him with one good eye and a dead eye—none of the pictures in his office was quite square with the wall. If one was never entirely sure where Baruch was looking, one usually knew what the man was thinking and feeling. He was an emotional man who regarded the courtroom as a battleground: he was there to defeat the enemy, and the enemy was anyone who threatened the interests of his client. He was not afraid to cajole, to complain, to pressure, to carp or to whine—the kind of lawyer who would do what was necessary. A short trim man with a gray mustache, he had the sudden movements and alert gestures of a wary soldier, fancying himself as someone not easily fooled. Smart, shrewd, quick, passionate, resourceful and a street fighter, he believed in tenaciously defending anyone who employed him, regardless of what he thought of the client personally. He was proud of his credo and committed to practicing law by it—up until this point in his career.

Mary Bailey told Patti repeatedly to get her own lawyer and when Mary insisted on something, people tended to pay attention. The lawyer Patti hired was a handsome, solidly built, athletic-looking man named Don Rubright, who didn't fit the devious cardboard image of an attorney at all. He spoke simply and directly (although he didn't tell a lot of the Orange Country lawyers he associated with that he was a longtime member of the hard-core, pro-environmental Sierra Club). He was friendly, accessible, masculine without being macho, and somehow conveyed the notion that he was nothing more and nothing less than what he appeared to be. In a land of quick-draw artists and a county in which everything appeared to be for sale, he came across as a stable and trustworthy force. Watching him in the courtroom, one had the feeling that if more attorneys behaved as Rubright did, there wouldn't be such an abundance of lawyer jokes.

In early October Rubright began talking with his client at length—the first adult male other than David Brown who had ever done so—and laying out a legal strategy. The D.A.'s office had decided that although Patti was seventeen at the time of the murder, she would be tried as an adult and tried with Brown. If convicted, she faced a life sentence. When informed of this, Patti became number than she already was. Rubright wanted to separate her case and Brown's and began looking for an alternative, something that would help him pry Patti away from the man. In most murder cases, an attorney's initial step is to waive his client's right to a speedy trial; in California the accused is guaranteed a trial within sixty days. Waiving this right gives a lawyer more time to do research and prepare for the courtroom. Rubright knew that Baruch would follow this pattern, and he did, which meant that Brown would not come to trial for months or even years. Rubright's plan was to get Patti scheduled for trial quickly, a clever and effective way to split up the two defendants. The lawyer didn't really want her to be tried anyway, but to plead guilty and get the best deal for herself, regardless of how that affected Brown. In Patti's mind, this concept was revolutionary—she'd never done anything for herself, let alone anything that went against the man who had supported her for the past seven years. She didn't immediately accept Rubright's ideas, but she did consider them.

As Patti sat in the Orange County jail, a curious thing began to take place, the same thing that had already happened to Cinnamon. Patti began to think for herself, or at least to admit the possibility that she could do this. Throughout her life, when someone had asked her or told her to do something, she'd done it. Rubright was the first man she'd ever met who didn't want anything from her except the truth. The young woman barely knew how to talk to someone like him, and when they spoke she couldn't look directly at him. Or at any male. If she tried to, her eyes shot to one side or down at the floor or off toward the wall. It wasn't just men she mistrusted, it was everyone, but she was most frightened of the opposite sex.

The lawyer assumed that she'd come from a difficult background, but he didn't yet know that she'd been given to David Brown in exchange for money, been abused by her brothers and, at the age of five, begun playing a game with David called "Cinnamon Kisses." The game took place when Cinnamon, age three, came to visit her father in Riverside and Patti was living next door. Brown would kiss the girls on the lips, and the object of the contest was to see who could hold these kisses the longest without laughing. When she was eleven, Patti began performing oral sex on Brown, who had explained to her that if she wanted to become a woman—to grow breasts and menstruate and eventually have a baby—she had to do this to him. It was perfectly normal, he'd explained to her, a part of growing up. At fifteen, she started having intercourse with him. It happened when he drove her to school in the morning or when Linda was out of the house or when she was home and sleeping or when she was taking a shower.

The reason that Cinnamon had been sent outside to sleep in the trailer in the winter of 1985 was so that Brown could come to Patti late at night and find her alone in her room. "A million other girls would love to take your place," he would say to her when she feebly tried to resist. I wish they would, she often thought, but never spoke the words

146

to him aloud. If she refused to have sex with Brown, he would threaten to send her back to her mother's. Patti knew she would find little sympathy there. When she was fifteen and thinking of moving back in with Ethel, the woman suggested that Patti hit the streets and earn a living as a prostitute.

After getting to know his client, Rubright compared her to a rabbit frozen by the headlights of an onrushing vehicle, too terrified even to jump. But over time the attorney observed a shift within the young woman: the longer she was physically removed from Brown, the more she began to change, to open up, to cry, to discover her own emotions, to feel hatred and shame and guilt and anger, to talk, to relive the past, to think about what had happened. Everyone agreed that she was still a mess, but she was no longer just the sullen denying child she'd been when arrested. Slowly she was being deprogrammed.

While Baruch and Rubright interviewed their respective clients, the detectives retrieved and reexamined old police reports, filed right after the murder. Three and a half years earlier, the evidence indicated that both David and Patti had handled guns at or very near the time of the crime. When the results of the same illumination tests were studied again, the opposite conclusion was reached: neither had apparently touched a firearm on March 18 or 19 of 1985. This piece of information, combined with the fact that right after the murder Cinnamon had confessed to things that only an eyewitness could have known, raised a new round of questions.

On October 27, Jeff Robinson visited Cinnamon at CYA to prepare her for the hearings. While he was there he asked her to tell him the story of the night of the murder one more time. He explained that if Cinnamon wanted to help her cause, now was the time for the truth and nothing but the truth.

In the weeks before the hearing, Rubright arranged for his client to listen to the September 22 audio tape of Brown telling Newell and McLean that he was frightened of Patti and that she was responsible for the murder. Patti was shocked and hurt and number still, remembering what her husband had told her about spouses not being able to testify against each other—one more lie. It was becoming apparent to the young woman that she was going to face her trial alone, with both Cinnamon and David aligned against her. Brown had lately been using the prison mails to inform her that his health was failing terribly and that if he was not released from jail soon, he would die or kill himself and Krystal would grow up without a mother or a father. Manuella Brown also visited Patti in jail and told her that Arthur, her husband, had suffered a heart attack and been hospitalized, all because of the stress created by having his son unjustly accused of murder. Arthur was also about to die. Manuella implied that if Patti would simply step forward and take the blame for Linda's death, as she had once said she would, David would be set free, Arthur's health would improve, some pieces of the family might be salvaged and Krystal would have a home. That was the decent thing to do for someone who had done so much for her. Patti was torn; where did her obligations really lie—with her husband and Krystal or with herself? Secretly, she didn't want Krystal to be left with Manuella because she did not trust the woman to raise the child lovingly.

Shortly after Manuella left the jail, Rubright came to talk with Patti and she repeated to him the story about Arthur Brown's ill health. The lawyer interrupted her to say that he'd just spoken with Mary Bailey, who had told him that Arthur was in the lobby of the building and appeared to be in fine shape. Patti received the news with a jolt—another surprise from the Brown family. Rubright tried to explain to her that it wasn't only Cinnamon and David who were conspiring against her, but the entire family, all of whom were under the control of one person.

On October 28, the day after Jeff Robinson visited Cinnamon and reminded her of the crime of lying under oath, Patti wrote her husband an angry letter, asking how he could have turned on her so quickly and completely after his arrest. It was the first time she'd ever openly confronted him with his treatment of her or allowed herself to show him any of her anger, the first crack in his absolute hold over the young woman. As soon as she'd done this, a curious thing happened to her, a thing she would describe several years later:

"David always said to me, 'No one's gonna like you for you. If you be this way and this way and this way, they'll like you.' I though that was true until a girl approached me in jail and said that she liked me for who I was. It was really strange, because I realized I wasn't being someone that David wanted me to be. I was being myself."

XII

While Patti was writing her letter to Brown, Cinnamon was trying to phone the D.A.'s investigator, Newell. On Halloween day, he made the trip to CYA, where he had lunch with the girl. She once again described to him the night of the murder—how she and Patti had watched MTV in the living room after the others had gone to bed, how they'd gone into Patti's room and fallen asleep, how her father had come into the bedroom sometime later and suddenly awakened them, saying that it had to be done that night.

"He was, to the effect, saying that if I loved him that I would do it for him," she told Newell. "I asked him why it had to be done tonight. He just said, 'You know. Otherwise, I won't be here anymore. Linda is going to kill me.' Patti and him exchanged a few words. Then he told me to come with him. I followed him and we were at his bedroom now. He told me to wait at the door and be quiet. He went in and got some bottles and brought 'em out. Like prescription bottles. He went into the kitchen and I followed him and he told me to get a glass and put water in it. So I did. At this time we were in the pantry. I took 'em, the pills he had told me to."

"How many pills did you take?" Newell said.

"I don't know."

"No idea?"

"Two or three," she said, referring to the bottles.

"Then what happened?"

"He told me to take 'em and I took 'em. He told me that after Linda was shot to shoot myself in the head with the gun."

Newell made a sound—something like laughter or disbelief.

"How were you supposed to do that?" he asked.

"He said that if I shot myself just to—where I would knick my head and make it look like I tried to kill myself. But I said no. I was too afraid.

He said, 'You girls take care of business while I'm gone.' He handed me a pillow. By then we were in the living room. He told me to hold the pillow over the gun. It was a little brown pillow that he had on the recliner to help his neck. He was talking to Patti and I wasn't listening."

"You don't have the gun yet?" Newell said.

"No. Then he was saying good-bye and then he left. Patti and me went back to her room. Patti was already sitting down and off the gun, with a bath towel, I guess. I seen her loading the gun. I was watching her. I wasn't saying anything. I was just watching her. She finished. She handed me the gun and she goes, 'Daddy told you what to do with the pillow.' I said, 'Yeah.' She said, 'Well . . . ' She was trying to explain to me to hold it over it, but I didn't ask her what it was for. I just did what she told me to. I'm not sure if she pulled the hammer back . . . She told me to fire the gun, otherwise daddy would be hurt."

"Okay," Newell said. "What then?"

"I took the pillow with me too. I went into Linda's room. I don't know where I was standing in the room because I was too scared. I just fired the gun. The pillow got stuck in the gun when I fired it and I got scared. I didn't know if I'd broken it or what I'd done, so I ran back into Patti's room. Patti had the baby in her hands. She was standing in there with the light on. She's helping me pull back the hammer and take the pillow out, even though she had the baby in her hand, and somehow I pulled the trigger. I don't know if I was just shaking and pulled it or what happened. It hit the tapestry on her wall and I panicked. I was afraid I'd hit Krystal because she was right near the end of the gun. Patti mumbled something about that wasn't supposed to happen.

"We heard Linda crying in the other room. Patti goes, 'She's not dead.' I go, 'Well, what do I do?' And she's telling me to go in there again. She had handed me the baby and I handed her the gun. She did something with the gun and handed it back to me and I handed her back Krystal. Then she told me to go—go in there. So I went in there. When I entered the room, I didn't hear anything. I just did what I was told to and I fired it again and the noise happened again. My ears were ringing and I couldn't concentrate. I remember I was scared and I dropped the gun. I didn't understand why I did it. I don't know. I was confused and I threw the gun down and I ran out and I got the note like my father told me to before he left—out of the trailer, where I was staying. I left the trailer and went to the doghouse where we had said I would go afterwards and I stayed there."

It was not true, she said, that she burned the other notes that night or that her father came outside after the gunfire.

Why, the detective asked, had she lied to him about these things in the past?

"Because I'm ashamed that I loved my father enough to shoot Linda. I'm ashamed of it and I didn't want to admit it or accept it."

On November 7, a week after Cinnamon's latest revelations, the authorities told Patti about her confession. The burden of being the shooter was removed from Patti, they said, but she was still a conspirator in the crime. She was also the only one who could help Newell and Robinson hold Brown responsible for the death of his wife. Cinnamon's testimony alone would never convince a jury. She had told to many lies. A jury would not convict him of first-degree murder without testimony that corroborated Cinnamon's.

Patti alone could provide that, if she was willing to tell them what she knew. She thought about what they were saying and she listened to Rubright, who had spent weeks trying to convince Patti that regardless of what Brown had promised her in the past or was promising her now, he would do anything to avoid a guilty verdict. Patti considered her choices and indicated that she was ready to talk.

Newell, Robinson and Rubright met with the young woman at eleven a.m. in the jury room of the Orange County Court House. She was very uncomfortable. Patti, who did not care much for Robinson and his remarks about "white trash," was one of the few women who had formed a bad first impression of the handsome attorney. Robinson was a tanned, well-dressed, well-proportioned ex-college-football player with a capacity to make females swoon. His eyes were dark and deep-set, his smile boyish and charming, his clothes tailored and his shoes shined. By turns his manner was gentle and childlike or petulant and annoying. Some people wanted to mother him and others wanted to scold him. Men were not as taken with the lawyer as women. In one moment he acted like a highly competent and successful professional on his way to becoming the District Attorney of Orange County, and in the next he came across as a youngster who could not quite stop himself from causing unnecessary trouble. As time passed he would reveal a curious desire to be tongue-lashed in front of other people.

Newell began the session by asking Patti to state for the record that neither he nor Robinson had promised her anything in return for her confession. When she said they had not, the detective asked her to think back to early 1985 and tell them every relevant thing she could remember because the men now wanted "the absolute and complete truth."

"Sometimes," Newell said, "it may hurt to say things and if it does, tell me it's hurting. But you have to say it anyway. Okay?"

"Okay."

She said that she'd lived with David and Linda since the age of twelve and in the early years the family seemed "normal" and "pretty happy." Then one day, when they were returning to Yucca Valley from a shooting expedition in the desert, Brown suggested that the gun Patti was carrying in her lap go off and shoot Linda.

"It's like it suddenly came up out of the blue," she told the men. "But . . . nothing happened. I thought he was just joking around. Like, ha-ha. My mom used to always make jokes like, 'I'm gonna kill you, you brat,' and that's all I figured it was."

Newell asked if Linda was present when Brown made this remark.

"I think she went into Del Taco or something to get a drink and he said, 'Wouldn't it be funny . . . ?' or just made a joke out of it. But I . . . did have the gun on my lap because he didn't want it on the floor or one of them didn't want it on the floor. But that was the gun that, I think, Linda was killed with."

The last conversation about killing the woman, Patti said, came on the day before the murder, Monday, March 18, when the family had plans to go back into the desert near Calico and take target practice but were rained out. The idea was for someone to take a running charge at Linda and shove her off a cliff. That, according to Patti, "was the whole intent of going out to Calico . . . Sometimes he [David] would talk to me all day about it and then the next day Cinnamon would be part of it and he'd make me tell her what he discussed with me, so she understood."

She brought up a number of other conversations that were held about killing Linda, including one that took place during a visit to a local hospital, the same one that Cinnamon had mentioned earlier. Arthur Brown, Patti said, was present on certain occasions and acted as a lookout to make sure that Linda did not overhear them. Patti acknowledged that she suggested different ways to carry out the murder, bringing up suffocating her sister and poisoning her with cyanide-laced Tylenol capsules. This last option was something that had just been portrayed "on the news," she said, "and all of us just looked at each other and thought, Why not? I mean, it would just be dismissed as one of those . . . He [David] got a lot of ideas from watching the news."

One night Brown awakened her and told her that if she "just went into the bedroom, stuck a pillow right there while her [Linda's] back was turned, and if I put the pillow there and just shot her, then nobody'd hear anything and it'd be done and over with . . ."

"Okay," Newell said. "When did he come and say this to you?"

"I don't know. It's—all this started when we moved to Garden Grove. We lived there for about a year and a half."

"Okay . . . Can you tell me about how close it was to the time that she actually did get killed?"

"Cinnamon wasn't living there at the time," she said, going on to speculate that it was "a few months" before the murder.

Newell asked Robinson if there were things he needed to clarify.

"For a period of time," the lawyer said, "when David was suggesting these things, you say that you weren't taking him seriously. Is that correct?"

"I wasn't taking him seriously."

"All right. But there definitely was a time . . . when that changed. When did you take him seriously?"

It changed, Patti said, when she went into the bedroom to kill her sister.

Newell asked her about that night.

"I was asleep and he just said that Linda was getting real moody and everyone else was getting moody," she said. "That he was just afraid that something was going to happen. And I wanted my family to stay together . . . He just said, 'Okay, you know you can go in there. You can get the pillow, hold the pillow, hold the gun with the other hand and you can shoot her and not very many people will hear it. And then you can just—we can claim somebody came in and robbed—whatever you want to say.' "

"Okay . . . Did you actually have a pillow in your hand at one point?"

"Uh-huh."

"Where did you get that?"

"Off his bed. They always had a pillow up there and another one down at the foot of the bed."

"Did you get the pillow or did he give it to you?"

"I don't know."

"Okay. Did you actually have a gun in your hand?"

"Yes."

"Which gun?"

"I don't know. I'm pretty sure it's the same one that she was killed with . . ."

"Okay," Newell said. "Was he standing with you during this time?"

"He was standing around the corner right there. His— their bedroom's right there and, like, there was the office. He was standing on the other side of the office 'cause he couldn't take to see it . . ."

"How far in did you get—how far did you go with that?"

"I was right next to her . . . I was right there. She was facing the other way. And then I walked out and I said I couldn't do it. He said, 'Okay, then, just go to bed. Just forget it. It's not important.' And then, apparently, a few minutes later she turned over or something. And he came and he said, 'Good thing you didn't because she turned over and that would have been real yucky . . . a real terrible scene to try to explain.'"

Robinson asked when she agreed to go along with the killing.

"I never agreed," she said. "It's just the fact that he hands you the gun and I did take him serious then, but I never actually agreed . . ."

"He continually laid this business on you about keeping the family together, the guilt, he would be gone, so on, so forth," Robinson said. "Is that true?"

"Yes."

"Was that something that made you go along with some of this stuff?"

"Yes."

"All right. After he laid all that guilt on you about keeping the family together . . . did you, along with Cinnamon and David, agree and participate in the planning to kill Linda?"

"Yes."

"And did you feel that you were doing something that was right?"

"Yes and no. To be honest, I really didn't think it was ever gonna happen. I mean, it was like a science fiction story. You went through all the way to the end but nothing ever—"

"But . . . you knew that he wanted her dead. True?"

"Yes and no . . . I guess you could say I didn't understand the terms of death."

"You're kidding!" Newell said.

Patti didn't respond.

Newell asked her whose decision it was not to pull the trigger when she was standing over Linda's bed.

"Mine."

"Okay. He didn't try to stop you."

"No . . . The next morning when I woke up, he goes, 'Well, I'm sorry that I put you in all that. I was just kidding. I just wanted to see' . . . I didn't know how serious he was until after she died . . ."

"Did he tell you whether or not to discuss these plans to kill Linda with anyone?"

"No. He never said anything. Once in a while he'd say, 'Well, don't tell anyone what we just discussed,' or Linda would be back in the kitchen and then she'd come back out and . . . it'd get real quiet and she goes, 'Well, what's the matter? Why did everyone suddenly get so quiet?' And he'd laugh and say, 'Well, I just told her a joke and she didn't get it.' Or something off the wall."

Newell asked Patti to talk about the night of the murder and not "hold anything back . . . even if it's hard."

"Okay."

"Now's the time to do it."

She described the visit to the house by Brown's parents, the dinner, the card game and how she and Cinnamon went to sleep in her room.

"Me and Cinnamon were later woke up by David, telling us girls that something had to happen tonight or else he was going to leave."

"Uh-huh," Newell said.

"And we went out to the living room and talked about how was the best way for it to be done . . . I know he sat in his recliner, talked to me and Cinnamon, and said, 'We got guns, you guys can do it that way.' I mean, he did the suggestions . . . Me and Cinnamon would say it was a good idea, a bad idea, whatever."

"Okay," Robinson said. "Had you seen the gun at this point?"

"No . . . He said he didn't want to be in the house when it happened and he was going to have to leave when it happened. For the purpose [that] if the police did come after she was killed, the car would have to have been warm so his alibi would've been true that he was at the beach."

"Okay," Newell said. "You say 'alibi.' Did he—are those your words or . . . ?"

"If the car was warm, then that would cover him."

Newell asked if she had seen the gun yet.

"I don't know where the gun came in or anything . . . He told me I had to get Krystal so nothing would happen to her."

"Uh-huh."

"And I went—I couldn't reach Krystal 'cause it was up and over the crib and I didn't know how to put the crib down. And I didn't want to wake her up. But he went in there. He helped me get . . . Krystal up out of the bed and then I walked halfway out to the living room and he said he was leaving."

"Okay. And then where did you go from there?"

"My bedroom, to try to get Krystal to go back to sleep . . . I think Cinnamon was in there."

Newell asked if she had seen the gun by now.

"No. Uh, like I said, I don't know where the gun came in. I think it was on the couch . . ."

"Did you hear, before David left, any instructions about how to shoot the gun?"

"He once—he made a comment that the first shot might not kill her. We might need two . . . He made that comment when he took us girls out of the room. Saying, 'Well, if

159

you guys shoot her, one shot might not kill her. She might be able to get us all separated from the family.' ''

Before Brown left the house, Patti said, he told Cinnamon that she was "going to have to use the pillow so no neighbors would hear . . .''

"Did you hear David say that?''

"Yeah.''

"To her?''

She nodded. "Because I had to hand Cinnamon the pillow.''

What pillow? Newell asked.

"It's a long brown pillow . . . that he always had on his recliner.''

"Okay. Did she have the gun at that time?''

"I don't know. I don't know where the gun came into the . . .''

"Had Cinnamon taken any medication by that time?''

"I don't—I don't know . . .''

"Did you see Cinnamon take the medication or see—?''

"No.''

"Or see David give her the medication?''

"I didn't see it. I know David told her where it was. And I know David said it'd make it look like a suicide.''

When did he say that? Newell asked.

"In the prior conversation when he called us girls out into the living room . . . He just said it would make it look like she tried to kill herself [and] that she couldn't live with what she did, so the authorities would go real light on her. And . . . he used to tell me, if I tried to kill Linda then I'd have to shoot myself in the leg or somewhere to make it look that I was trying to commit suicide, 'cause I couldn't live with it. I mean, it was always in the leg, in the head, or take the pills and make it look like you tried to kill yourself.''

Newell asked if he'd ever told Patti to shoot herself in the head.

"Yeah. He said if I did that, then Linda would feel guilty about her little sister getting upset and Linda would go . . .

160

in a state of shock or something . . . and maybe it'd be too much on her and maybe she'd die that way."

While the three of them were in the living room, did the subject of suicide notes come up?

"Notes were discussed that night, yeah, but notes were discussed before on different occasions . . . He had us write on notes like what you've got there . . . he'd make it look like a suicide note."

"He had you write notes also?"

"When I was supposed to kill Linda, yes."

Newell asked her to return to the moment when she and Cinnamon and Krystal were in her bedroom and Brown had left the house. "Does Cinnamon leave—go out of your room?"

"Yeah. She left my room. She said, 'Okay, Patti, I'm gonna go get it done and over with.' "

"Okay."

"And I didn't—I don't know where the gun was, how she got the gun. After she came back, like two minutes later, she said, 'Patti, the gun don't work.' I got up off the bed with Krystal on my hip and went over to her and the gun went off. I don't remember what I touched—if I even touched the gun . . . The gun went off and I—we both said, 'Oh, my God,' and I said, 'Oh, my God, Cinnamon, you better go.' And she went and—"

"Good," Newell said. "Explain that a little more . . ."

"I don't know what I meant. I mean, now I would say that I meant for her not to go do it."

"Wait a minute," Newell said. "You just confused me." The men were aware that Patti's story didn't agree with Cinnamon's. One had wondered why, if Patti was telling the truth, the first shot hadn't awakened Linda.

"Well, I mean, I didn't really think anything was gonna happen . . . but it was serious."

"Okay. You sound like you're having a hard time discussing this part of it."

"Yes," Patti said.

"You're having a little bit of a tough time—"

"Well, I told her, 'Oh, my God, go.' I mean, I don't

know what I was thinking. I mean, I can't say that . . . my intent at the time was for her to . . . go to Linda's room.''

"And what?'' Newell said.

"Well, the gun went off. I would imagine the conversation was for her to kill Linda.''

"Okay. And it's . . . hard to talk about something like that. I can see that. But . . . we need to get it down now. All right. That's why I keep going back to that area. Okay. So you did—you told her to go . . . in and do what the plan was for that night, then.''

"Yes . . . I heard a shot about a minute, maybe. I don't know. It seemed like a long time. I heard a shot and then I heard another one.''

"You think you heard two shots.''

"I know I heard two shots.''

Where, Newell asked, returning to the same question the two men had been posing throughout the session, did the gun come from?

"I think it was on the couch. I don't know. I don't know where the gun came from or anything.''

Newell dropped this line of inquiry and asked her to continue with her story.

"I was scared. I stayed on my bed. I walked around. I thought I heard things. I don't know.''

"Did you ever go into Linda's room?''

"No.''

"How soon after that did David come back?''

"About . . . an hour, hour and a half . . . I heard someone outside. I peeked out my window. I realized it was him. I got out of my room. I met him halfway in the hallway. And he goes, 'What's the matter?' I was crying and I said, 'Something did happen,' and he said, 'Oh, my God.' And he says, 'Calm down, relax,' and he started to go back to the back bedroom and I told him don't go because I really think something happened. And he asked where Cinnamon was and I said I didn't know. And then he went in the kitchen and got on the phone and he called 911 or whoever he called . . .''

"Did David say any more about the plan and it getting carried out or anything?"

"Nothing. I mean, I was crying and he kept on telling me calm down and he kept on taking Krystal from me and then giving her back to me . . . and then the officers came and one of them asked me to sit in the dining room and Krystal stayed with me once in a while, then she'd go over there with David. And then his mom showed up and got Krystal."

"Did you and David ever discuss what should be said or shouldn't be said?"

No, Patti replied, but then added, "He said if something was ever to happen it was because her [Cinnamon's] daddy's life was threatened or . . . Linda didn't like Krystal or wanted Cinnamon out of the house or whatever reason. I was always told Linda hated me. But then Linda said, 'Don't worry, Patti, I don't hate you.' And I was always put in the spot that Linda didn't like me, so that was my reason to do it, if I was to do anything."

"The night you went in with the pillow—a few months before this—was there a discussion as to what you'd tell the police about that?"

"No . . . He told me all day that Linda hates me, she wants you out of the house . . . but nothing was ever discussed about what I was supposed to tell them. He said for me to make up my own story . . ."

"Some of the things that you testified to [at Cinnamon's trial] weren't the truth," Newell said. "Is that right?"

"Yes."

"Recently, when you and David went up to see Cinnamon and Cinnamon talked to David, did David come back and tell you Cinnamon had talked to him about wanting to tell the truth?"

"He came back . . . and said, 'Cinnamon's going real far. She's depressed. I think she's gonna kill herself, Patti. We need to trade places or do something to get her out of there before she blows it for all of us . . .'"

Robinson said, "Did David, when you went up there, plan to get you to . . . go along with her?"

"Well, he asked me if I was the one that killed Linda because she said she didn't do it, and that's why she was so upset . . . He asked me if I'd be willing to trade places. And that's when I said, 'Well, if it's gonna help you and her, then yeah, I'll trade places, but as long as someone will take care of Heather and Krystal.' "

"Did he explain how you would trade places?"

"Me to make up a believable story. Either lie or whatever—make up a story."

"What you've told us here is—?"

"Is the truth," Patti said.

"Uh-huh."

"Ah, the best that I remember," she said.

"Okay . . ."

"He said that he'd stand behind me and he'd still let me see Krystal and still let me see Heather, and Cinnamon would be happy . . . He told me, 'There's no way Cinnamon did it. She's too good of a person to hurt Linda. There was too much love there.' Or, 'I know my daughter better than that.' And then he told me, 'Well, it must have been Larry or Alan [Bailey].' "

"Well, and was this all a lie by him?" Robinson asked. "In other words, when he was saying this stuff, you knew that he knew what had happened, right?"

"No. I didn't know he knew that Cinnamon did it. I didn't know."

"Well, you knew that Larry or whoever didn't do that."

"Well, I mean . . . before she got killed, there was a time on the driveway that he'd say, 'Well, Linda and Alan and Larry are out to get me.' But I mean, I never took him serious. And then, after it did happen, then he started telling me more and more that maybe it was them, maybe it was them."

"But you knew that night," Robinson said. "You were there."

"Yeah."

"Okay."

"And I knew that there was no way that it could have been Larry or Alan."

164

"Yeah."

"But, I mean, just the power of suggestion of someone else taking it—I guess—taking the blame [was] appealing. I don't know."

"Was appealing?" Newell said.

"Well . . . yeah."

"Yeah, well, I want you to be honest about it . . ."

"Well, I mean, he started saying, 'Larry got released two hours before Linda was killed and I know in my heart that Cinnamon didn't do it, so if Larry just got released, then Larry has more of a motive for killing Linda because Linda wouldn't bail him out that night that he was in jail.' I mean, just the power of suggestion, I guess, made me believe that it wasn't Cinnamon and that it was possibly him. But I do know that it was not Larry or Alan because Cinnamon was in my room."

Don Rubright spoke for the first time, addressing Patti. "And nobody else was in that house that night?"

"No one was . . ."

"So that Alan-and-Larry thing came up out of David's mind?" Robinson said.

Patti nodded.

"Okay," Newell said, and there was a pause, the men exchanging glances and sorting through what they'd just heard.

"So," Newell said, "just rehashing some of this. You feel that . . . when you went to help Cinnamon fix the gun . . . do you know what was wrong with it?"

"No idea," Patti said.

He asked if she'd pulled back the hammer on the pistol.

"Yeah. I don't know. I mean, I want to say yes, but I want to say no. I mean, I want to say no because I don't think I did, but I want to say yes because there's a part of me that thinks I did."

"Or could have," Newell said.

"Yeah . . ."

"You could have pulled back the—"

"The hammer, yes," she said.

"Do you remember doing something with the gun?" Robinson said.

"I remember getting up and walking to her [Cinnamon] by the door. And standing next to her with Krystal on my hip. I'm not sure if I touched the gun, reached over to it or what. But it was like, thirty seconds later, the gun went off."

"Did Cinnamon have that pillow that you had handed her with her at that time?" Newell said.

"I don't know . . . ."

Whatever became of the brown pillow? the detective asked.

"David had it up until about six or seven months ago. And it was finally so worn out that it got thrown in the trash . . . ."

"Do you know where that bullet went that night in your room?"

"No. My ears started ringing. Krystal seemed upset. And like I said, I told Cinnamon she go—she's got—she's got to go—I mean she's got to go . . . ."

"Got to go finish what she was supposed to."

"Finish what she was supposed to do," Patti said.

"Yeah," Newell replied.

"My ears rang. I didn't even think about the shot when the police was talking to me about it. I didn't even think about it and then I remembered in the middle of the interview that a shot did go off in my room."

"So your ears were still ringing when Cinnamon left the room."

"Yes. Ringing for a long time . . ."

"Patti," Robinson said, "your last words to Cinnamon before she left—when you, in essence, told her to go finish Linda off—why did you want Linda dead at that time? What were your reasons? Was there something for your own selfish reason or was it because David had—?"

"David had us believe that . . . the family was the most important thing and she was gonna disrupt the family and we'd never be able to be a family once again . . . My family was never a family. And this was our one true chance of being a family and having everything that a family was supposed to have. And she was going to interrupt that if he was to leave or they were going to get a divorce. Then we'd never be a family again. And, I guess, I needed the fact to know that there was a family."

"Did you believe then that by you guys killing Linda based on everything he told you over and over that—?"

"We'd all stay family . . . He said Cinnamon wouldn't serve that much time. We'd all be happy, the four of us. We'd come back and be a family the way we were supposed to be. With no 'I'm leaving' or 'I hate you' or 'I want a divorce' or none of that. We would always be a family, forever from that day forward, no matter what."

She told the men that before the killing she was aware of only one life insurance policy on Linda, which David had purchased from Annie Blanks's father, Robert. Patti did not say how much it was for. Money was a vague subject for the young woman; during her years with Brown, he'd never allowed her to have bank accounts of her own, and when she'd received money from car accidents or her relatives, she had to endorse the checks over to him. That money was often used for household items, like furniture or a new refrigerator.

"Can you think of anything else?" Newell said. "Is there anything . . . that we haven't discussed that—things may have come up to your mind and we never did get to them or—?"

"No."

"Patti," Rubright said, "do you realize now that you feel like you were duped?"

"Hell, yes . . . I didn't think any—I mean, I knew someone was gonna die, but I didn't realize that it was gonna be so close to home."

"You didn't realize . . . what it was gonna feel like afterwards?" Rubright said.

"Yeah. I didn't realize that this is . . . what it was gonna be like. I honestly believed that the four of us were gonna maintain being a family because I didn't have a family with mine. And I honestly believed that the four of us would maintain a decent family and nothing was ever gonna tear us apart.''

"That you'd live happily ever after, after Linda was killed?" Newell said.

"Yeah, like a little fairy tale . . .''

"And," Rubright said, "in summing everything up—I mean just so we can clarify—what you did, you realize, was wrong?''

"Yes.''

"All right. And in retrospect," her attorney said, "you feel that you did it for . . . reasons that you thought at the time were right but now you know were wrong.''

"Yes.''

"Do you feel remorse or sorrow," Rubright asked, "for taking part or participating in the killing of your sister?''

"Yes. After she died, I felt so bad, so upset . . . I couldn't live with it. I mean, I lived with it, obviously, but there is several occasions that I did try to kill myself because I couldn't live with it.''

XIII

David Brown's preliminary hearing, which is the California equivalent of a grand jury, was set to begin on the nineteenth of December. As that date approached, word came back to him through his lawyer that Patti had spoken to the authorities and would be testifying against him at these proceedings. If the judge at the hearing ruled that there was enough evidence for a first-degree murder trial, Brown would be facing these charges alone. That came as a shock to the man. Throughout his life, Brown had done virtually nothing by himself. As a child he was surrounded by brothers and sisters. At an early age he had physically left his parents' home, but he'd never emotionally left his parents. From seventeen on he had not been without a wife or a lover or both or, occasionally, more than one lover. All of the women who knew him said the same thing: he was terrified of being alone. When faced with the prospect for even a day or two, he would call old girlfriends or potential new ones and invite them to stay at his house. He would not go shopping or run an errand by himself and would almost never go for a drive without others in the car. He had to have people nearby who would listen to his stories and act upon his demands.

When Brown was well into his thirties, it wasn't unusual for him to insist that his parents come over simply to keep him company or do housework. His father always wanted to help with the computer business and his mother liked to clean—she would vacuum a carpet with very little prompting. After the murder Arthur and Manuella moved in to please and placate their ill son. They felt needed and he felt more secure in their presence. Until his arrest, he had never been separated from those in his innermost circle, those he trusted and turned to with his latest ideas and plans. Once he was living in the Orange County Jail, he acted like someone who was unaware that there were people who did not think as he did and who were not as malleable as the members of his family. He made little or no distinction between dealing with the teenage girls he was financially supporting and dealing with longtime convicts, although he did quickly take on the vernacular of whomever he was talking to. Brown's peculiar sense of innocence—his belief that he could control everything—was profound and unshakable.

Don Rubright put it another way: "David is just smart enough to be really stupid."

Brown spent a lot of time talking with other inmates about his past and what had led to his arrest. He would trade stories and, like most other prisoners, tell anyone who would listen that he'd been unjustly accused of a crime. One of those he opened up to was Joe Drake, a veteran resident of the Orange County Jail and a good listener. Brown told him that his wife had been killed while he was away from the house on a late-night ride to the beach; he'd been set up by his daughter and sister-in-law, who were only interested in his money; to this day he didn't really know what happened the night she died, only that he was facing a trial and a possible death sentence for something he had no part in. Under California law, "murder with special circumstances" can lead to death by the gas chamber; "special circumstances" means that one has been convicted of killing for monetary gain. He had a lot of cash buried out in the desert, Brown told Joe Drake, and if he could only get out of jail he would share it with those who were on his side.

In prison money is power. It can buy lawyers and hope and protection from other violent cons and perhaps even freedom. Money gets the ears of prisoners, especially if one can prove that he has it on the outside. Brown was a persuasive talker and spoke with authority. In the past few years, he'd owned two different models of Mercedes, including a big champagne convertible 560 SEL and a tan 190E; he'd purchased a $480,000 house with a swimming pool and hot tub; he'd had bank accounts holding hundreds of thousands of dollars, having collected $835,000 after the death of his wife; he'd torn up the desert on a Honda motorcycle, a Ford Bronco and a Honda Odyssey; in his safe at home were rare coins valued in the thousands of dollars apiece; in his possession were expensive paintings, lithographs, Oriental ivory, jade sculptures and bronze and marble figures appraised at half a million dollars, plus whatever cash was in the ground out by Yucca Valley. When he talked of things he had owned or still owned, some people could not help paying attention. Joe Drake was one of them.

Jeff Robinson, the prosecuting attorney for Orange County, and Joel Baruch, the lawyer for David Arnold Brown, did not like each other. A lot of legal squabbling is purely a professional exercise; lawyers say things to one another in court because they feel that the situation requires it or because they want to make certain that their client, who is watching their performance, knows they are putting out and willing to sweat for their fee. Like professional wrestlers, attorneys are notorious for attacking one another in front of a judge and spending the evening together over a drink. It's part of the job and often the most fun and exciting thing that happens to them professionally after all of their pretrial grunt work and hours of tedious research. Most lawyers will admit there is some ham or thespian inside them. In Los Angeles in recent years, this idea has become a business. Actors give lessons to attorneys on how to be more dramatic and persuasive in front of a jury. In California itself, the competition between the state's 122,000 lawyers has become intense and many of them will try anything to get an edge on their legal foes. One out of seven of these attorneys, according to 1990 statistics from the State Bar, can no longer handle the pressure and has developed a substance abuse problem.

None of this applied to Robinson and Baruch. They didn't have to rehearse their emotions or work up any false animosity. They just didn't get along. Baruch was by nature a hand grenade in the stately halls of justice. He looked like a man who was always waiting for his feelings to be hurt. He might go off at any time and there were bound to be people whom he rubbed the wrong way. Robinson had a more subtle and mysterious personality. When he was charming, he was fairly irresistible, acting just like a successful attorney with plenty of self-control. When he slipped out of control, he became adolescent, confused and lost. If either he or Baruch perceived anything resembling a threat, each one went for the jugular. One of the first things Robinson did during the preliminary hearing was to refer to his opponent as the "dirtiest and most unethical lawyer I have ever seen," although his professional ethics had never been called into question. Baruch counterpunched by calling Robinson a "buffoon." Robinson labeled Baruch's conduct "improper and contemptuous."

Baruch told the bench, "I'm sorry for that [for losing his temper], but I want the court to realize that from my standpoint Mr. Robinson is trying to push certain buttons. Yesterday when I called him a name in the court, he had stated on no less than three occasions without a response from me that I was playing to the press. That's an unfair accusation of this district attorney . . . I've been in this county a dozen years as a practicing lawyer and today was the first time that I've been found in contempt of court by a judge."

"It may not be the last," the court replied.

Another lawyer might have interpreted this statement from Judge Floyd M. Schenk as a victory for the prosecution, but Robinson didn't win easily. He stood up and said, "I want the record to reflect the fact that the court has been more than fair with Mr. Baruch, and I feel that I only responded after Mr. Baruch has gone into visible and audible tirades, challenging the court, challenging the prosecution, challenging the witness. And Mr. Baruch, like a spoiled child when he doesn't get what he wants, goes off into this tirade. I don't think it's proper in a courtroom and I'm only asking the court to treat both counsels the way that an advocate should be treated.''

''Shall we proceed?'' the judge sighed.

Baruch stood and declared, ''Your Honor, my client has requested that I furnish him with a couple of Tylenol for a very severe headache.''

''That's all right with me,'' the court said.

Throughout the hearing, Judge Schenk, a patient man, had his tolerance stretched by several sizes. He was forever telling the men to calm down and grow up. On the record both attorneys asked for the other one not to smirk. Brown watched the proceedings from the center of the courtroom, taking notes and saying little, yet at times it appeared that his curious influence on people had spread to the lawyers, who acted as if they wanted to skip the legal niceties and choke each other. When Cinnamon or Patti was testifying, Baruch made a point of standing right behind Brown, so the young women had to look directly at him as they answered the attorney's questions. On several occasions when Mary Bailey came to the hearing to make a show of support for the women, Baruch stood in front of her—Patti and Cinnamon could not see the most sympathetic pair of eyes in the courtroom. The lawyer didn't realize that the young women were nearsighted, but his ploys were still effective.

''Why are you intimidated by your father?'' he asked Cinnamon on December 22, several days into the hearing.

''Because he's sitting there looking at me.''

''I've heard you say that before,'' the lawyer said. ''I don't understand what you mean.''

''It's—it brings back the power of him sitting there staring at me. It hurts.''

''What power?''

''Like in '85 and '84. I mean, he'd look at me and it just reminds me of the same thing over again. I can't—I'm uncomfortable with him sitting there looking at me. I feel threatened by it.''

She went on to say that she was so uncomfortable with the situation that she never wanted to see her father again. More than once during the hearing, the young woman left the courtroom in tears.

When the lawyers held private conferences with the judge, away from Brown and whoever happened to be testifying, things became even more personal. Baruch went so far as to tell the judge that because he—Schenk—did not like Baruch, he was prejudiced against his client and should remove himself from the case.

Baruch: ''Mr. Robinson, out in the hall at lunchtime, came up in full view of several people, called me an unethical attorney outside the courtroom and said I'm going to be in jail someday. He threatened—''

The court: ''Just a second now. Are you indicating that the court heard that?''

Baruch: ''No, I don't think the court heard that. That was outside.''

The court: ''Wait a minute. You don't think it did?''

Baruch: ''I don't think you were there.''

The court: ''That's right. I wasn't there and I don't want any innuendos to in any way indicate that I was anywhere near you two at lunchtime.''

After a brief consideration of Baruch's argument, Schenk decided to leave himself on the case.

One of Baruch's key tactics was to remind Cinnamon repeatedly that if her father was convicted, he could go to the gas chamber. Did she realize that she was sentencing her own father to death? Did she really want to do that? Or was she only doing it to help herself? Baruch also told the young woman that the penalty for perjury in a death-sentence case is also death. Was she willing to keep lying in the courtroom with that prospect facing her? Jeff Robinson, raised a Catholic and morally opposed to the gas chamber, was disturbed by these tactics. He had accepted the death penalty as a possibility in this case only because he felt that Brown's actions were so heinous. The prosecutor found

Brown's actions were so heinous. The prosecutor found Baruch's courtroom performance both legally and personally objectionable and spent considerable energy telling this to Judge Schenk.

That was exactly what Baruch wanted him to do. After announcing that Robinson was prejudiced and unfit for these proceedings, the defense attorney initiated an unusual legal procedure known as recusal, which seeks to remove a lawyer from a case. If the judge granted Baruch his wishes and Robinson were dismissed, Brown's possible trial and conviction would be pushed back even further and things would become even more confused and entangled than they already were. "There has never been," a beleaguered Robinson said at one point, "a more convoluted case than this one." As with most legal requests, the court had no choice but to take this one under consideration. Until the issue was resolved, there was a chance that everything that had so far occurred could be nullified. Baruch was on the offensive and Robinson was dismayed. For months he'd been working closely with Newell, anxious to convict Brown and win this highly emotional and highly publicized case. If he were removed, not only would he be disappointed, but replacing him with someone who had a comparable knowledge of the murder would be time-consuming and virtually impossible.

For three days the hearing was stopped and the judge considered the recusal motion. More legal minds were brought into the courtroom to offer opinions and argue their way toward a resolution—a lawyer's paradise. Jack Earley, an attorney who worked with Baruch, represented his man, and Tom Goethals, from the D.A.'s office, represented Robinson. Goethals accused Baruch of trickery and Baruch admitted that he'd hoodwinked Cinnamon, asking her false questions on one subject in order to elicit information from her on other subjects. Baruch accused Robinson of intimidating Patti into testifying against Brown. Robinson accused Baruch of letting it be known within the Orange County Jail that Patti Bailey Brown was snitching on her husband—the same thing, in Robinson's view, as giving Patti a death sentence. Emotions uncoiled and anger flew. Robinson's cheeks flushed and Baruch trembled with indignation. The bad blood got worse. At the end of three days, the judge ruled that Robinson could stay and that it was time for everyone to settle down. Baruch, unruffled, conceding nothing, said that in order to protect his client and ensure that justice be done, he would appeal the ruling. The proceedings stumbled forward.

"This hearing," Baruch declared late one afternoon, "is going to last forever."

"It may," the court replied.

The hearing lasted for weeks and produced thousands upon thousands of pages of testimony, the great majority of them containing information that the women had already revealed, although there were variations on many of the details. Robinson's central challenge was not to derail what some regarded as a solid case against Brown, while Baruch's goal was to establish that Robinson had nothing but a few facts surrounded by a wall of lies: Cinnamon and Patti weren't just casual liars but were fundamentally incapable of telling the truth. Cinnamon's only motive was to get out of prison, while Patti's was to avoid the gas chamber—it was still Baruch's contention that she was the killer—and send Brown to his death. The lawyer let no one forget that during Cinnamon's original trial both of the women had repeatedly lied under oath. Robinson watched Baruch's performance and listened to him with all the patience he could muster, but at one point he could not stop himself from saying that his opponent had a "ridiculous mind."

In the first weeks of the hearing, Baruch asked Cinnamon, "Are you lying now to cover up the lies you told to the police about the lies you told just after the killing?"

"I don't remember," she said, using a phrase she would employ 173 times as Baruch fired off his endless questions. She said, "I don't know," at least that often.

"I told so many lies," she said to the defense attorney during the hearing, "I don't remember the lies that I told before."

On the sixth day of January in the new year, Baruch asked her, "Did you wrap the ribbon around the [suicide] note because you were happy to kill Linda?"

"I doubt it," a weary Cinnamon replied. "I think I was just bored."

Throughout her testimony, Cinnamon reiterated that Patti had loaded the gun and handed it to her before she shot Linda, a process that intrigued Baruch. He couldn't help wondering what passed through Cinnamon's mind after she took the gun and prepared to walk into her stepmother's room to kill her.

"Did you love Linda at that moment?" he asked.

"Yes," Cinnamon said.

"Were you angry at Linda at all for anything?"

"Not that I know of," the young woman shrugged.

Patti was next on the stand. Ever since Brown had learned that she would be testifying against him, he'd been sending her more letters about marital loyalty and telling his parents not to visit her or bring her any gifts until she changed her mind. He persuaded a Mormon minister to go to the jail and attempt to talk her out of her plans and, finally, he insisted that she write to him in jail, keeping open their lines of communication. When Rubright learned about this last request, he demanded that Patti turn Brown's letters over to him and that she stop writing the man. After more guilt and tears and anguish, the young woman once again listened to her lawyer.

For years before the hearing, Patti and Cinnamon had perceived each other as enemies. Cinnamon, in particular, saw Patti as someone she had quarreled with when they'd all lived together, someone who had lied to her in the past, someone who had come between her and her father, someone who had played a role in the murder of Linda but had never taken any responsibility for her actions. As Cinnamon had told Robinson and Newell the previous summer, she didn't care for Patti at all. By the end of 1988, her feelings had seemingly begun to change. It wasn't just that she wanted Patti to cooperate with the attorneys and corroborate her own story or just that she wanted Patti to help make the charges against her father stick. It was more than that. By the time the hearing had begun, Cinnamon had been away from her family for a long time and had started to confront at least some of what had happened to her as a child and adolescent, some of the guilt and shame. More than anyone else, she knew how difficult it was for Patti to speak up and face the possibility of sending Brown to prison—or to his death. Cinnamon knew what Patti was going through now and how deep her father's hold was on the young woman. Over the holiday season, she did something that would have been inconceivable only a short time before: she sent Patti a Christmas card and offered her support. Patti was thrilled to get the card and returned the favor. She needed all the help she could get.

When she took the stand, she shook just like her mother, hands shaking, lips shaking, head shaking, words shaking, pure terror looking out at the courtroom and speaking in a soft voice. She had asked Rubright if she could be hypnotized for this ordeal, but he said no. Patti repeatedly denied that either she or Cinnamon had been given any kind of a deal to testify, although she had lately been placed in protective custody. Baruch, who could distract a toughened convict with his badgering style of inquiry, used everything he'd learned at law school and some other skills that he'd picked up in less elevated environments to turn Patti to mush. Sometimes it worked.

She sat quietly and listened as the defense attorney called her "promiscuous" because of things she'd done with Brown when she was eleven (inside she wasn't quiet at all, and privately she said, "I shouldn't let these things bother me, but being called that is like your worst fear. I mean, no one would have believed me if I would have told the truth back then, and I feel like nobody believes me now"). Patti told the court that she never actually heard her sister speaking on the phone with Alan Bailey about killing David, but only "assumed" that was what Linda was talking about that night in the kitchen.

Patti said that Brown was "surprised" in the early hours

of March 19, 1985, when he came home and she informed him that Cinnamon had fired a gun several times in the house. After learning what had happened, Patti said, the man was "casual." She explained to the court that David had spoken to the police who first arrived on the scene in such a loud voice so that she could hear him across the room, repeat what he was saying, and their versions of the events would square. One thing Patti didn't tell the judge or assembled attorneys was why there was no gunshot residue on her fingers. While detectives were roaming every corner of the house, she asked if she could go to the bathroom and was told yes, but ordered not to wash her hands. A policeman stood outside the bathroom door to make sure there was no water running within. He heard nothing when Patti dipped her hands in the toilet bowl, rubbed them together and dried them with a towel.

The most striking thing about the testimonies of both Cinnamon and Patti was their innocence. They seemed completely innocent—not innocent of the crime of killing Linda Brown, but innocent in a stranger and more mysterious way. Despite what they said in the courtroom, they didn't seem capable of planning and carrying out the execution of their stepmother and sister. On the stand, while being coddled by Robinson or hounded by Baruch, they were not at all sinister or devious. They were, most of all, vague—vague about details, vague about the past, vague about their motives, vague about when things had occurred, vague in their language, vague in the same way that Brown himself was vague. Throughout the years leading up to the murder, nothing was ever clearly and sharply defined in their own minds, but everything flowed along like one ceaseless television situation comedy that at some unknown point had become real and serious.

Was there really any connection between the dead woman and the two nice innocent young women who marched into the courtroom and told their stories? Watching them, one had the feeling that they'd become different people since being separated from the man who had raised them. His influence was not just subtle and pervasive, but far more powerful than one might have first guessed. Throughout the hearing, the impression was slowly being created that he had never given specific orders for how his wife was to be killed. That wasn't necessary; all he had to do was talk to the girls and then go for a drive. Brown didn't simply control things in his household. He didn't just manipulate others or get them to act out his ideas and schemes. He introduced them, to their own hidden rage and capacity for evil.

XIV

On Christmas Eve of 1988 a new prisoner came into the Orange County Jail. Richard Steinhart had been a high school football star, an amateur wrestler, a soldier in Vietnam, and was a member of the Hessian motorcycle gang of California, a drug abuser (using up to $1,000 a day of cocaine), the owner of a criminal record, a certified grandmaster in karate, a violent man and what many people would regard as a terrible human being. Round, wide and heavily muscled, he sweat profusely and usually needed a bath. His dark ponytail was stringy and his black goatee was unkempt. He had a repugnant attitude and even his laughter was menacing. Intimidation came naturally to him and he liked using his fists. His belly wobbled, his biceps were meaty and he wore tattoos in places not generally visible. Blue jeans, leather and boots were his chosen attire, and he looked something like the legendary late-night radio personality, Wolfman Jack, but this was Jack with a lot of twists and kinks, Jack on dope, out of control and ready to rumble, a louder, brutal Jack with a strong desire to punish his own body and the bodies of others. Steinhart had not only done a lot of ugly things—robbed and pillaged and assaulted— he liked to brag about this behavior. In addition to his other disturbing traits, he talked too much and too fast and claimed to have taken part in twelve murders.

He was arrested for violating his parole from a previous drug charge: he enjoyed speed and other illegal substances. For a man who was drawn to amphetamines, he didn't seem to need an artificial boost. He was naturally jumpy, unable to sit in a chair, or at least not sit as most people do. He squirmed, he writhed, he flailed. When he told a story sitting down, he swung his arms with enough force to hurt a grown man. When he walked, he looked like two truck drivers who were about to engage in a brawl. It was hard to say what struck one the most about Steinhart—his swaggering movements, his nonstop mouth or his nasty point of view. When he was in a room, even a crowded room, eyes landed on him and were fixed. Despite his appearance and his frequent bad intentions, something about the man was charming. He had what is loosely called "heart."

When he was arrested, because he was scheduled to be a witness in an upcoming triple-murder trial involving the Hessian gang, Steinhart was placed in protective custody. Brown first saw him on Christmas Day when he was giving a karate demonstration in the jail. It wasn't a planned demonstration but an impromptu one, the way the biker did most things. He felt something and then roared into action. Using his feet, he was showing an inmate how to hurt someone, and this captured Brown's fancy. Although David himself was in protective custody, he was still afraid of many people inside the walls. He needed a shield and it had suddenly appeared in the form of this twirling nightmare.

When the demonstration was over, Brown went up to Steinhart and introduced himself, complimenting the man on his martial arts skills and flattering him at length. They began to talk and Brown was soon spending time with him in the "day room" section of protective custody and telling him his story. In the jail Brown hadn't been known as someone who possessed a smart mouth. If one uses provocative language in prison, one needs to be able to "walk that talk," as cons say. Brown couldn't walk anything and he knew it, but Steinhart . . . he was something altogether different. Nobody wanted to get in his way. For one thing he looked very tough, and for another he was obviously crazy, likely to do something dangerous at any moment. Before long Brown was taunting others in the day room—"Sit down, punk"—big Richard swelling at his side.

It occurred to Brown that his new friend was more than protection. Steinhart was scheduled to leave the jail soon, and once he was gone, he could work for Brown on the street. He might even be a way out, probably the last best way out. When the two men met at the end of 1988, Brown was counting the days until Patti took the stand at the preliminary hearing. Once she'd decided to testify, he could no longer sustain the notion that he controlled what she said or did. He believed that Patti had cut a deal with the district attorney's office, and after she'd testified and portrayed Brown as the puppeteer behind the killing, she would be released from jail. That, in David's mind, made a new plan absolutely necessary. What he was thinking of required more than a sympathetic ear or a set of parents who would lie for him at will. It took more than he would ask of anyone in his immediate family. It took daring and boldness and a devil-may-care attitude that not everyone had. Brown was pretty sure that his new friend fit into that category.

Just as he had done with Joe Drake, Brown told Steinhart that he had coins, diamonds and other valuables stashed in various places and a lot of cash buried in the desert. Inside one of the safes in his home, he said, was a set of maps that showed exactly where the loot was hidden, and a second set of books that showed all the money he'd earned and never reported to the IRS. Brown told Steinhart that he owned twenty-five acres in Australia and if the biker would help him break out of the Orange County Jail, they could fly to that distant continent together and ride motorcycles down under. David, naturally, would pay for everything.

Steinhart was nothing if not suggestible—he couldn't help listening to the offer and thinking about spending someone else's money. He and Brown and Drake began eating their meals in a huddle at the prison and talking low, trading information about an escape route and starting a new life in another part of the world. The talk flowed freely, as it does when there is little else to do, and Brown was quickly the center of their attention. He had a dentist not far from the jail, he told them, and if he arranged an appointment with the man and was transported to the office by a couple of cops, he could have someone waiting there who would shoot the policemen and help him escape. Would Steinhart be willing to do this for $50,000 or $100,000 or whatever Brown was offering that day?

There were people inside the jail who knew that Drake was a snitch who moved among the inmates and listened to scenarios for escape or violence or other things that were being planned. When Brown first entered the prison he had been told this, but in the excitement of meeting new friends and laying out new strategies he ignored the information. He enjoyed talking about his latest ideas even more than Drake enjoyed listening. When Brown first opened up to him, Drake tried to shut him off, but that was impossible, so the snitch did what he believed would help him get out of jail sooner. After each gathering of the trio, Drake went back to his cell and wrote down everything he could remember from their conversation, including logistical details for escape and direct quotations. On January 13, 1989, as Patti was testifying in front of Judge Schenk, Drake went to Jay Newell and divulged what he'd been plotting with the men.

The original plan was for Drake's girlfriend, Cecilia Palomino, to get arrested on a traffic-ticket charge and be taken into protective custody at the Orange County Jail. Brown said he would pay for any expense she incurred for her trouble, and to prove his sincerity, he managed, through Western Union, to slip her $500. Once she was inside the jail, her path would cross Patti's and Cecilia would befriend the young woman. Steinhart, for $50,000 in cash, would kill Newell and Robinson, and another woman would be sent into the prison to kill Patti. Cecilia would come forward and inform the police that Patti had confessed to her in jail that what she'd said about Brown at the preliminary hearing was a lie—he'd had nothing to do with the murder and she'd only said those things in court to exonerate herself. Before this scheme could unfold, Palomino changed her mind and announced to Drake that she didn't want any part of David Brown.

That is where things stood on January 13, when Drake reported what he'd learned to Newell. After speaking with the detective, Drake went to Steinhart, confessed that he was a snitch and that the police knew everything he and Brown were planning. At first the biker was enraged. He hated snitches and expressed his feelings to Drake very clearly. In time he calmed down and decided that the only way to save himself from a much longer stay behind bars was to do what Drake had done.

On the nineteenth of January Steinhart spoke to Newell and said that he'd initially advised Brown to drop his jail-house scams and try to beat the charges in court, but Brown wouldn't listen. "He got obsessed on this thing," Steinhart told the detective. "It snowballed . . . to the point where he wants to participate in killing you. It's hard to keep a straight face—he's something else . . . He keeps insisting he's innocent. At first I thought he was a nice guy who got stuck . . . I think he [David] is lying. He knows he's going. He's the kind of guy who'd go out and hire somebody to—he worked himself into a frenzy. He gets that look in his eye. I think he did get his daughter to do it . . . When he gets going, he tells me every single thing. He's just like a god-damned magpie."

Newell wanted Steinhart to talk to Brown while he was wired, just as Cinnamon had done, and if the biker went along with this plan, he would find himself on the streets much sooner than he'd imagined.

"You'll be an agent for us," Newell told him.

As he thought about what he was going to do, Steinhart listened not only to his sense of decency but also to his stomach.

"I have a couple morals left," he said. "I want a pizza and a beer so bad I can't stand it, man."

* * *

Baruch had left Cinnamon in tears on the witness stand and was even more exhaustive in his questioning and more relentless with Patti. One wondered if he were being paid by the question.

When Patti had been on the stand for several days, Baruch asked her about the visit she and Brown had paid to CYA on the previous August 27, their second trip to Ventura. "You knew that David didn't know who did the killing," he said. "Isn't that right?"

"No," Patti said.

"Did he know?"

"Yes, I told him."

"When?"

"When all of this first happened."

"You did?"

"Yes, I did."

"You're lying now, aren't you, ma'am?"

"No, I'm not."

"You're committing perjury right now, aren't you?"

Robinson interrupted the questioning. "If the record could reflect that Mr. Baruch is yelling at the witness— burning red in the face."

"Yes." Baruch turned to him. "My client is faced with a death penalty. You bet I am."

"Gentlemen," the court said, "one second. Now just lower your voices and let's control ourselves, Mr. Baruch. Don't ask the question in that tone; just ask your question and we'll proceed . . . We're going to be on recess now until tomorrow morning, and you'll both have a nice sleep and you will come back and you won't be yelling, right? I can see that . . ."

The following day, Baruch began insisting that the district attorney's office had bought Patti's testimony by making a deal with Patti that would greatly lessen her time in prison. Robinson not only denied this often and vehemently, he finally offered, on the record, to bet his legal opponent a thousand dollars that no such plea bargain had been struck. Baruch did not put his money on his opinions and eventually moved on to another issue.

"My theory is," he said, looking at Patti, "this woman is a seductress and a manipulator . . . This woman is the one that orchestrated the killing because she wanted her sister out of the way so she could be with him . . . This woman, during this entire period of time, was sleeping with everybody in town."

"Everybody in town?" the judge said.

"Pretty close," Baruch replied.

After many other questions, the lawyer took another unexpected detour.

"Now," he said, "on the night of the murder, you injected cocaine into Linda, didn't you?"

"Hell no," Patti said, glancing at the judge. "I'm sorry. I didn't know Linda was on drugs until she died and David was the one that told me then . . . In my opinion, Linda was my best friend and also my mother."

"You did intend to hurt your sister that night, didn't you?" Baruch said.

"No, I didn't."

"You did intend that she die?"

"No."

"You did want it to happen?"

"No. I was scared for David."

"But in being scared for David, you intended that your sister die that night?"

"No. I didn't understand why he couldn't just leave."

"But you said you were involved in the murder."

"Yes, I was."

"Then you wanted it to happen?"

"No, I didn't."

"You were acting of your own free will?"

"No. I was acting on what David asked us to act upon."

"Right, but you had your own free will to resist that."

"What do you mean?"

"Well, you just stated that you didn't understand why David couldn't have just left, right?"

"Yes."

"So you then were able to weigh the pros and cons of

what you were doing. Do you understand what I'm saying?"

"No."

"You were able to weigh the yes and the no of what was going to happen. Is that right?"

"I didn't weigh anything. All I know is I was scared that something was going to end up happening to the family."

"But you, at the same time, didn't understand why David couldn't leave?"

"Yeah."

"You've testified about an occasion sometime before the murder where you went in the room and made a conscious choice not to pull the trigger. Is that right?"

"Yes."

"That night did you make a conscious choice to prevent Cinnamon from pulling the trigger?"

"What do you mean, 'a conscious choice'?"

"Did you try to stop Cinnamon from doing what you knew she was going to do?"

"No, because I didn't know she was going to do it any more than anyone else."

Baruch changed course, asking Patti about her revelation that she'd made two attempts on her life following the murder, the first time with sleeping pills and the second time with a knife.

"Why did you try to commit suicide?"

"Because I was upset and confused."

"About?"

"Linda's death . . . I didn't do it right."

"What do you mean?"

"David once told me if I was ever to kill myself, make sure it was on the main artery. I guess I didn't get it on the main artery . . ."

The judge interrupted Baruch on a number of occasions, telling him that he was being argumentative with Patti and needlessly dragging out the proceedings. Baruch was unapologetic and proud of his legal gyrations, describing one of them this way: "You take a report and get the witness to agree that she said four different things and impeach her

188

thereby. And then you pick up the report when you want to slip in something she never said but that you know is helpful to your case, and the witness, by that time, is so conditioned and she says that she said it, even though it is never in the report. Now, that is a time-honored tactic by the defense attorney. It has been going on one hundred and fifty years. Abe Lincoln did it. You know, I really—"

"You told us a few days ago that you were older than you looked," the judge said, before admonishing Baruch to move forward.

Baruch plunged on, questioning Patti about the night of the murder, after Brown had awakened the girls and they were standing in the living room talking about different ways to kill Linda.

"What suggestions did you make?" Baruch asked the witness.

"Stabbing her . . . suffocating her."

"When you mentioned stabbing, what was her [Cinnamon's] response?"

"She just said it would be too messy . . ."

"What, if there were any, were the other methods that were discussed?"

"Just shooting her."

"Whose idea was that?"

"David's . . . He just said that we can shoot her but one bullet might not kill her. We'd have to make sure that we used two."

"Did he direct Cinnamon to do the shooting?"

"No."

"Did he direct you to do the shooting?"

"No."

"What did he tell you?"

"He didn't tell me anything. He was just talking to both of us at the same time."

"Wait a second. Are you saying that he didn't tell you to do the shooting?"

"Yes, I am."

"And he didn't tell Cinnamon to do the shooting?"

"He didn't tell her point-blank, no."

"He didn't tell you to tell Cinnamon all the details of how it was to happen?"

"No."

"Did he tell you to do anything about Krystal?"

"Yes."

"What did he say?"

"He told me to get Krystal out of bed and keep her with me."

"To where?"

"In my room."

"So that left Cinnamon to do the shooting while you were holding Krystal. Is that right?"

"Yes."

"Did he tell Cinnamon that she should be hiding out in the doghouse?"

"Yes."

Patti adamantly denied wiping off the gun before handing it to Cinnamon and said once again that the pistol misfired in her bedroom before Cinnamon left to go into where Linda was sleeping.

Baruch had finally reached the end of his inquiry and sat down.

Robinson stood and addressed Patti. "What is your belief as to what David is as a human being?"

"Confused . . ."

"Well, you said you hate him too."

"Yes."

"Why do you hate him?"

"Because if it wasn't for his discussions, my sister probably wouldn't have been killed."

"How do you see David Brown at this point in your life?"

"Twisted . . . I knew no other way to live except his way."

On the eighteenth of January, the judge ruled that "the special circumstances are found to be true for the purposes of the bind over."

Brown would be going to trial for the death of his wife and, if convicted, he would face the gas chamber.

XV

On February 2, at eleven-thirty a.m., Steinhart met with Brown in separate bird cages in the basement of the Orange County Court House. Each cage was a small wire-enclosed basket in which prisoners were held before going upstairs to a courtroom for their judicial proceedings. The men were placed next to each other and Brown was happy for the company. He liked to talk and he especially liked to talk with Steinhart, who had enthusiasm for almost everything, particularly if it was illegal. Brown wanted the biker to burn the motor home next to his house on Chantilly Street, which would not only make it look as if someone were trying to kill David but would also provide him with some fast insurance money. Since his arrest Brown had increased his coverage on his home and its properties. He asked Steinhart if he would kill Patti, Newell and Robinson, which would both delay the trial and throw a considerable monkey wrench into the prosecution's legal machine. Was the big man ready to show Brown how tough he really was?

"I'll go—I'll do it for you," Steinhart told him.

"There's no—there's no problem, right?"

"There's no problem . . . taking 'em out."

"Okay."

"I'll kill 'em."

"Leave me out," Brown said.

"Oh, yeah."

Steinhart did have some qualms about torching the motor home, particularly if Ethel Bailey or any other family members were in it. "See," he said, "I don't want to kill anybody if I don't have to."

"I'm getting them out of there as soon as I can," Brown said. "It doesn't have to be a total wipeout."

They also discussed the dentist plan—in which Steinhart would spring Brown when he was taken outside the jail to have his teeth worked on.

"I may have to kill a cop or two," the biker said, "and I just wanted to let you know."

"Better them than me," Brown replied.

"I'm gonna ask you something professionally . . . I have to ask you this—see where your head's at. The two cops [Newell and Robinson] . . . you want 'em dead or hurt?"

Brown laughed. "Dead."

"Dead. Okay. Just making sure your head is in the right spot, man."

"Is that a piece of cake?"

"Yeah . . . As long as you can live with yourself after I kill the cops."

Brown laughed again. "They won't but I will."

"They won't." Steinhart joined in the laughter. "All right. You smart-ass. I think you like this."

"No, I don't. But when it comes down to survival . . . I'm not egotistical at all. I think you know that. But I think I'm worth more than they are."

"There you go. That says it all. It works for me."

"I think that's the best attitude to have. You know, the only reason I could make that decision is because my little girl, the four-year-old . . . She is a sweet kid."

"Yeah, she is. I've talked to her."

"A wonderful kid," Brown said.

"She laughs too much."

"I know. She loves me to death. She does. I'm a joker.

I had her laughing from the day she was born . . . You may not see it so well here, but I'm a real ham when I get out . . ."

"Killing cops ain't funny but . . . that's cool. We should get some lunch."

"I think I've got a lot to contribute and I don't think it's fair, considering that the girl is the one that got rid of her mother. I don't think it's fair for her [Krystal] to lose a father without even getting to go to Disneyland, fishing and all that."

"Right on," Steinhart said.

Brown took the conversation in another direction, speaking of how, if he were found guilty on the murder charge, he planned to tie up his sentencing process for a long time. Bringing him back to the murder-for-hire scenario, Steinhart said, "I get [Patti] Bailey first, right? Okay. I'm getting released today. How soon you want her offed?"

"Yesterday."

"Yesterday. Okay, I got it."

"Don't you think? The least times she has to talk to anybody, the better off I am."

"Okay. So she's first, then the cops?"

"Right."

"Okay. No problem. Let's have lunch."

"Let's do lunch," Brown said, laughing once more.

As soon as Steinhart left the jail, he followed Brown's instructions and picked up the $600 that Manuella had stashed in the glove compartment of one of Brown's cars, which was parked near the Summitridge address. The money was to be spent on the throwaway guns used to kill Newell and Robinson. On the evening of February 3, Steinhart and Brown spoke again, this time by telephone. Unbeknownst to Brown, the biker was in custody at the Huntington Beach Police Department. Brown had called him collect and when a woman answered the phone, he was immediately suspicious. Steinhart explained to him that he was staying at the house of a man named "Animal" and Animal's "old lady" had picked up the receiver. In reality Brown had reached a specially arranged dead-end number at the police station. After the biker assured him that it was all right to talk freely, Steinhart said that he'd been doing his homework in preparation for burning down the motor home. Brown indicated that the payment for these efforts would come through his older brother, Tom, but he was still working out the details. After a while, David loosened up and recovered his sense of humor, especially when giving a physical description of the people he wanted dead. Robinson was "well-groomed. He's getting a bit of a tummy. You can tell he hasn't played [football] for ages. I guess you would consider him a good-looking guy."

Brown wasn't so kind to Newell, who was "older, receding hairline. Mustache again. Scruffy mustache. Ugly as sin. Looks like a giant rat." Patti had a "bubble nose. It looks like two ball bearings on the end of her nose."

Steinhart, who was displaying a talent for deception in his new role as a police informant, showed a lot of emotion on the phone.

"I miss you," he said.

"I miss you," Brown replied.

"I miss your fat face."

"Yeah, I miss your fat ass."

"Don't get personal." Steinhart laughed. "I'm all ass."

"Yeah, and it's chubby."

Brown shifted the subject to what Krystal had said to him earlier in the day on the telephone. "We have this ongoing thing," he explained, "where she says, 'Dada, you coming home?' "

"Yeah."

"And I tell her, 'Well, I can't wait until somebody tells the policeman that I can go home.' And she goes, 'I can't.' You know, she's been doing this for months . . . Today when I called home, she said, 'Dada, come home.' And I said, 'Krystal, somebody's gotta talk to the policeman.' She said, 'I did!' "

Steinhart chuckled. "God bless her."

"Oh, God, I—"

"She's such a doll."

"I got goose-bumply and everything."

"You're a lucky man, there, David."

"Oh, God."

"You're a gas," Steinhart said.

The next morning at eleven-thirty, when the men spoke again by telephone, Steinhart said that he'd arranged for a woman to go into the Orange County Jail and kill Patti, but before she would make the hit, the biker had to show her $10,000 in cash. This was earnest money—once she'd seen the cash, she'd know he could be trusted and would carry out the execution. Otherwise, the deal was off. Brown had no objection to showing her the money and was scrambling for cash. He'd ordered his brother, Tom, to sell one of his cars and sent him to the office of Joel Baruch, who was in charge of David's assets and various bank accounts, to pick up a first installment. This money, Brown had told his brother, was for bodyguard services for himself inside the jail and for protecting Krystal on the outside. Tom Brown, like his parents, was willing to help out a member of the family, and his job in this endeavor was to get the $10,000 to show the woman and an extra $1,700, which Steinhart would use to purchase the weapons for murdering Newell and Robinson. The only roadblock to this plan was named Baruch. The lawyer did not like the sound of all this and was opposed to giving Tom Brown the money. He argued with David, but during the argument he was up against someone—or something—that was more powerful and more persuasive than his own instincts about what a lawyer should or should not do for a client. When David told him that the money would be used to buy rare coins, Baruch fell in line.

When Steinhart and Brown spoke on the telephone, the biker told him he'd found two professionals to help him kill Newell and Robinson but they were businessmen first and hit men second. For his part, Steinhart explained, he would be willing to kill the lawyer and the cop for nothing, but his partners wanted $20,000 for their labor. This was fine with Brown, who said that he would have his brother sell one of his rings to generate more cash. Money was no problem, Brown reiterated. The more critical thing, he said, was that none of the steps Steinhart was taking on the outside could ever be traced back to him. During their conversation, when Steinhart outlined all the things he'd been doing for Brown, the prisoner turned sentimental.

"I love you to death for it, man," David said, before asking Steinhart for another favor.

"Anything you want," the biker said.

"Would you tell me . . . what you believe the chances are that these phones are listened to?"

"None."

"Okay . . . I was just trying to be a professional."

"Yeah, I know. You know what, David? If I had any doubt that I thought the phones were being listened to, I sure—I'm not much of a professional—I sure as shit wouldn't say anything on them."

"Okay . . . You gave me lectures about being supercareful."

"I know, I know. Well, I am."

"And I believe everything you say."

Steinhart, picking up a tone in Brown's voice, said that the man sounded "kind of bummed."

"I'm getting aggravated," David said, "because I can't get people to fucking move when I want them to."

"Dammit!"

"You know what I mean?"

"I know."

"You know, especially people that are saying, 'Hey, your mind is all fucked in there. You don't know what you're doing.' Goddammit, I've always known what I'm doing . . ."

"I miss your face," Steinhart said.

"I miss your face."

"Miss the jokes, miss the you-know-what."

"No, what?" Brown said.

"I hate to admit this, but I miss the sittin'-at-the-table bullshit."

"Yeah . . . I don't have any regrets about what needs to be done. None, and I will have no regrets, okay?"

"Okay."

"I care about you, man. I don't want nothin' to happen to you, even if I end up getting the pellets dropped on me. As long as you're okay, I'll be all right."

"You know, I'm not—I'm old, but I think I have got one last one in me . . ."

"I'm gonna stick by you like glue," Brown said. "We're gonna have some good fuckin' times too."

"Right on. Well, you can't hardly get rid of me."

"I ain't gonna get rid of you. Goddammit, you drop me, you're gonna see one depressed motherfucker."

"Oh, come on," Steinhart said. "Oh, sure. I do this every day. I go out killing cops every day for people."

That afternoon Steinhart called Tom Brown and asked if he could meet him and Animal at a parking lot adjacent to a Bennigan's restaurant at the Westminister Mall near the 405 Freeway. The biker said he would be driving an old beat-up blue Camaro, and Tom's car was a chestnut-colored 1979 Mustang.

"How about we make it five o'clock dead up," Steinhart said, "because of traffic and rain?"

That was fine with Brown.

When Steinhart called David and told him that he was rendezvousing with his brother to pick up $1,700, the prisoner was delighted, but his mind was already working on the next phase of the plan. "I really want that motor home gone," he said.

At a few minutes before five, Steinhart and Animal, who was better known as Officer Bob Moran, met Tom Brown at the mall and took the money from him.

"You're better-looking than your brother," Steinhart told him as he was thumbing the cash. "I'm gonna tell him."

* * *

Two days later, on the sixth of February, Brown called Steinhart to discuss the woman who would be going into the jail to befriend Patti. Her name was "Smiley" and her job, after Patti was dead, was to claim that Patti had lied in court. Brown and Steinhart also talked about payment for the men the biker had lined up to help him shoot Newell and Robinson. Steinhart said that his partner, Animal, had located the home addresses of the lawyer and the detective and discovered what kind of cars they drove, but he wouldn't hand over this information unless he received $10,000 up front. Brown was impressed with Animal's research techniques and didn't argue with the money. He said that he had more than $500,000 in bags in the desert and Steinhart could drive out there and pick it up.

The biker was to keep $200,000 for himself and to save the remainder, which would be used after David was out of jail and the two men were traveling around the world. Steinhart wanted to know exactly where the money was located, but Brown was characteristically vague. On February 8, they spoke again and Brown said that as soon as the killings were done, he would tell Steinhart precisely where the cash was buried. In the past, David confessed, he'd lied to him, saying that it was near Barstow when it was closer to Yucca Valley.

Steinhart called Tom Brown to ask if he'd picked up the next installment of $10,000 from Baruch and the answer was yes. Tom agreed to meet Steinhart and Animal at the same place as before at three o'clock that afternoon. As Tom was handing over the money at the Westminister Mall at three-fifteen, Steinhart said they needed another $10,000 right now and wanted to know when Tom could get it from Baruch, a request that made Brown queasy.

"I had to beat the lawyer over the head just to get this," he said. "I'm nervous because he [David] didn't tell me there was supposed to be another ten thousand. His biggest mistake is letting his lawyer control his money."

Animal wasn't interested in such talk—he demanded the money by six o'clock the next morning.

That evening Sally Jacobs, an undercover policewoman who went by the name of "Smiley" and was posing as a friend of Joe Drake's, paid a visit to the Orange County Jail. Drake had told Brown she was coming and David had arranged for his parents to be there at the same time and to sit next to her in the visiting area. When David gave the signal, Arthur and Manuella switched positions with Smiley so he could speak with her about Patti. The switch left no record on the prison files that the woman had ever spoken to Brown. Smiley told him that she'd been in custody in the jail before and knew Patti. Brown was riveted by the woman's dark hair and dark eyes and had difficulty keeping his mind on the business of murder.

"The point is," he said, "that Patti and I aren't really married. She knows I'm worth over five million dollars and that's why I didn't want to remarry. Now what I like about you—what I've heard—is that your preferences are a lot like my wife's were. We had a dynamite marriage."

"She didn't seem like that kind," Jacobs said.

"She's deceitful. I loved my wife. I loved my family. She set me up."

"So, I think I'm following you. You want me to go to your attorney and tell him that Patti told me that she was lying and she did it because they are gonna let her go. Your attorney—is he cool?"

"You can't tell him about this."

"Patti and me—we talked a lot, but we didn't talk about you. I didn't know any of this shit was going down."

"No offense, but you don't look anything like . . . You're beautiful. I guarantee I'll take care of you. I'm worth it."

She asked if there would be more money for her when everything had been done.

"If you want to get to know me better," he said, "I can take care of you for the rest of your life."

Brown spoke in a soft voice, often using one of his favorite turns of speech—"Honest to God"—and telling the woman how Krystal cried to him on the phone and how she, Smiley, could help reunite the little girl with her father. He explained to her that it was Patti who'd talked Cinnamon into pulling the trigger, and he gave her Joel Baruch's name so she could call the lawyer with her story. Jacobs announced that it was time for her to go and Brown protested, saying again that she was very pretty and he was willing to take care of her. When he asked if she thought their conversation was being recorded, she said that wasn't possible. She promised to call him soon and rehash the details of their plan.

In the morning Brown called Steinhart and told him that Smiley—whom he called "Happy Face"—not only was a "looker" but was definitely interested in him. He complimented the shape of her mouth and said that God had done a superior job of putting her together.

Steinhart said that Smiley was in the Orange County Jail now and just waiting to hear the news that Robinson and Newell were dead before she moved on Patti. "I've got a sneaking suspicion," the biker went on, "that she's [Patti is] going to back up on a knife or something."

"Good," Brown said. "That's good. That's what I want. I want it to be for sure."

The most important thing, Brown reminded his partner, was that events unfold quickly and nothing could be traced back to him. Steinhart was reassuring, optimistic and ready to go—he and his associates were "planning on hittin' them tomorrow morning." As often happened at the end of their discussions, the men talked about pizza, a food they both liked and something they joked about eating together one day when Brown was free and they were on the lam.

"Anything you want," David said. "I'm here for you."

"I'm here for you too."

Steinhart and Animal stayed in the Huntington Beach Jail, where they were fielding the latest round of collect calls from Brown and preparing for the final act of their drama.

The prisoner phoned regularly, anxious to know what was going on, anxious to pursue his romance with Smiley, anxious to set up the next delivery of money through his brother, anxious to learn that Robinson and Newell had been shot. On the morning of February 12, the men talked about financing the operation by having Steinhart dig up the hidden treasure in the desert near Yucca Valley, the biker pressing again for the exact route to the cash and Brown deftly refusing to be specific.

"You don't need to get it all at once," David said.

"No, I don't want it all at once."

"Okay, just as long as you know where it's at and you can mark it your way."

"So I'm gonna find out where it's at? How am I gonna do this?"

"Uh, I figure that once everybody is done and all that and you're back, that's the next question . . . The biggest problem is that I think you will need a four-by-four [vehicle] because I put a—I drug a substantial rock over it."

"Oh, right on. I'll definitely get a four-by-four. That I can do."

"Yeah, and a chain."

"And a chain—oh, for the rock?"

"Yeah."

"David, why can't you use a bank?"

"I think you know the answer."

"I know, I'm just—I just don't like manual labor but we got to do this . . ."

They spoke of other things, of inmates at the jail and who had lately been released from prison and who had been rearrested for new transgressions on the outside. Steinhart eventually circled back to the money and the best time to dig it up.

"I really think," Brown said, "from my experience, 'cause I lived up in Yucca Valley for a while, your best day to go would be, like, Friday."

"That's cool. Why?"

"The reason is very simple, because most everyone that goes to visit family is—you know, relatives or something—they leave up there on Friday afternoon and come down here to San Diego or wherever their family is."

"Oh, right, so hardly anybody is up there."

"Right. And nobody goes up there until Saturday to ride in the desert or to visit their relatives . . ."

"You have, like, a primitive road—like a blacktop road? How hard is it going to be for me to get there?"

"Remember, the street I told you is Twenty-Nine Palms."

"Yeah."

"Okay. That's paved."

"Okay."

"But you're gonna need to follow it . . . like I did, or right next to a . . . riverbed."

"Okay. That's off that paved road."

"Yeah, directly off the paved road."

"Does it run parallel to it or across from it?"

"No, it runs across."

"Okay. So it's a dry wash."

"Yeah, and it's a very loose sand . . . I would recommend that you follow above it, you know, on the ridge . . . From there I'll give you the distance and the landmarks."

"Okay, good. Yeah, we'll do that as soon as they're hit. I'll just—I'll tell you when they're done . . ."

"Okay. I'm gonna call him [Baruch] and try to get him to get the extra thousand. I'm sure that will cover your expenses."

"No problem. I can't see it being more than that."

"Yeah. It will probably cost you two days of pizza and beer."

"Yeah, well, that doesn't include the pizza and beer . . ."

"How's your stomach?" Brown said.

"It's fucked."

"Ah, come on."

"It's been pretty fucked, only 'cause of stress. I'm waitin' to get this done for you, you know."

"Are you all right?"

"You kiddin'? I'm just waitin' for you to get out. I'll be a lot better when you're safe."

202

"Yeah, but you quit exercising, didn't you?"

"No, I didn't, as a matter of fact. Every time I get done eating a dinner or lunch over here, I take a walk."

"Do you really?"

"Yeah, I do. It sure beats going around in circles . . ."

"You were in here for what—three weeks?"

"Forty-five days."

"Forty-five days?"

"Yeah. How time went by when I was there, huh?"

"God," Brown said, "no wonder I miss your fat face."

"That's right."

"Son of a bitch. God, it didn't seem like it. It really didn't."

"It did to me. It does when—now that I'm out, it seems like it. It seems like forever."

"God, it feels like you've been gone a month."

"Isn't that weird?"

"Yeah, it does," Brown said. "Shit, I miss you . . . I really do love you and I miss you."

"I love you too."

XVI

The next morning at eight-thirty, when Steinhart was at the Huntington Beach police station, Brown called him collect. Between outbursts of laughter, the biker announced that Newell and Robinson were dead.

"David," he said, "it's done."

"Say what?" Brown replied.

"I'm done."

"Oh, really?"

"We're done, we're fucking done. Animal is in the garage right now, out torching the pieces. He's melting the fuckers down right now. How did we do, huh?"

"You did great . . ."

"Is that hot or what?"

"Yeah, it's hot . . ."

"He's in there with the acetylene torch melting away the throwaways. We're gonna dump them so they can't tell. He's got all his shit packed. He's getting ready to go. Hey, man, how did we do, huh?"

"Wonderful. You're a good man."

"Wonderful. Is that all?"

"Huh . . ."

"Tell me I did good."

"You bet your ass."

"We got them both, man."

"You're fantastic."

"Got them fucking both. You had—you should have been there."

"Huh, next time . . . Buy yourself an extra pizza on me."

"I'm gonna, I'm gonna. Hey, I'm real nervous still."

"Yeah, I can tell. Are you all right?"

"Yeah. It went like clockwork. Bang, bang—right in the back of the head. Both of them . . ."

"All right."

"Capped 'em both. I didn't have a chance to give them any last words from you, though, or anything."

"No, that's all right."

"They're both gone. So that should hit the paper probably tomorrow or actually probably tonight or this afternoon."

Steinhart asked Brown to call his brother and tell him to bring the next installment of cash—$11,000—to the Westminister Mall at ten-thirty a.m. sharp. As soon as he received the money, Steinhart said, he would buy a few supplies and drive out to the desert, where he would dig for the hidden money.

"I love ya," Brown said.

"I need—right now can I get basic directions to where I'm going?"

"Yeah. Are you ready?"

"Yeah, I'm ready. Go. I've got a pencil."

"Okay . . . It's right after Twenty-Nine Palms or Joshua Tree. I don't know what landmark it is, but it's the first one past the bowling alley, heading east, after you're leaving Yucca."

"Okay."

"I wish my memory was better on street names . . ."

"Well, just get me the most detailed instructions you can, 'cause I don't want to dig up a desert."

"Oh no, no . . . Turn left on that street. You will pass the wash. It is less visible on the left than it is on the right-hand side . . . You're gonna be heading north. Okay?"

"All right."

"On the far side of the wash, you'll see . . . like a five-six-foot-high . . ."

"Like an embankment?"

"Yeah, on both sides of the wash. That's how I identify the wash."

"All right."

"Okay. You want to take the north side of the wash."

"Okay."

"Find a path up there . . . You will go exactly, on my odometer on a Nissan pickup, one and three-quarters miles . . . Then you head exactly north again—you may want a small compass for that, because I made sure I was heading due north."

"Okay . . . exactly north."

"Exactly one and three-quarters miles . . . Three-eighths of a mile thereabouts, you'll see a boulder and a yucca tree. You know what a yucca tree looks like?"

"Yes, I do . . ."

"You will see the—I call it a boulder because it's a heavy motherfucker."

"Well, how big in diameter around?"

"Uh, probably three—maximum four feet around . . . It is directly under the boulder."

"Okay. Is this on your property or government property or what?"

"Well, it's property that I owned at the time, but I made sure that it's near a survey marker so . . . it's within a couple of feet of a survey marker. So if anybody was gonna fence it in, they wouldn't have any reason to dig or move that boulder."

"Do you own the property now or no?"

"No."

"You know who does? I don't want to—it's one of these deals if I got to go out digging on their property—"

"It's open," Brown said. "There was no barricade. The only thing there was, like I said, the survey markers, little wooden sticks with the red flags."

"Right. Okay. I think I got it . . . Is there anything else I need to know?"

"I wish I could get excited for you right now, but I can't."

"You better get excited for you. You're gonna be out here with me pretty soon."

"You bet your ass. God, I love you, Richard."

"I love you . . . Anything else I need to know?"

"No. Uh, I did think of something last night that I was gonna warn you about."

"Which is what?"

"But apparently you didn't need it."

"What? Oh, it don't matter, then?"

"No."

"Well, what was it anyway?"

"The investigator [Newell] was armed."

"Oh, yeah. They both were."

"They both were?"

"One had one in his briefcase and one had one on him."

"You serious?"

"Uh-huh."

"I never noticed it on the attorney."

"Well, I'll tell you what. Don't matter now, does it?"

"No."

Steinhart made another pass at getting more precise instructions for his journey into the desert. He asked Brown for the old address of his property in Yucca Valley, but the man could remember only that it was five digits long. When Steinhart inquired about the name of the road leading toward the cash, Brown would say only that the money was near a lone yucca tree. He promised to call his brother and tell him to go to the mall with $11,000, and then promised to call the biker later in the day, at high noon.

"I love you, man," Steinhart said.

"Thanks. I love you too."

After hanging up, Brown found Joe Drake in the prison and shook his hand, whispering to him that his archenemies were dead. Drake nodded, revealing nothing, but a few days later he told Newell that although David seemed pleased that the killings were done, he acted surprised and even alarmed that his wishes had actually been carried out.

208

"He looked liked somebody was bleeding," Drake said. "He looked like a cooked lobster."

At ten-twenty that morning, the thirteenth of February, as a cold winter rain fell on Southern California, Tom Brown arrived in the parking lot of the mall at the same time as Steinhart and Animal, and before their transfer of money was completed, all three of them were rushed by the police and arrested. Steinhart and Animal were hauled off and Brown was left by himself with the cops, who explained to the bewildered man as they were cuffing him that he was being charged with murder.

"For murder?" he said.

"Get out of the rain," they told him.

They took the $11,000 he was transporting and escorted him, shocked and outraged, to the police station. There he was frisked and the only weapon he was carrying, a small pocket knife, was confiscated. For thirty minutes he was left by himself in an interrogation room, where he squirmed and pondered who had been killed, but then Newell and Fred McLean arrived, removed the cuffs and began to explain to him some pieces of the mystery and to ask a few questions. How much money had Tom recently delivered for his imprisoned brother? He told the detectives about the $600 that he and his parents had given to Steinhart several weeks earlier, leaving it in a car near the Summitridge address.

"I still want to know what this is about," he said. "I haven't done a goddamned thing except what I've been told to do."

"From what I can see," Newell said, "you've followed some pretty simple instructions. Is that right?"

"David told me he needed to pay these guys for his protection. That's all I know."

Whom did David need protection from? McLean asked.

"The Baileys," Tom said. "If you've ever met 'em, you'd know why."

Newell told him that the money wasn't to be used for

protection but for murder and that a murder had in fact occurred, but the wrong person had died.

Tom was further shocked. "All I know," he said with disgust, "is that I was supposed to say that the money was for protection."

"Your mom and dad didn't know about this, did they?" Newell asked.

"No. They knew what I did—that it was for protection."

Newell said that he was considering releasing him, but only if Tom promised not to call his brother at the jail or to take any collect calls from him, because that might endanger other lives.

"If I ever thought somebody would get killed," the man said, "I wouldn't have anything to do with it . . . I just want to get out of here to pick up my son at one o'clock so he doesn't have to wait out in the goddamned rain."

They let him go.

At noon that same day, David called Steinhart once more from the Orange County Jail, his last chance to reach the outside world, because the authorities were about to issue an order that would prevent him from using the prison phone system again. During their final conversation, he told the biker, "If I don't trust you, I'm an idiot."

"If . . . you don't trust me," Steinhart said, "I'm an idiot,'cause I just killed two people for you."

"So I, you know, obviously I trust you with my life."

"All right . . ."

"I don't think you're gonna burn me," Brown said.

Two days later, when Joel Baruch was vacationing in Florida, he learned that his client had set him up as a funnel for money to be used to finance the deaths of Newell and Robinson. Baruch was livid and even hurt. He wasn't accustomed to dealing with people—including those accused of serious crimes—who treated him so shabbily. The lawyer was upset both personally, because Brown had violated their trust, and professionally, because he felt that all of his work on David's behalf had just been destroyed. Even after the preliminary hearing and Judge Schenk's ruling that there was massive evidence against Brown, the lawyer was convinced that once the trial started and he had another opportunity to reveal Patti and Cinnamon as inveterate liars, he could win the case. But not now. What had happened in the past few weeks was beyond his previous experience as an attorney. During his career he'd represented those charged with the worst crimes and defended nineteen other alleged murderers, but this behavior—plotting the deaths of lawyers and detectives—was indefensible. Perhaps it was time for Mr. Brown to find a new attorney.

The lawyer had one other thing to think about: he did not want to be included in the illegalities or held liable for aiding and abetting an attempted murder. While still on vacation, he called Ed Rudd, an investigator in the Orange County District Attorney's office, and said that yes, he had been in control of a trust fund for Brown at the Security Pacific Bank in Newport Beach, but he'd known nothing whatsoever about any criminal intentions when he'd given money to Tom Brown. His client had sworn that it was to be spent on rare coins. Baruch went out of his way to distance himself from the prisoner and to express his concern for his recent bitter courtroom rival.

"If you see Jeff Robinson," he told the investigator, "give him my regards."

"Okay . . ."

"Robinson is—or at least was—a friend of mine before this case broke."

Rudd indicated that he would pass along those sentiments.

The sting operation performed on David Brown had been completed and Steinhart was set free. In the Orange County Jail, Brown was stunned to learn that not only were Newell and Robinson alive and well, but he himself, in addition to facing the upcoming trial for the murder of his wife, was being charged with three counts of conspiracy to commit murder, three counts of solicitation to commit murder, solicitation to commit perjury and conspiracy to commit arson.

XVII

In May of 1989 Patti pleaded guilty to the charge of first-degree murder and officially decided to testify against her husband at his trial. Before reaching this decision she went through months of agony, more than once concluding that she could not say things under oath that might send Brown to the gas chamber. More than his welfare was on her mind. If she chose to testify, wouldn't he try to kill her again? Weren't there people in the Orange County Jail at this moment waiting to jump from the shadows and stab her? And what about Krystal? How could Patti live with herself knowing that it was she who, at the very least, sent the little girl's father to prison forever? And Arthur and Manuella? What would they do if she presented damning evidence against their son when it counted in front of a jury? What was worse—facing her fears of speaking out or hiding what she knew and perhaps turning Brown loose so he could unveil another round of bizarre and violent plans?

She listened to the advice of her attorney, who told her to go into the courtroom and speak the full truth, something she had not yet done. When Patti pleaded guilty she believed that she would be treated by the law as an adult—she was now twenty-one—but on the recommendation of lawyers on both sides of the case, she was dealt with as a juvenile, just as Cinnamon had been, and sentenced to imprisonment at the California Youth Authority until age twenty-five. At that time, her criminal record would also be expunged and she would be free. Two months after making her plea, she was transported to CYA, which she entered as the oldest inmate at the facility. She had a lot of idle time at the compound and filled part of it by looking into the procedures one would follow in filing for a divorce. Like Cinnamon, Patti did not ever want to see Brown again, although he continued to write her, asking for pictures of Heather and telling her to "watch out" in prison. Six weeks after deciding to testify, Patti still tormented herself with whether or not she was doing the right thing—wasn't she about to harm the only father figure she'd ever had?—and she almost called Rubright and changed her mind. At CYA she began to menstruate again for the first time in nearly a year.

By the time Patti arrived at CYA in July, she and Cinnamon had exchanged a series of friendly letters, the bond between the two of them growing stronger. This was partly because they were older, partly because they were both female, partly because they were having similar experiences as inmates and partly because they shared many memories before Linda's death, but there was one other reason for their feelings. They realized they had something else in common now—Brown had tried to kill both of them, Cinnamon with Darvocet and Patti with Richard Steinhart. In recent months Patti had discovered another piece of information which she could contemplate while sitting in prison: Jay Newell had told her that just before she and David were arrested, Brown tried to talk Annie Blanks into throwing an appliance into the tub while Patti was taking a bath.

Five days after Patti pleaded guilty, Steinhart was arrested again on a drug charge, this time in Huntington Beach. He went back into the Orange County Jail but stayed away from David Brown, whose thoughts had turned in new directions. The recusal appeal, which Joel

Baruch had filed during the preliminary hearing, was scheduled to be heard in court in the second week of July. If Baruch won the ruling on this motion, Robinson would be dismissed from the case, a possibility that a few months earlier would have filled the defense attorney with joy. Since learning about Brown's murder-for-hire plot, things had changed for Baruch. He was still representing Brown, but not with the same fire; he didn't speak with as much intensity or pace as much in the courtroom. All of this left the emotional lawyer distracted and bored. When he felt inner pressure he cricked his neck, and his neck had been busy lately. In the past few months he'd also dropped twenty pounds, and while he'd been on a diet during this time, he attributed some of the weight loss to his sobering encounter with David Brown. The ex-foot soldier in Vietnam had lost his passion for getting Robinson out of the courtroom, and passion was what he ran on. He was thinking of leaving the case. Any doubts that remained about his view of Brown faded when he got wind of another scenario unfolding at the jail. The prisoner not only intended to pay two inmates $70,000 to go to the authorities and claim that Steinhart had lied about the solicitation-for-murder plans, Brown again expected his lawyer to be the conduit for the money in this transaction.

The recusal appeal went forward, but Brown, sensing the change in his attorney, fired Baruch. In mid-August, before a ruling had been made on the appeal, Brown began parading attorneys through the jury room at the courthouse, looking for a new one. He finally retained the services of Gary Pohlson, another Orange County lawyer, but one without the same relish for legal street-fighting as his predecessor. Pohlson was smoother than Baruch; some people called him more reasonable. He was certainly less volatile and more willing, at least in these circumstances, to cut a deal if one should present itself. After looking at the evidence in the case, he advised Brown to skip a trial and accept a plea-bargain agreement of twenty-five years to life, with a chance at parole after seventeen years. Pohlson felt so strongly about this that when his client rejected the suggestion, he made Brown put his refusal in writing. It was not an optimistic gesture. If convicted now, Brown had no chance of ever leaving prison.

Unlike Baruch, Pohlson had no personal vendetta against Robinson, and one of his first actions was to offer a compromise to the district attorney's office: if Robinson would drop the option of a death-penalty sentence for Brown, Pohlson would drop the recusal appeal and a trial date could be set. All of the parties liked this solution, but Robinson was especially pleased with it. Not only did it remove the possibility of his sending a man to the gas chamber, which he disagreed with in principle, it gave him the chance to convict someone who'd ordered him to be shot in the back of the head. The prospect of sending Brown to prison for the rest of his life delighted the lawyer. The trial was set for early 1990.

Outside Ventura, in the cottage she occupied at CYA, Patti continued to sweat and hyperventilate, to cry and to scream in the night. She was moved several times and given sedating drugs, but they left her sluggish and did not deaden all of the pain. A psychiatrist at the institution suggested that she relive the killing and pretend that she'd been shot, just like her dead sister, as this might lessen some of Patti's agony. She tried it, but the guilt did not go away. One day she broke a bottle of nail polish and sliced her wrist with a shard. In the past she'd flirted with suicide, but this was a more serious attempt and left a much deeper and redder scar on her flesh. She still doubted that she had the courage to testify against the man who had raised her. If Cinnamon had had the opportunity in recent years to make some peace with herself about her involvement with her father and the murder, Patti was just beginning that process. In some ways she was much younger than the other woman and much rawer.

In the Orange County Jail Patti had finished high school, and at CYA she began a program of college studies, the first of Ethel Bailey's children to matriculate beyond the twelfth grade. Patti's mother, who visited her only once at the compound, was proud of her, telling people that her daughter had survived "the firing furnace of David Brown" and would eventually go on to a better life. Mary Bailey drove to CYA for visits as well, bringing along Heather, who had turned into a blond-haired, brown-eyed little girl who seemed to embody childhood health and to radiate innocence. Patti kept a picture of her daughter on the wall of her cottage. When she felt like making another attempt at suicide, she looked at the photograph to remind herself that she was part of something larger than her own despair and had at least one reason to live.

A psychiatric report filed on Patti at CYA, which referred to Brown as a "modern-day Svengali who used young ladies one after another for his nefarious, perverted and egregiously selfish purposes," was unflinching in its assessment of her: "Patricia appears to have been completely under the control of this cruel and ingenious psychopath for most of her life. He manipulated her by instilling fear, withdrawing love, threatening to do harm to loved ones or whatever else he could do to keep her under his complete domination. As a result, Patricia is a tragically disturbed young woman. She is guilt ridden over her part in the murder of her sister, and has no sense of herself other than as an instrument which David Brown used for his own gratification . . . I believe that incarceration comes as a relief for Patricia. She sees herself as no longer under the control of David Brown. Additionally, she can now receive what she sees as just punishment for her part in this terrible crime. She sees it as a new beginning for her. She appears grateful to her co-defendant Cinnamon for finally revealing the truth . . . As soon as she was liberated from the constricted and isolated world inside that house of horror, Patricia's madness began to evaporate. Her shared delusions could not withstand the light of day . . . Patricia makes absolutely no attempt to justify her actions or to lessen her responsibility. She expresses an extreme measure of guilt. She is filled with remorse. Patricia feels a marked need for punishment, so much so that she believes staying in Youth Authority 'only' until she is 25 years old is not nearly enough punishment. She expected and wanted life imprisonment . . .

"Patricia has only recently been released from her captivity. She was a psychic prisoner to her master, socially isolated with all of her loyalties directed to the man who bought her . . . Patricia Bailey needs as intensive psychotherapy as we are able to provide. Initially, this needs to be supportive. Subsequently, she has a cauldron of severe emotional issues that will need to be worked through. She is depressed, blunted, emotionally confused, cognitively dazed, the product of a lifetime of neglect and abuse. She has dimensions of hate, rage, despair that she is only dimly aware of. All of these aspects and many more will have to be faced and worked through. It will be a long, long road."

In private, Patti's anguish was tangible. Speaking with a visitor to CYA in the summer of 1989, she talked about the futility of bathing three times a day in order to feel clean and about the death of her sister.

"I just want to get rid of this dirt," she said, "and this shame that I feel. This disgust. I can't do it. I feel like even my blood is dirty. I want clean blood. I keep thinking of Linda, my own flesh and blood, and then marrying my sister's husband."

On the wall of her cottage/cell at CYA she kept a picture of Linda and a picture of Heather, but she disfigured a photograph of David, writing the words "Devil A. Brown" next to it. In group therapy sessions at CYA, she wrote angry letters to Brown and to her mother, asking why the woman had sold her years ago, but she couldn't bring herself to mail them. During the therapy meetings she didn't show much emotion, and the most difficult word for her to pronounce was "manipulate."

"I can't cry in front of other people," she said at that time. "I'm afraid someone is going to take advantage of me."

When asked about her past suicide attempts, she said, "I was thinking about Krystal. I was thinking about Linda. I wanted to feel the pain Linda was going through. I was thinking about how bad it ruined Cinnamon's life. Everything. I have so much anger that I want to take it out on someone, so I take it out on myself. I let the ultimate sacrifice happen. Let's face it. I'm a murderer.''

PART FOUR

XVIII

Mary Bailey plays with Heather as she does with all children, teasing her, touching her, talking to her constantly with words the little girl does not understand but seems to enjoy, the woman acting perfectly natural and at ease. The two of them are in the air-conditioned living room of Mary's Riverside home on a humid, dripping day, and the little girl stares up at her surrogate mother, smiling and blushing and looking as if she very much wants to please. She runs into her bedroom and brings out a picture of her real mother, Patti gazing out from the photograph with her determined jaw, broad mouth and turned-up nose, the pretty features that originally drew Brown to her. She looks too young to be in prison, too strong to be involved with killing her sister. "Mommy," Heather says, pointing at the image in her hand. "Mommy, mommy." The child is beautiful and wears a white dress with red roses and white sandals, a red ribbon in her hair. She has her mother's eyes and perfect skin. Mary towers over her, wearing a loose blue dress and very light lavender fingernails. She picks the girl up and hugs her with mock ferociousness. "It's fun being Heather," she says, swinging her. "I swear to God it's a blast." The child squeals and wants more. They dance across the floor, swinging their hands and laughing at each other, Heather's cheeks growing redder with each step.

Mary stops and glances at the photograph of the child's mother. "Patti hates it up there," she says. "She just wants company."

If Brown is convicted of first-degree murder, the woman says, he may be sent to Chino, a prison not far from Riverside. Mary has friends in the Chino pen, both guards and inmates, and she believes that they would make life very rough for the man, a prospect that delights her.

"Child molesters and wife-killers," she says, "are dead meat in jail. I want to see David get the gas chamber and I want to go watch that. I would have no problem with that, no nightmares or anything. But that won't happen. He'll be cooped up somewhere and that will be worse than death. He hates to be controlled by people and now he will be. He'll try to play the same games there as in his living room."

In Mary's backyard, which is bordered by oleander and heat waves, are the dogs that Brown once owned. When one reaches out to pat Ziggy, a golden retriever, the dog falls to his belly and whimpers, ears dropping and eyes wary, looking for punishment, the behavior of an animal that has been beaten. He reminds one, in a queasy sort of way, of Patti when she is introduced to a man and unable to look him in the eye or hold her shoulders straight. She also cowers but, unlike the dogs, she quickly recovers and acts tough, shrugging and swearing and laughing in a painful way.

"David hit that dog because it would chew things," Mary says, looking at Ziggy. "I watched him kick that dog's ass and my mouth fell open. If you raise your voice to that dog, he goes down in nothin' flat."

Things have come full circle for Mary and her husband, Rick, who is at work this afternoon. Mary has a later shift at a local shopping mall, selling uniforms and footwear to doctors, nurses and the elderly. "I'm kind to the old people I sell shoes to," she says. "They got these eighty-year-old feet and need some consideration." Fifteen years earlier, Mary met David Brown in Riverside and her first impression—she is the kind of person who trusts first impressions—was immediate: "I didn't like him the minute I met him. I had a problem with a married man hangin' around two young girls. Rick and I hated it, but no one paid attention to us. If I really don't like somebody, I can instantly feel them around me. I could always sense when he was around before I saw him." Several years after Linda met Brown, she moved in with Rick and Mary so she could get away from her mother and carry on a love affair with the man. Now another Bailey offspring has moved in with the married couple so she too can be surrounded by a family.

Mary has found an old photograph of Linda and is studying it with an expression of dull shock.

"I loved her," she says. "After she died, David made her out to be a junkie but she wasn't. She wasn't compulsive. Linda liked to party, but she only did cocaine to lose weight after she had Krystal. She once pulled me into the bathroom after the birth and showed me her flat stomach. She was jazzed about that.

"Part of David's attraction for people—for women—was the romance part. He could work you into a situation, but he couldn't work me. I don't do nothin' for nobody unless I want to, and I wasn't one of his patsies. He knew that and we had a good understanding."

Her husband comes home from his job near a blast furnace at a steel-manufacturing plant. Rick is perspiring, his clothes are dirty and his hands rough. He sits on the living room floor and smokes a cigarette. He is a handsome man and Mary makes constant jokes about how happy she is to have a good-looking husband. He glances away, chagrined yet pleased by her attention, a man who has agreed to be overmatched, at least in public. Rick is nearly as quiet as Mary is outspoken, but beneath his silence a lot appears to be simmering, waiting to come out when there is a space in the conversation. He has a small mustache and a kindness in his eyes that becomes more prominent when he is talking with his two children or playing with Heather. He's the sort of person who thinks more than he talks.

"When we first met Dave," he says, "I knew that he

didn't do anything for anybody unless there's something in it for him. I saw right away that he was manipulative. My first comment after Linda died was that he had done it. He doesn't have to do much to get things the way he wants them. He gets everyone to do his dirty work for him and bring him the information he needs, and he just sits back and watches things happen."

"Patti wouldn't be alive now," Mary says, "if she and David hadn't been arrested. He would have gotten her too."

"I think Arthur is just as guilty as the rest of them," Rick says. "He was there when the plans took place. I don't know why they haven't arrested him."

"Rick has a real problem with that." Mary looks at her husband.

He nods and glances at the floor.

Mary is proud of the fact that she talked Patti into getting her own lawyer. "Rubright got her to confess and come clean," she says. "He didn't cut no bullshit with her and that was the best thing he could have done. He played those tapes [the videotapes made of Brown during his initial interview with Newell and McLean on the day he was arrested] for Patti where Dave talks about her and accuses her. That crushed her. She was still in love with him at that time."

Rick puffs his cigarette.

"I think it's a crock of shit that Dave has money out in Yucca Valley buried somewhere," Mary says. "But people in Rick's family believe that."

The man looks at his wife and takes another puff, not responding for a while. Heather has wandered back into the room and touches Mary's hand, the woman taking her fingers and caressing them, the two of them looking into each other's eyes and laughing.

"The family's done a lot of arguin' about that," Rick says. "I just don't know."

Victorville, a couple of hours to the north and east of Los Angeles, gets hotter than the devil's anvil of Riverside. It is another California town that has been stuccoed and malled. The surrounding land is as flat as a spatula and the air is a light shade of beige, which goes well with the pinkish-brown color of the prevailing style of architecture. The town feels desolate, perhaps because it's so far away from all that money in Orange County and L.A., or it could just be the heat. Dust in Victorville swirls in cones and dies on the wind. At the edge of town are ranches and beyond the city limits is Apple Valley, where there are no apples but an asphalt park with row after row of blazing trailers, trailers with tin roofs that reflect and absorb the naked sunshine all day long, trailers that shimmer and bake, trailers on very small plots of ground surrounded by gleaming chain-link fences. When a shoe steps on the trailer-park asphalt, it gives, and in the distance the tar sends up waves that vibrate in the sun. Ethel Bailey lives in "Bear Valley Mobile Home Park" and her trailer is yellow, a color that blends well with the rest of the high desert. The air is quiet but the buzz of the heat is audible.

Her small, un-air-conditioned mobile home is surprisingly cool. A small American flag hangs on one interior wall and Merle Haggard sings on the radio about the virtues of the United States. Ethel has sixteen grandchildren and ten children left. Pictures of her offspring are everywhere, and three of her grandkids, who were fathered by Larry Bailey, are playing outside the trailer in a piece of shade. Ethel stands in the middle of her trailer and shakes, her hands and arms and chin jumping with each breath. Tim Bailey, a brother of Patti and Linda and Rick, sits in the trailer's kitchen quietly looking on. His mother, Mary Bailey and Cheri, the oldest of the Bailey siblings, are in the living room passing around a photograph album. Tim's belt says "Harley-Davidson," and he's as thin as the rest of the Bailey males, all beard and bone. Cheri is also thin and soft-spoken, her blue eyes pretty and thoughtful. The living room features a large picture of Patti, several tributes to motherhood and an image of Mary and Jesus. With long fingers, Ethel picks up a photograph of Linda and stares at it, the thing trembling in her hand. "She was a beautiful girl," she says.

The other women nod.

"After Linda and Dave were married the first time," Ethel says, "dear darling Dave decided he wasn't making enough money to have a wife, so he dropped her off at my house one day like a bag of potatoes. He said he'd be back when he made more money. Then he went off and got married to someone else. That guy is a low-down conniving rat." She looks at the other women and speaks as if no one has heard the stories before. "Then they got married again. One time Linda and I didn't even talk for a year. All over Dave. He wouldn't let her do anything for me."

Ethel's basic expression is a wince, which may be the result of all the cigarette smoke that's drifted around her eyes. She has a good wide smile but it never lasts for long. The matriarch of the Bailey clan has a certain presence and command of the room she is in, not so much because of her looks or what she says or does, but because one realizes that this woman has borne eleven children, lived through divorce and abandonment, consumed rivers of drink and canyons of smoke, endured violence and murder, and although she often looks weary, the frog in her throat is full of life, she's light on her feet, proud of her children and grandchildren and friendly to strangers. She talks openly about the past, long gone now, yet alive when she and the other women turn it over and over inside the trailer, reexamining what might have been, reliving old tales and anecdotes, smiling as they recall how pretty Linda was and that she liked to race her black convertible Mustang with the vanity license plate ("327 FLIES") and have a good time. The women enjoy keeping the memories fresh, but one senses there is more to the reminiscing than nostalgia or even heartache. A lot of anger is also present in the room, anger on the edges of their voices, anger in Tim's silence and sad eyes, anger in the trembling of Ethel's hands, anger that really has no focus until they bring up David Brown. Then the emotions slip out into the trailer and the air seems a little cleaner and for a moment everyone feels better.

"That last year when Linda was alive," Ethel says, "I was down there and she and I got very close. It was misery on both of us. We talked a lot. We spent time at the kitchen table and we knew something was wrong, but never in my wildest dreams did I think he'd go to murder." She pauses for emphasis and laughs through a wave of smoke. "Dave always said he wanted to be retired at thirty-five. Well, he's gonna be."

She coughs deeply, the sound wracking her shoulders and filling the room. "We knew Patti and he were doing something together. We wanted Patti to go to a counselor, but Dave put the brakes on that."

Ethel lights another long cigarette. "I could see that Cinnamon and Patti were under some kind of control in that house. But no one could argue with that man. His word was law."

Cheri, who is sitting on a padded footstool, leans forward and says, "I told Linda, 'You've got to get tougher, woman.' She was just starting to get tough with him when . . ."

There are a few moments of silence, the sound of children playing coming in through an open door.

"I think Linda was planning on leaving him," Ethel says, and the women nod again. "The last time I saw Cinnamon and Patti together, in January of 1985, I was staggered. Cinnamon was talking to Maynard all the time and petting him, and Patti was Dave's maid. When he said jump, she jumped. He always had her on that beeper. Beeper, beeper, beeper. We left once for fifteen minutes and he beeped her. She came back and she was so mad she was gonna leave. He said, 'If you leave, you'll leave with your clothes and nothing else and you'll never see Krystal again.' She didn't leave."

They bring up the seventeen car accidents and the money the wrecks generated.

"David would drive along," Mary says, "and slam on the brakes and someone would rear-end him and he'd get banged a little bit and collect on the insurance. He'd do this all the time and control it so he'd never really get hurt.

Linda knew he was involved in insurance scams, but . . . He almost got in a head-on one time but he chickened out. After they staged a car accident, they'd take an ambulance ride to the hospital and then go to the chiropractor and then start collecting. David had fraud down pat. Linda went to a palm reader once and the woman told her she would die young and in a violent way. Linda figured it would be in a car accident.''

Ethel says she wants to write a book about the influence of Brown on her family—her title is *Shattered Lives*—and as she speaks another wave of memory and anger penetrates the room. Ethel shakes harder and looks as if she might cry, but her grandchildren race into the room and she compliments one of them and lightly scolds another, back in the present again.

''Our lives,'' Cheri says, ''will never be the same. We were very close when we moved out to California from Nebraska years ago, because we were all we had. But our family, as a unit, is ruined.''

''Some people won't come visit us anymore,'' Mary says, ''because of Heather. They feel that we're wrong to be raising a little girl whose mother's in prison.''

''The one thing I can't understand,'' Cheri says, ''is that Patti stood in that room and heard Linda dying and waited for him to come home. She didn't even dial 911.''

''I have trouble understanding or forgiving that,'' Ethel says. ''She didn't even call a paramedic.''

''Patti heard Linda moaning and didn't even go in that room,'' Mary says. ''I still have a problem with that. I always felt—I could tell by watching Patti at the funeral— that she knew everything that had happened. She knew that Cinnamon had shot her. Patti's face was swollen and she looked as if she'd been suffering.''

''She knew everything,'' Cheri says. ''At that funeral home, after Dave got all the rest of us out of that room where Linda was, he went in there with Krystal. I'm sure that he just stood over her casket and laughed.''

The women nod in unison.

Tim, who has been playing with the children and listening

to the adults, walks into the living room and talks in a voice so low that it's muddy, almost impossible to understand. Someone tells him to speak up.

"I'm just emotional and bitter about all this," he says.

XIX

The parking lot outside the Orange County Court House reflected much about Southern California. The vegetation was attractive and exotic: palms, eucalyptuses and the delicately shaded purple leaves of the jacaranda tree, glowing in the sunshine and giving a royal touch to the slab of asphalt covered with cars. These weren't just any cars, but lawyers' cars, very successful lawyers' cars. Gary Pohlson, who was picking up roughly half of Joel Baruch's original legal fee of $300,000, was driving a red Porsche, and Baruch himself, who was often seen in and around the courthouse, had a Mercedes with a lot of dents. He appeared to drive as aggressively as he practiced law. Jeff Robinson had a more modest Acura with gold-rimmed wheels, but Newell was occasionally seen behind the wheel of a big white Mercedes, which he steered with authority. Even in a white Mercedes he looked like a bulldog, a man who would just as soon have been putting people in jail as going for a Sunday drive. The whole parking lot was crowded with expensive machinery, many of the cars wearing vanity plates. The most creative one belonged to a prosecutor whose view of his job and what he intended to do to the local criminal population was summed up in the seven letters on his plate: "TOASTER."

After a number of delays the trial began in early May of 1990. The presiding judge in the eighth-floor courtroom of the Orange County Court House was the Honorable Donald A. McCartin, a frail-looking, sleepy-eyed gentleman who bore some resemblance to a reptile that occasionally awakens from a nap and kills an insect with one swipe of its tongue. The insect in this particular case was usually Jeff Robinson. Courtroom observers said that McCartin's son and Robinson were good friends and that the judge himself was quite fond of the young deputy district attorney, but at times one wondered if that was true. His Honor snarled at Robinson and sometimes he growled. As he had done at the preliminary hearing, Robinson seemed hell-bent to protest certain minor points of law or legal etiquette, asking questions repetitively and seeking constant assurance that he was doing something right and that his opponent, defense attorney Pohlson—who came to the trial each day with a sidekick and adviser, Richard Schwartzberg—was doing something wrong. Pohlson overlooked most of Robinson's outbursts, although he did take exception one morning when Robinson referred to Schwartzberg as "a slob." Pohlson was much less willing than Baruch to get into a cat fight, but there was another reason he stood aside from Robinson's behavior: his best defense—some might have said his only defense—was to give Robinson a chance to annoy the jury.

If Pohlson generally refused to take the bait, the judge was not so passive. It was, after all, his courtroom, and he controlled the atmosphere. He was mercilessly impatient with Robinson and appeared to take a subtle pleasure in saying things to him like, "Let's get on with it, goddammit."

The judge kept photographs of his dogs in the courtroom. Under his robe he wore blue jeans. He parted his hair down the middle, walked slowly and was as soft as iron.

"The judge is irascible and eccentric," Don Rubright said during the trial. "His words are less tempered than most judges'. In every case he picks a whipping boy and in this case he picked Robinson."

McCartin often had the appearance of a man just waiting to get irritated, and Robinson gave him many opportunities. The lawyer was unable to read the judge, or unwilling to. When silence was the best strategy, he argued. When swallowing an opinion was prudent, he coughed it up. When it was time to be gracious, he attacked. One could only imagine the courtroom repartee had Robinson and Baruch gone at it in front of McCartin. They might still be arguing.

The trial was not nearly as heated as the preliminary hearing. Some of this could be attributed to Baruch's absence and to the more low-key style of Pohlson, but some of it was because Patti and Cinnamon had had experience testifying and most of what they said at the trial had been said many times before. The one great, final revelation had come from Patti in the year between the hearing and the trial, although she'd made passing references to it before, but not for the record. To her lawyer and to the opposing attorney, she had acknowledged that she'd maintained a lie about the sequence of shots that Cinnamon had fired. The first shot had not occurred in her room but in Linda's, and it was after that explosion that the gun had jammed. Cinnamon ran into Patti's room and asked for her help in fixing the pistol, and as they were trying to unjam it, the gun fired again, blowing a hole in the tapestry on the wall and in the wall itself. As the two girls stood in the dark bedroom working on the gun, passing it back and forth, they panicked, Patti juggling Krystal on her hip, Cinnamon trembling and crying, both of them frantically wondering what to do next. They heard Linda moaning in the master bedroom, moaning and heaving up surges of air in a semiconscious and severely wounded state. As they listened to her cries for help, Patti told Cinnamon to go back in and shoot her again, and this time to make sure that she was dead. Cinnamon did as she was told.

As Patti began testifying against Brown at the trial, revealing this last piece of the puzzle, she experienced something new.

"I'm not afraid of David anymore," she said. "It's scary when it hits me that I'm doing this in court against him, but I'll be okay. If I don't face up to him now and look him square in the face, I never will.''

Throughout almost the entire trial, Brown was silent and motionless. At a small table in front of the judge, he sat next to Schwartzberg and Pohlson, who sat next to Newell and Robinson, the four legal authorities lined up in dark suits like schoolchildren before a master. On occasion Fred McLean was present—red-faced, smiling gently and sporting neckware adorned with tiny American flags. When he spoke he barely moved his lips, and his teeth were better than those of most of the people he arrested. The ex-Marine looked more like a dentist or a minister than a cop. His eyes weren't shifty, as if he were waiting for someone to jump him.

Pohlson and Robinson were the best dressers and Pohlson's ties were world-class (his wife picked them out). Schwartzberg was built like a fire hydrant. Nearly as thick as he was tall, he had the appearance of a man who was so solid, both intellectually and physically, that he had never lost an argument or been knocked off his feet. The most arresting thing about him was his Argyle socks, which seemed out of place on such a grave and scholarly presence. Throughout the trial, he claimed to be reading an obscure book on Roman history. Newell, true to form, dressed in various shades of brown and ambled across the courtroom with the quiet determination and confidence of a tortoise that always wins the race. If one looked very closely at the man, one might have detected a small hint of satisfaction in the wings of his mouth because David Brown, at long last, was on trial for first-degree murder.

The defendant wore pastel shirts, provided by his parents. His hair was dirty and hung over his shirt collar. He was heavier than ever and appeared exhausted, as if standing up would empty him of breath. Pohlson had advised him not to dress up any more for the occasion and not to get a haircut so he would look somewhat ragged. The jury could see firsthand that sitting in prison was not good for someone with his delicate health: David was already suffering greatly, and if the ladies and gentlemen who were sitting in judgment of him convicted him, he would suffer even more for the remainder of his life. Pohlson had also advised him against testifying in his own behalf. He told Brown that Robinson, who was considered very good at cross-examination, would shred him on the witness stand and the best thing he could do was keep still and hope for deliverance. Before the trial started, to make his point more graphically, Pohlson took Brown into an empty courtroom and videotaped the defendant being tormented by Schwartzberg. After watching his own performance, Brown agreed to remain silent.

There was no eye contact at all between Brown and the two men he'd instructed Steinhart to kill. They sat six feet apart, the prosecutors acting as if the defendant were invisible and vice versa. Throughout the trial Brown took notes on a yellow legal pad, even scribbling during pauses in the testimony. Some people thought he was making a word-for-word transcription of the proceedings, but others claimed he was working on a science fiction novel. Pohlson would not reveal what his client was doing and said only that the man was very alert to what was taking place around him.

Brown looked as if prison did not agree with him, although Patti said it should have, because in jail he was brought his meals three times a day, he did nothing but sit and talk about his fantasies, and he was waited on constantly by the guards. The man looked pasty and sluglike. His bodily processes seemed to have slowed down in jail and then come to a halt. He was so pale he seemed almost featureless. His back, shoulders and stomach were massive, his lower body stunted. When he walked he moved in slow, determined steps, the walk of a man who is going to have his way, no matter what.

Looking at him, one might be moved to pity until you realized that he'd captured that great gold ring that so many people in California pursue. He'd had the hot tub and the swimming pool, the home computers and VCRs and Mercedes-Benzes; he'd had affairs with many pretty women and married the young blonde with the drop-dead body—

twice; he'd fathered two beautiful children in Heather and Krystal and then thrown away every speck of it. David Brocon's problems had never been physical.

The most striking thing about him was that he did not react at all to the things that were being said in court about his behavior during the past decade. One kept waiting for him to show a glimmer of embarrassment or shame or some recognizable emotion, but these never came. He didn't appear nervous or upset, didn't sweat or drum the table. He didn't look self-conscious. He was more than distant from the proceedings. He was fundamentally disconnected—the bubble had been sealed. His eyes looked directly at no one, except when an attractive woman came into the room, and then they bore in on her. But even then they were wary, skittery, retreating, uncertain, full of fear, staring blankly, or quick flat eyes that did not let in or reflect back much light. He did not appear to be aware, on an emotional level, that other people were as real as he was—the rest of the world was a TV set that he could ignore or switch off at will. Brown was completely self-involved.

He drank a lot of water and occasionally asked to be excused from the proceedings because he did not feel well. The judge told him to stay put. Even when he raised one eyebrow, he looked as if he were scheming. At no time during the trial did Pohlson or anyone else question Brown's sanity, and that was perhaps the most intriguing thing of all. In some ways he seemed perfectly sane: he was articulate, bright, financially successful and in control of his mental faculties. As he'd told Steinhart during one of their phone conversations, he not only always knew what he was doing but planned and controlled the outcome of events, or at least he had in the past. Brown was, Pohlson said in private, more intelligent than most of the people he'd defended, but for that reason he was also more impenetrable and mysterious. He was just like a lot of other people who wanted to defraud insurance companies or make love to their wife's sister or who thought about getting rid of someone who'd become an impediment, except he had no inner mechanism that checked him and until now there had never been boundaries he could not violate.

"David," Joel Baruch once said of his ex-client, "is very childlike."

"In everything he deals with," said Rubright as the trial progressed, "his motivation is uncontrolled self-gratification, along with money and power. There isn't any defense in his murder case. He is Machiavellian. I don't think he's insane at all in a legal sense. He understands what he's doing and chooses to do it. I wouldn't call him mentally ill, but evil. People have compared to him to a chess player, but he's the antithesis of that. He only looks two moves ahead, not five. He doesn't tell his lies looking far enough ahead."

One got the feeling that something was missing from the man, something intangible and elusive. It should have been in his eyes, but it wasn't there. It could have been in his words, but it wasn't there either. Brown had never admitted to any involvement in his wife's death, and beyond that, one felt that he'd taken dishonesty to another level: when he spoke of his dead wife, his eyes filled with tears and his voice trembled. When he said something that was provably false, he didn't act as if he was lying, and in a sense he wasn't. He believed what he was saying. He had become the lie, wore it like another layer of skin (in the courtroom, Robinson told the jury that Brown always tipped off his lies by prefacing them with the phrase "Honest to God").

What was missing from David was that something that lets one feel that other people are alive and significant. It's something holds back one's impulse to be absolutely selfish and keeps one from breaking all the little annoying rules of society. While watching Brown's non-response to the trial, one felt that, after the weeks and months and years of attention that had been given to the man, after the thousands upon thousands of papers had been filed and refiled on the case, and after countless dollars had been spent to bring him to justice, nothing that happened within the courtroom would have any effect on him at all. To him the trial was irrelevant. He had been deadened in a place that was deeper than anyone could reach through legal debate.

The most dramatic witness was Richard Steinhart. Since his latest arrest a year earlier, the biker had undergone a radical transformation, a shift so bizarre and unexpected that it carried with it a certain ring of truth. He'd become a passionate Christian and sworn off drugs, alcohol, violence and crime. In June of 1989, while sitting in the Orange County Jail, he'd suddenly fallen to the floor of his cell and been shaken by a force that was beyond his power to comprehend and nearly beyond his power to talk about. From that moment forward he was a different man. He stopped threatening people and hitting them. He didn't swagger as boldly anymore, and he thanked Jesus when people told him how glad they were that he was no longer so dangerous. He began attending Bible-study classes at the jail and even teaching a little on the side.

When the biker first began proselytizing within the walls, the inmates thought it was a scam that would help him escape, but after a while they realized that he was serious and a few of the cons decided it was time they went to chapel. Born-again experiences leave some people quiet and rather predictable, but not Steinhart. He went at promoting the Gospels the same way he'd once gone at riding his Harley or closing a drug deal—with verve. He wanted to save everyone in the jailhouse.

Despite his sudden conversion he still looked like a hellion in his black leather vest and blue jeans, but he'd added a twist to his skin. On one of his huge bare upper arms the word "Jesus" had been needled into his flesh, and on the other was written "Is Lord." When he talked he moved his hands like a windmill and was sort of a freewheeling advertisement for Christianity. He didn't go anywhere without a big red Bible or without his new wife, a large soft-spoken blond ex-heroin addict named Pat who was as religious as her man. At the trial she also carried a ruby-red Bible. Her long nails were painted white and she wore earrings made of leather and bone. When she and her husband entered a room, heads swiveled. They made a formidable pair of missionaries, and some people found themselves agreeing with their ideas simply because they looked so bad. After his release from jail, Steinhart had taken up residence at a Christian drug-rehabilitation center near Lake Elsinore, California. Everyone there was given a nickname, and his was "Liberty."

From the witness stand, he weaved in his chair, swallowed often and announced that he had AIDS, which sent a shudder through the courtroom. During his testimony he asked the judge if he could leave the room to take his medication, and the request was granted. While his soul was in good shape, Steinhart told the jury, the rest of him was composed of "junk body parts." Some people took his medical opinions lightly. Baruch, upon learning of the biker's claim about AIDS, said that the man had been predicting his death from this disease for years and that he was just as healthy and ornery as he'd always been. "Steinhart," the attorney said, "is the biggest liar I've ever heard of." The biker maintained that he was very ill but did acknowledge that he was the only known case in the annals of science of an AIDS patient who was consistently gaining weight.

"God bless you," he told the courtroom at the conclusion of his testimony. "Praise the Lord. I feel a lot better now."

Brown did not look at his ex-friend or acknowledge him in the courtroom; the big man might as well have been a ghost. The defendant kept writing on his legal pad or leaning over to whisper in Pohlson's ear. The lawyer would nod and go back to watching the trial. There was a hint of resignation in the attorney's posture and in some of his remarks. He didn't call many witnesses and he didn't pursue anyone with the ferocity of Baruch. His best chance in the case was breaking Cinnamon and Patti apart in front of the jury and making them look like pathological liars, but he didn't appear to have the stomach for that. He acted like a man who was performing a professional service, not like someone on a crusade. Brown had gotten rid of the kind of lawyer who would have gone to extremes to defend him, just as he'd alienated Joe Drake by telling him things that he really didn't want to know, just as he'd turned aside his sister, Susan Salcido, many years before with his sexual advances and then his brother, Tom, by involving him in something criminal. After discovering the true nature of the sting operation that had led to his brief arrest, Tom Brown said that from that moment forward his brother ceased to exist. In the end the only people who were loyal to David were his parents, but that bond raised at least one uncomfortable question. Were they committed to him because of affection, or because they never wanted him to reveal what he knew about their involvement in his schemes?

With the exception of Steinhart and his bride, the trial, which lasted five weeks, proceeded without many ripples, although the final arguments brought out a few bursts of eloquence and passion. The prosecutor especially spoke as if he meant what he said, meant it in a way that went beyond his duties and obligations as a lawyer. Like most attorneys, Robinson had a bag of professional tricks—smiling at the jury members as they filed in and out of the courtroom or making jokes at his own expense to keep them alert when he was talking—but during his closing argument he dropped his ploys and spoke from the heart. He didn't exactly mention that the defendant had personally wanted him dead, but his feelings about being a murder target came through. He wanted to win. He wanted to put the man away forever. He called the defendant "Mansonesque," a remark that shot Pohlson out of his seat.

Manuella Brown was at the final argument, along with Krystal, but Arthur was absent, claiming to be ill. Susan Salcido, with short dark hair and intense dark eyes, was also in the courtroom with her mother. A few Baileys were present, including Mary and Rick, but they did not look at the Brown family. The media came out for the occasion, wiring and miking the room for the evening news, and any number of courthouse visitors wandered into the chambers to look at the defendant and listen to the attorneys. There was an underlying sense of excitement in the room, not so much because the lawyers were saying something new, but because finally, more than fifteen years after Brown had come in contact with the Bailey family, something was going to be resolved.

Robinson had never looked better. He was more tanned, better-coiffed and better-dressed than usual in a dark suit and a red paisley tie. His shoes were serious and his movements quick, betraying a certain nervousness. He led off the arguments by thanking the nine women and six men of the jury (three were alternates) for their time and raising the central question he wanted to address: did Brown have "consciousness of guilt?" Was he aware that what he had done was wrong in a legal sense? Robinson began by calling the events they had come together to sort through a "modern-day tragedy" and an "atrocious set of facts." David Brown, the attorney said, his voice quivering, "enlisted his own flesh and blood in this crime . . . By his own admission, Mr. Brown is a coward. He has others do his bidding because he is the ultimate coward. As he always says, 'Leave me out of it.' He wants and wants and wants without ever taking the responsibility for it. As he tells Mr. Newell in the interview, he doesn't have the stomach for it. What a father. He sweetened the pot by overinsuring his wife so he could come into a windfall after her death. How could one man take part in all this?

"Long before this murder, Mr. Brown preyed upon Patti Bailey for many years. He promised her a new life, taking her out of a home where the best day was bad. The promise had to do with money, clothing and food, all basic things. What kid wouldn't want out of that jail? Patti said, 'He was my life support.' Mr. Brown made very sure that he remained that way. This is like the story of Cain and Abel, where a brother kills a brother. For a sister to take a sister's life is a horrible thing. Two of these people, Cinnamon and Patti, have 'fessed up. You're going to have to decide on the third.

"What would have happened if Cinnamon didn't vomit? You would have had the perfect murder. The daughter is dead with a suicide note that extricates you. The wife is

243

dead. The sister is with you. There are no witnesses or dying confessions and there is no evidence to connect you. All of this—if the stomach doesn't vomit. He has selected the suicide note, rejecting others as too corny. And even if Cinnamon lived, she was willing to sacrifice herself for him. She didn't even ask if she was gonna die. What kind of father would ask his daughter to shoot herself in the head and just nick herself?

"This man doesn't have a conscience. This man is the typical sociopathic personality. Everyone in his life is just a pawn. He can justify anything because he believes he's worth it. Isn't it the ultimate confession of guilt to try to kill those who are trying to restrict your freedom—the prosecutor and investigator who know the most about his case? And trying to kill his wife, his betrothed, because she could testify against him? He is clearly conscious of his guilt. David is charged with count one—murder—and count two—conspiracy to commit murder . . . This case is all or nothing. Either Mr. Brown is guilty of murder or he is not. This is a textbook case of first-degree murder. This was an act that was considered for a long, long period of time."

During this speech, Newell's expression—one of flat disbelief at the things that human beings do—never changed. He looked as he always did, as if he were holding something in and as if he secretly wanted to reach down the table, take Brown by the scruff of the neck and shake him. Newell looked restless and like a man who very much believed in crime and punishment.

Brown, in a pink shirt and gray slacks for the final arguments, looked put upon and as if he had a bad headache. His mouth sloped downward in a steady leer. He looked intelligent and afraid of everything, every movement around him, every word, every change in the air, every whisper, as if all of it needed to be controlled. Even his hands looked frightened. Brown was fascinating to observe, but not because of his physical appearance. The fascination was connected to something vaguer: the common belief that there is something bad in the wind, a free-floating thing that can strike at any time and create havoc in people who are com-

244

pletely unsuspecting. The thing has no name and no face and no clear identity, but is a force that seems to hover just beyond the reach of human understanding. Sometimes one person comes along and appears to embody it. Brown was fascinating because he was like a man in a fable, a man who walks into town one day and changes everyone around him by doing nothing but distorting the truth, through vagueness, through inference, through suggestion, through planting small ideas and repeatedly dropping one piece of information into the minds of those who don't have great powers of discernment. He was a master at inserting the wedge of fear.

"In that home," Robinson was saying, "the girls were vying with each other to come up with a plan to kill Linda . . . Those kids were more obsessed with saving David than killing Linda. He used the word 'family' over and over again. He said, 'We've got to do this to save the family.' A lot of good kids would act like this under these circumstances. Cinnamon Brown is not a hardened criminal. The defense attorney wants to blame this on the puppets, but who's pulling the strings? It was a weird existence. Patti wore a beeper. They went to the chiropractor together. Their friends were limited and restricted. They went everywhere in the car. David knew how to manipulate the kingdom of Brown. He was juvenile in some ways and a genius in others. He's had one hell of a reign."

While arguing his case, Robinson said that he believed that it was only during Cinnamon's testimony at the trial, when she had cried on the witness stand, that the young woman fully realized that her father had intended to kill her. Until that moment she had never really confronted that possibility. During his speech, the lawyer also made a reference to the Bailey family, calling it "less than fortunate." During a recess, Jeff Bailey, another thin, wiry sibling who had come to the courtroom, took offense at this description and stomped out into the hall, acting as if he were going to hit something. When he was approached by the press, he became quiet and inward, like someone who had never been encouraged to talk in public. In time his anger passed and he went back into the chambers, but like many of the Baileys, he still appeared to be seething. Alan Bailey was also present, looking skittery, but he quickly left because he couldn't stand being in the same room with Brown and wanted to beat him up.

"They are not," one courtroom observer said of the Bailey family, "the Brady bunch."

As Robinson continued to speak, his rhetoric loosened up. He told of how the defendant enjoyed sharing stories about how much his wife or other women were attracted to him. "David always says that Linda is all over him," the attorney said in a sneering tone and pointing at the man. "This is the love god, David Brown."

The defendant glanced away.

"David said that he had a 'dynamite marrige' with Linda," Robinson went on, "but he would not go in and check her pulse when she's been shot. He doesn't call 911. He calls his dad. Why did he call his father? Because he'd committed murder. Why did he stall for time? Because he was waiting for Cinnamon's medication to kick in. Why did he send Patti out with the baby if he thought, as he said, that a murderer was out there [in the backyard]? Because it was a lie, lie, lie."

Pohlson gazed up at Robinson as if he admired his performance, although he did frown a while later when the attorney called Brown "a real creep."

"He's a poor excuse for a human being," Robinson said, pointing again. "It's all money, sex and I, I, I."

After several hours, the attorney paused and drew a long breath before facing the jury again. "I'm only gonna ask you for another fifteen minutes," he said, "but those are lawyer minutes."

Laughter blew away some of the tension and seriousness.

"Consciousness of guilt," Robinson said in conclusion. "Are these the actions of a man with a guilty conscience? Does an innocent man arrange to kill three more innocent people? That's a guilty conscience . . . You may find David Brown despicable. Despicable people sometimes do despicable things . . . Don't feel guilty for judging him guilty."

He ended by praising his legal opponent and calling Pohlson a good lawyer. Then he sat down and rested.

Following a lunch break, Pohlson took the floor. The one and only thing that he agreed with in Robinson's speech, he told the jury, was the man's assessment of him as an attorney. This brought more laughter, but when it stopped, Pohlson went on the attack. He moved around the room with short quick steps, which added a dramatic flair to his words. For years the compact red-faced lawyer, with his blond thinning hair and an attractive open smile, had wanted to be an actor. Before his son was born he'd worked at community theaters in Long Beach and Cypress, and when he sat in his law office and recalled playing the Robert Redford role in *Barefoot in the Park* and Jerry in *The Zoo Story*, he looked proud of himself and a little wistful. Like a lot of successful professionals, he would, on occasion, chastise himself for not having the courage to pursue his dream of a career in the arts. Yet he looked at home in a courtroom and happy speaking his mind at length in the closing arguments. The more he talked, the faster he talked and the more articulate he became. One sensed that he, like most attorneys, got to do plenty of acting in his job, especially when it came to hiding his feelings.

"I want to talk to you about the emotions of this case and all the sympathy we've felt for the little girls," he told the jury. "I want you to think this thing through as human beings. So I'm gonna approach this not as a lawyer but as a human being . . ."

He approached it by saying that Steinhart had preyed upon Brown's weakness and that "in jail, David does something terrible, but that doesn't make him guilty." He approached it by sarcastically referring to Cinnamon and Patti as "two little angels."

"Cinnamon fired from between six and fifteen inches," he said. "These are not two little innocent angels. We're talking, in the person of Cinnamon, about a disturbed fourteen-year-old girl. She was shunted back and forth between her parents and she's finally landed where she wanted

247

to be: with her father, who's making good money and buying her good things. And Linda is a threat to all that. And Cinnamon has been kicked out of the house and was living in the trailer . . .

"And there's Patti. She may be manipulating David Brown. We're not talking rape here. We're talking consensual intercourse."

Some disapproving noise passed through the courtroom.

"The only thing that stands between Patti and what she wants is Linda," Pohlson said. "It was Patti who said to them, 'We have to get rid of her.' You don't have to make a decision here about who did the killing. They told you who did it . . . These girls have been lying for years."

Pohlson told the jury that, by choosing to testify, Cinnamon would get a very good deal from the authorities. If Brown was convicted, she might get to walk out of CYA soon, and that was obviously her motivation for saying what she did on the witness stand. And Patti, he claimed, had told so many lies in the past that it made no sense whatsoever to believe her now.

"The prosecution's case," Pohlson said, "is built on these two little angels who have admitted they lied and admitted they killed and who had reason to lie and reason to kill."

Pohlson paced and talked and smiled at the jurors, poking fun at himself. He slowly built a good argument, raising questions that no one could answer, planting small doubts and cultivating them thirty minutes later, using the word "unreasonable" to describe things that had been said about Brown, portraying his client not so much as innocent but the girls as guilty. All three of them—David, Cinnamon and Patti—had joked about murder for months, but to Brown's surprise, went Pohlson's argument, the girls actually killed her. The attorney did what he could, treading a fine line between attacking the credibility of the two young women and attacking them as individuals. His speech was neither as long as Robinson's nor as impassioned, but he raised several fundamental issues for the jurors to consider when they retired to make a decision. Who is ultimately responsible for what an individual does? How deep is the psychological hold of a parent on a child? Or of an adult lover on a teenage girl? Is the guilt of controlling one's mind or emotions as great as the guilt of pulling a trigger? Is it much greater?

"David doesn't even know who did it," Pohlson concluded. "These two girls, of their own motives, killed Linda Brown. After it happened, David felt guilty. When he came back home, the first question he asked was, 'What's the matter?' That is not the question of a guilty man."

XX

On the day of the final arguments, because the burden of proof is on the prosecution, Robinson was to have the last say of the trial after Pohlson had sat down. The arguments ran on so long that the judge suggested that Robinson do his final rebuttal the following morning. The lawyers agreed to this and everyone filtered out into the courthouse, a lively place full of women in high heels, noontime health fanatics jogging in the stairwells, attorneys cutting deals in whispers and thugs wearing ill-fitting suits. The building rocks with activity and is reminiscent of an old-fashioned grade school where all of those who have been disruptive in class have to go out and stand in the hall. Walking through the courthouse and taking in the flurry of people moving in and out of elevators, one can only conclude that crime is flourishing in Orange County.

The next morning Robinson began his speech by turning his attention to the legal strategy of his adversary.

"When you don't have the law or the facts on your side," he said, "you try the prosecutor. Mr. Pohlson is a good lawyer. I loathe the day I have to try a case with Mr. Pohlson when we have equal facts. I'd be up a creek.

"The last thing the defense wants you to do is have any

feelings about this. Your gut is going to tell you that Mr. Brown did something wrong. Bad people do bad things. You're not just computers. You do have feelings and life experiences and common sense . . . David Brown wanted people dead who were working on this case. Innocent people don't actively participate in the killing of other people. He actually wanted to take human life. Guilty killers take human life. What kind of a man can kill his wife, Patti? A guilty man . . . A diabolical man. Mr. Brown doesn't do anything without a noble cause. He always takes care of people. Mr. Brown is worth more than anybody or anything. He knows what the carrot is for different individuals. For adults, it's money. For Cinnamon, it's her family. He always has what somebody wants and he knows how to use it to get them to move. Is there no end to this? Are you, ladies and gentlemen of the jury, about to finally say no to him? As a man thinks, so he is. When a man is with so much garbage—''

Pohlson jumped up from his seat and asked for a meeting with the judge, out of earshot of the jury. The defense lawyer, Robinson and McCartin gathered at the bench and conferred for several minutes; then Robinson again took the floor and spoke even more forcefully than before. The defendant stared up at him, giving him his full attention for the first time.

''Patti wanted her sister dead,'' Robinson said. ''No question about it. She and Cinnamon lied till the cows came home. I think Cinnamon Brown should get out. I think she's paid for this, but they're [the parole board] not interested in my opinion.''

Brown looked away and shook his head, as if in disgust.

As he'd done several times during the trial, Robinson said that on September 22, 1988, when Brown was first interviewed by Newell and McLean, he'd admitted mixing a concoction for Cinnamon and giving it to her to drink. Although he'd told the detectives that it was nothing but aspirin and baking soda, this admission, according to the prosecutor, ''left him dead in the water.''

Robinson faced the jury box, cleared his throat, squared his shoulders and paused for effect. He smiled at them.

"This is it," he said. "My fear is that I have a knack for tweaking people. That's just my personality. If I've done anything to offend you, don't hold it against the people of California. Justice has not been served for five years. He's had a long and evil reign and it's time that justice be served. In history and plays, there is a time when people rejoice at the dethroning of an evil king. It is time for that. Cinnamon is in jail. So is Patti. Krystal and Heather are without mothers. Think long and hard about everything this man has done. Cinnamon and Patti have their just rewards. It's time for Mr. Brown to have his."

Judge McCartin then did something extraordinary. Declaring that the prosecutor had had an entire evening in which to prepare his final remarks, it was only fair that the defense be given another chance to speak—and then Robinson could briefly speak once more. This decision infuriated Robinson, who had just completed his courtroom performance in excellent fashion. His last speech was his best and he was unprepared to say anything else. As he stood and vigorously protested the judge's ruling, his deep California tan became crimson. He looked as red as if he'd been slapped.

The judge was unbending—Pohlson would get another chance to speak. When Robinson began another round of protests, McCartin's face grew pale and his manner severe.

"You made your point," he said to the attorney, "and you lost."

"What else is new?" Robinson shot back before sitting down, his words echoing through the chambers and jangling the sedate legal atmosphere.

The defense lawyer stood and looked at the jury. "You've all been sentenced to life in this courtroom," he said.

Pohlson, after thanking the judge for the opportunity to rebut Robinson's rebuttal, was brief and direct: "If you dislike Mr. Brown intensely, fine. That does not make him guilty of this murder. Child-molesting does not make him guilty of this murder. If you want to convict him, convict him on the facts."

He paused and looked at his client. "David isn't a charming guy. He isn't an Adonis."

Brown's head jerked up toward his attorney, and for the first and only time during the trial he noticeably flinched.

"But you can't convict him of that," Pohlson said. "He may not be charming and he may be lacking in good looks, but that does not make him guilty of murder."

After Pohlson sat down, Robinson stood and once again complained to the judge about giving the defense another opportunity to speak. To the prosecutor this was an unprecedented gesture and he wanted the record to show that.

McCartin snapped, "That is improper, Mr. Robinson, and you should be aware of that. That is my last admonition."

Robinson's voice was shaking. "This charade," he said to the jury, "has gone on long enough. Please have the fortitude to end it. Don't be afraid to follow your heart in this case."

He was finished. When ending a monologue, the attorney usually smiled at the jury, but this time his face was frozen except for his cheekbones, which were pulsating beneath his tan.

"I've had to admonish you before in this case," the judge told him. "Anyone with an IQ over seventy would understand what I was doing."

Robinson looked at the table, the back of his neck bright red. This time he remined silent.

Before sending the jurors into their private chambers to decide the case, the judge read them page after page of instructions, which they were to follow in reaching a verdict. The instructions were written in mind-numbing legalese and were virtually impossible for a non-lawyer to comprehend. Throughout the hour of McCartin's droning reading, only one sentence stood out: "You must not feel pity for the defendant or be prejudiced because he has been arrested."

Before court was adjourned, Pohlson asked the judge if Brown could be absent during the deliberations (defendants are supposed to be in the building itself while the jury is deliberating, so that once a verdict has been reached, the accused can immediately be brought into the courtroom, the verdict announced and the jurors sent home). Brown wanted this requirement waived. Without much enthusiasm Pohlson explained to the judge that his client wasn't feeling well and would prefer to stay in the jail.

The judge would have none of it.

The jury filed out, McCartin disappeared into a hallway behind the bench, where he quickly shed his robe, and the lawyers mingled outside the courtroom, trading friendly looks and anxious expressions. There was nothing to do but wait. A reporter asked Newell, who was standing next to Robinson, about the computer service that Brown had once run, Data Recovery, which had earned him hundreds of thousands of dollars just a few years earlier.

Had Newell investigated that?

The detective nodded but said nothing.

Was it a complex technique that Brown used to bring back the apparently lost information on those disks?

Newell gave a partial smile.

What was the secret liquid that Brown wiped on the disks, the magical solution that he never wanted to reveal?

Newell shuffled his feet and looked strained, all of his mixed and volatile feelings about the media buried in this one tense expression. Most of the time his shoulders didn't seem quite coordinated with the rest of his body, but when he was asked a direct question or became annoyed, he looked very much intact.

What was it? the reporter asked.

He gave a full smile.

Well?

"All you needed to do David's operation," he said, "was a bottle of Ivory soap."

During the next three days the jury deliberated for a total of seven hours, a remarkably short period of time for such a convoluted case. On Friday afternoon, the fifteenth of June, a chilly unsummerlike day with an edge to the California wind, five years and three months after the murder of Linda Brown, the bailiff of the court, an amiable man named Mitch Miller, put out the word that a verdict had been reached and would be read within an hour. From every floor of the Orange County Court House and from many of the surrounding law-enforcement buildings in Santa Ana, people moved directly toward the chambers of Judge McCartin. When the proceedings began, no members of the Brown family were present, and no Baileys—Riverside was more than an hour away, even if one drove well over the speed limit. By three o'clock the room was full and the TV cameras were in place. A feeling of lightness and celebration was in the air, a lot of smiling and laughter and relief, as if something cathartic had already happened. Heads were turning and tongues were buzzing. A few moments before the final act of the trial someone whispered from the gallery, "It's showtime."

The judge entered adjusting his robe. Brown, wearing a pale shirt and slacks, walked in through a side door with short, childlike strides, his first gesture after sitting down to take another sip of water. The jury, made up mostly of middle-aged women and younger men, filed in and took their seats, all of them poker-faced. The place was utterly silent until the jurors were asked if they'd reached a verdict; the foreman answered yes and their decision, written on an off-white sheet of paper, was handed to McCartin. He read it in silence, showing no reaction at all. While Brown remained seated, the judge told Gail Carpenter, the court clerk, to announce the findings to the defendant.

"Guilty of murder in the first degree on count one," she said in a wavering voice.

Brown made no response.

"Guilty of conspiracy on count two."

He did nothing.

"Guilty of murder with special circumstances."

Still nothing.

The courtroom exploded in noise and movement, jurors turning to one another to embrace. Robinson smiled at Newell and the attorney's shoulders relaxed. Pohlson looked at Schwartzberg and then at the floor. The defendant, barely lowering his head, was quickly and silently taken away, disappearing through the side door from which he'd come in. There was a lot of gasping, sighing and milling; there was interviewing of the jurors, whose silence was broken after five weeks; there was note-taking and filming, there was handshaking and backslapping; but gradually people began to leave the room, and the celebration was nearing an end. The lawyers, their relatives, courthouse employees and an assortment of those who worked for the media drifted out into the eighth-floor hall and assembled in front of the elevators. They too began to disperse, the noise and movement fading away. The whole thing was oddly anticlimactic. Something was missing.

Only Robinson and a few jurors were left. When their deliberations began, the jury members said while standing in the hall, not all of them were ready to convict Brown. The group asked the court if they could see the September 22 videotaped interview that Brown had done with Newell and McLean right after he was arrested, an interview the jurors had already watched during the trial. Their request was granted. As Robinson had foreshadowed in his final argument, it was the few remarks that Brown made on the tape about giving Cinnamon something to drink that convinced all twelve of them that he was guilty.

The elevator door opened and Mary Bailey ran out into the hall, waving her arms and shouting. All at once she was happy and she was sad, jumping up and down, crying and laughing and filling the eighth-floor lobby with an overwhelming release of emotion, reminding onlookers that somebody in her family had been murdered and that David Brown, at long last, was finally getting his due. It was time to let out the grief and the joy for both the living and the dead. Mary whooped and screamed and wept. Veteran newspaper reporters looked at her and stopped writing. The remaining TV crews lowered their cameras and stared. For a moment everything ceased and everyone focused on this raw outburst of feeling, the one thing that had been missing from the trial and its endless legal analysis. Mary transcended all that. The woman had soul.

The elevator opened again. Rick Bailey, his brother

Alan and Alan's girlfriend emerged, and all of them grabbed Mary and formed a huddle, whirling around the floor, twirling and spinning and filling the hall with another round of cries and laughter. Rick's cheeks were wet and so were his brother's.

"I drove eighty miles an hour to get here!" Mary said to a group of observers who had backed away so the family had room in which to dance.

Alan Bailey, Linda's twin, fell to the floor and pounded the tile with clenched fists. He jumped up and spoke into a TV camera. "He's evil to the core!" he said, his face a brilliant red. "He ruined so many lives. He betrayed. He manipulated. He thought he was smart but he got away with nothing. Justice prevailed!" His arm shot up and punched the air. "Oh, that's so nice!"

All of the Baileys rolled on the floor, kissing, hugging and rolling some more in heartfelt jubilation. After a while, they stood and moved toward Robinson, Mary leading the way. When the lawyer saw her coming, he looked apprehensive. When she opened her arms and smothered him, he returned the embrace, giving the woman his happiest and most handsome smile. He looked deeply relieved.

Later that day, on another floor of the courthouse where things were much quieter and other cops and attorneys were going about their daily business, Jay Newell was walking toward his office when he was asked how he felt about the verdict. He paused and grinned a friendly grin.

"Now I can get a good night's sleep," he said.

Soon after the verdict, Mary Bailey drove to the cemetery in Newport Beach to place a bouquet of flowers on her sister-in-law's gravesite. A guard told her that nothing could be left behind on Linda's plaque without the permission of the deceased's husband. When Mary told him that the husband had just been convicted of killing his wife, the man relented.

In Victorville, when Ethel Bailey learned of the verdict, she yelled and raised her arms. "All right!" she said. "All right! What goes around comes around!"

Cinnamon and Patti received the news on Friday afternoon at CYA. Cinnamon cried, not so much because her father was going to prison for life—Brown had neglected her for five years and she'd grown used to receiving emotional blows—but because it was still hard for her to accept that her father was the kind of man he was. Patti had come in from swimming when she heard that the jury had reached a decision. She began kicking and screaming, furious that no one had called her. Then she burst into tears, but her response was more complicated than those of her brothers or sisters or mother. Half of her was ecstatic that the man had been found guilty and half felt sad, as if the part of her that Brown had always filled in would now have to be filled in by her. She felt as if half of her had died.

"When the verdict came in," she said later, "Linda was there with me the whole time. I said to her, 'Don't go, don't go away.'"

After leaving the swimming pool and changing her clothes, she phoned her mother's home collect to talk about the verdict. Tim answered and refused to accept the call, but Ethel finally did. The following day when Patti met Cinnamon at CYA, they sat down together and cried. A few days after that, Patti went to the prison librarian and began the long, slow process of researching the information needed to file for a divorce.

A month later Brown pleaded guilty to the murder-for-hire charges and received a six-year sentence to run concurrently with his other time. At his final courtroom appearance, in September of 1990, Brown wore a thick white neck brace, which he attributed to a recent fall inside the jail. Judge McCartin rejected a defense motion to lessen the charges and sentenced him to life without parole, saying he believed that if the prosecution had not bargained away the death penalty, the jury would have sent the defendant to the gas chamber.

"The circumstances in this case are unbelievable," the judge said. "I certainly hold that I gave Mr. Brown the benefit of the doubt. He had a fair trail. I rode Mr. Robinson into the ground as much as I could to make sure both sides got a fair trial. Certainly, he was represented by, in my opinion, one of the best, if not the best defense attorney in the county . . . Mr. Brown, you're a scary person. That's about the best way I can put it. I feel a little uncomfortable here. I never gave any special thought to my own safety, but I'll tell you that you look more normal than I am. Take Charlie Manson—take one look at him and he's crazy. Look at you and you're saner than your defense attorneys. I don't mean that facetiously . . . I've seen it all, but for you to be able to get one of your own children to kill your wife and your sister-in-law to assist in doing away with your own wife—it makes Charlie Manson look like a piker.''

XXI

Gary Pohlson works in an attractive office in Laguna Hills, and on his walls are pictures of John Kennedy, Abraham Lincoln and members of his own family. Visitors sit on chairs with plaid backs and the attorney himself occupies a large, handsome piece of furniture covered with blue leather. A small Jack Daniel's tin is on his desk; golf balls and a putter stand in the corner. On a shelf is a tiny golden basketball goal. Pohlson enjoys roundball and over a noon hour has gone one-on-one with Judge McCartin's son in the basement of the courthouse. For fifteen years he's been a lawyer, starting as a prosecutor with the Orange County District Attorney's office before moving to the other side— he's defended twenty-four people accused of murder. When asked about David Brown, he leans back, his fingers interlocked behind his skull, pauses before speaking and says only, "David thinks a little different from anybody else."

The subject shifts to Jeff Robinson.

"He looks like a male model. You have to admire him for dropping the death penalty in this case, where Brown tried to kill him. This was a big case and I enjoy trying the big ones, but this was not fun. I was uncomfortable a lot, because of the tension between McCartin and Robinson.

And David Brown isn't the easiest person to deal with. He has been more involved in his defense than any client I've ever had. He made a million suggestions. He's not a jailhouse lawyer, he just wants to participate.''

He pauses again. ''I'm not convinced he's guilty or not guilty and I don't get into that. But he said so many stupid things that it's hard to prove this either way. This was just not a guy who was going to be attractive to anyone.''

When it is suggested to Pohlson that he was much kinder to Cinnamon and Patti than some lawyers would have been, he shrugs.

''My compatriots tell me that I'm much too nice, but I'm not comfortable being another way. We had fifteen other witnesses subpoenaed but didn't call them because we wanted to steer the trial away from the facts and didn't feel these people would do us any good. If David had not made any statement at all when he was arrested and just said, 'I want a lawyer,' we could have won. It would have just been the two girls cooking this thing up.''

He arranges some papers on his desk. ''David is absolutely adamant that he didn't know this was going to happen. If he'd told that story right from the beginning, he wouldn't be where he is. But he had trouble being candid and that's what has got him in this position. You always have the picture of this mad scientist over in the corner, and he's a lot like that. You can be a genius in one area but not in all others. He didn't have social skills. Not at all. He surrounded himself with young people and he didn't have to have any social skills with them.''

Pohlson leans forward in the chair. ''I honestly don't know if the truth has all come out. I'm not sure David even knows how it came to happen. Things happen over a period of time. You get involved in talking about things you shouldn't be talking about. I've just tried to understand it as a human being. You talk and joke about things and then it all blows up. I don't think we're ever gonna know exactly what happened. There have already been so many lies told, so how can you ever know?''

* * *

It's a Friday afternoon and Joel Baruch is drinking Jim Beam at a Newport Beach watering hole. He's had a great day at the office—getting two acquittals on clients accused of murder—and after a triumph he likes to loosen up and talk. He's taken off his shoes, a decidedly unfashionable thing to do in a bar this chic.

The bar is full of well-dressed, well-coiffed, well-manicured men who look as if they have been making deals since sunrise. They drink, smoke and stare aggressively. In local parlance, they are known as "suits," because they wear dark suits, dark ties and white shirts and their clothing tells people that they are serious businessmen. Suits don't like to have their time wasted. Suits would rather fish than cut bait. Suits keep their shoes on when they drink in public. Baruch is surrounded by suits but he's playing with his socks, rolling them up and down.

Baruch is rolling, as talkative as Pohlson is circumspect, especially when it comes to David Brown. He takes a sip of Jim Beam and says, "After he did some of the stupid things he did, I got bored with the case. It became unwinnable." He shakes his head, incredulous. "In the first five minutes of meeting with the cops after his arrest, he tells them about making love to his wife that night. It's not like David was a six-foot stud. The next thing he does is tell them that he's always been afraid of Patti and he gives her up right away. That shows what type of person he is.

"He was the worst client I ever had. He was like a baby. He'd call at nine-thirty on a Saturday night and say it was an emergency and he wanted my help, just because a deputy moved something out of his cell. He's very dumb. How could you make so many mistakes? He's an idiot. He had visions of himself and Steinhart riding through Australia on Harleys."

Baruch laughs and takes another drink. "David was no match for the guys in jail. He won't last long in there. He felt that as long as he had the aura of big money in jail, he could use it as leverage to protect himself. He'll die after his money runs out. He'll be eaten alive in Folsom or San Quentin."

The attorney pulls out his wallet and displays a picture of himself in Vietnam in the mid-'60s. In the photo he has very long hair and a mustache, but he still looks like a tough foot soldier.

"Vietnam was easier than David Brown," he says. "I'd rather be shot at than defend him. At least in Vietnam you knew who the enemy was."

He puts his feet on the couch, reaching over to a nearby dish for a handful of mixed nuts. He looks much younger without his shoes.

"It was on my birthday," he says, referring to how he initially became involved in the case. "I was reading the paper and saw that David had talked to reporters in the jail. I turned to my ex-wife and said, 'Wouldn't that be an interesting case to handle?' She didn't like it. She said stay away from it. A half hour later my phone rang and it was David. At the start, I wanted to defend him. I'd been in the Orange County public defender's office for eight years, and only two years on my own. This case was an ego boost. And how many clients on a homicide case can pay you those kinds of fees?"

When asked if the case changed him, Baruch nods and takes another sip of whiskey.

"I will not represent anyone in a case anymore that I don't like. I did not like him right away. He's whining, demanding, manipulative, but there was the fascination of the case and the chance to get publicity, and those things are important in our business. David has no conscience. He doesn't care about anybody. Not his kids, his wives, his parents, not anyone. I met his parents—too many times. When he was a child, David was sexually abused by a male neighbor. I know that. And there is a suggestion that he was abused within his family."

He rearranges his feet on the sofa. "I had a forty-five minute conversation with David before giving him the ten thousand dollars for the murder-for-hire scheme. I talked to him and asked a lot of questions about what kinds of coins they were going to buy with the money. He told me and I believed him. I believed him. He lied to me. He lied to his brother. I have a good career. I'm gonna make a lot of money as a lawyer. I'm not gonna throw it away on David Brown.''

He eats some nuts, becoming more animated and combative. The man naturally spins drama around himself.

''If I had stayed on the case, I would have done a lot of things that Pohlson didn't do. I would have put Alan Bailey on the stand and had him say the things that he told me— that Patti is a whore and a liar. The Baileys and the Browns were two screwed-up families. I'd have brought in forty defense witnesses that said that Cinnamon was a liar and Patti was too. If Cinnamon and Patti told me what time it was, I'd get a second opinion. I'd have put on much more of a defense than Pohlson did.

''I don't think that on the night of the murder he sicced those girls on Linda. A scenario: Linda was getting rid of both Cinnamon and Patti, ready to move them out. David and Patti are having an affair. Patti is now better able to compete with Linda. David's been talking to the girls about the killing. He's flattered that when he suggests the murder to them, they take it seriously. Linda knows what's going on. She knows he's having an affair with Patti. She knows Patti is getting older. She knows that Patti is more of a woman now. Linda wants Patti and Cinnamon out and she's communicated that to both of them. They know they're living on borrowed time. There is a feeling that Linda was going to call her family the next day and ask them to get Patti out of there. The girls got wind of that and got rid of her.

''It wasn't supposed to happen that night. I don't think David is guilty of first-degree murder. I think he's guilty of conspiracy to commit murder. The girls did it for their own reasons. He wanted it done, but not that night. Cinnamon and Patti are both snitches. They're making it easier on themselves now by blaming someone else for what they did. I think David has grounds for an appeal. He wasn't a killer, but he would pay someone to pull the trigger. I respect someone more who pulls the trigger. I don't think David ever fully realized how seriously the girls took him.''

When asked his view of Jeff Robinson, he doesn't pause in his monologue.

"I like to work with him. He's a good prosecutor. He's got a way with the jury. He plays to the jury tremendously. He objects a lot and tries to throw off your rhythm and it works. We used to be friends, but things became personal.

"If David hadn't done the thing with Robinson and Newell, I'd have gotten Jeff off the case and tried it in sixty days and won. Robinson wanted the case badly. He saw it as a vehicle to stardom. There's nothing wrong with that. I'm the same way."

He takes another drink. "Several people told me that I looked ten years younger after I got away from the case. I felt very relieved. It was too much."

Baruch orders another round and rubs his feet, warming to the subject of talking about his work.

"I don't like to kiss ass," he says. "Not other lawyers' asses, not judges' asses, not anyone's. People deserve a good defense and they pay me for it. I'm a buffer between the state and the individual. The system needs good cops, good prosecutors and good defense attorneys. The nice thing about murder cases is that you can feel good defending the accused. You're not trying to get your client off, but to determine the degree of criminal responsibility. You don't want people to be overprosecuted. My job is to protect them from that. I feel very good about myself. I sleep like a baby at night."

XXII

In a conference room at the Orange County District Attorney's office, Jay Newell is awaiting the arrival of Jeff Robinson. Newell wears a gun, a large badge, suspenders and an inscrutable frown. He is quiet and doesn't seem particularly comfortable. One senses that he is more at ease dealing with convicts or those arrested for crimes than he is with others. It is only when he begins talking about the death of Linda Brown that he is once again immersed in his job as a detective and can relax. He says that the murder was suspicious from the beginning—"Just hearing about that fruit pie was suspect"—but he could do nothing with David until Cinnamon became a prosecution witness.

"I went up to CYA about three or four times before I really talked to her," he says. "I knew a lot about David and what he was doing, but I couldn't do anything without Cinnamon. I took pictures of Summitridge and showed them to Cinnamon so I could show her what was going on."

Robinson comes in, a few minutes late because of a battle on the freeway. He is as charming and fluid as Newell is not. The lawyer retains the air of a talented college athlete who enjoys the locker room, and one pictures him sitting around with attorneys and police, telling ribald stories and laughing out loud.

"Everybody thought from the start that David did it," Newell goes on. "One policeman went to his sergeant and said there were all of these inconsistencies, and the man said, 'We've got all this on Cinnamon and that's what we have. So let's go to the D.A. with this.'"

During Cinnamon's trial, Robinson says, her lawyer, Al Forgette, sat down in a local coffee shop with the prosecuting attorney in the trial, Mike Maguire, and told Maguire that he realized that David was involved in the murder. But Forgette was helpless.

"If she wouldn't budge," Robinson says, "there was nothing he could do."

Robinson smiles his tanned smile. "The miracle of all this is that Cinnamon is a normal kid. She's gonna make it. That sarcastic wit has kept her sane. She doesn't let herself get too attached anymore. Her wit lets her cope. She uses it with us a lot."

"Cinnamon went through my wallet once," Newell says, "because she said I knew everything about her and she knew nothing about me."

Robinson looks at his partner. "I don't know how Jay can always be so calm during these things. During cross-exam I was writing, 'Oh, shit,' on my pad when Patti was up there. Jurors always watch for your reactions. I was going through so much when she was up there, but I tried not to show it."

After several more exchanges, Robinson says, "Patti had more damage done to her than Cinnamon. We all suspect that David molested Cinnamon. Her denial of it is too great."

Richard Steinhart bursts into the room, his long black hair swinging behind him and two people in his entourage, both of them carrying Bibles. His wife, Pat, holds her Good Book from the trial, and the third member of the group, Tony, goes to the far end of the conference table and begins thumbing the Gospels. An ex-con, Tony is short and dark and muscular—while in prison he atoned for his sins by praying and lifting weights. He wears a chain with a six-pointed star. Sitting quietly and reading the Bible, wearing a black leather knuckle glove and moving only his eyes, he looks tougher than Steinhart will ever be.

The biker has begun talking, which is to say he's taken over the room. He's standing and testifying about Jesus and shouting, "Praise the Lord!" Newell and Robinson stare up at him, Robinson smiling at the man's wild energy but Newell maintaining his frown, although there is an occasional twitch around his lips. "If it wasn't for Jesus Christ," Steinhart says, "I wouldn't have gotten out of bed this morning."

His T-shirt reads, "Say No to Drugs, Say Yes to Jesus." A cross is hanging from one ear and a small pin depicting two silver feet dangles from his shirt. He wears a "Jesus" ring. On his wrist is a tattoo that resembles barbed wire. Steinhart claims to be thirty-six but looks fifty. He is telling everyone that before his conversion a year earlier, he had been characterized by a United States Attorney as "unspeakably wicked." This description makes him very happy.

"I accepted the Lord a year ago on June 22, 1989," he says. "I got on my knees and cried and put my head down and started singing a hymn. I asked the guys to say grace the next day and they thought I was crazy. I got rid of my drug connection and my perversions. Jay"—he looks over at Newell—"was real instrumental in helping me find the Lord, and he was a man I was gonna kill. I was gonna blow off the back of his head."

Newell stares at him.

Pat reaches over and rubs her husband's arm, a gentle touch. Tony reads the Bible and doesn't look up.

"I met David on Christmas," Steinhart says. "All I saw at first was a despicable person, but his money became real. I didn't care if he was a jerk. I thought he was pathetic. He would come to me and start to confide in me. He told me what he had—property here and there and money buried. He's trying to impress me. David said he'd supply cocaine to girls in the neighborhood. It wasn't his looks that got him where he was or his singing."

Steinhart whirls in his chair and keeps talking. For the half a million dollars that Brown once promised him, "I'da killed 'em," the biker says, looking directly at Newell and Robinson.

The lawyer grins, looking nervous and delighted, as if he got into this line of work just so he could meet people like Steinhart. Newell's eyes widen before quickly resuming their normal shape.

"Praise the Lord!" the big man says. "I don't drink or do anything evil. Pepsis are a lot less expensive than kilos. I've had an exciting life. I'm a jerk but God's good. I have lots of joy in my heart, although they say I've got AIDS. I feel good."

Unlike most people who have been detoxified, Steinhart claims that he is not a recovering alcoholic or drug addict. "I went cold turkey and prayed and I'm cured," he says.

Pat herself had six years of heroin addiction. "I prayed," she says, "and others prayed with me and I was healed."

"The only cure for drug abuse," Newell says, "is religion."

The men reminisce about their sting operation of the year before, when all of them set Brown up. Steinhart pulls the tassels on his Bible and slips into the past, speaking of the day that he and Newell were in a bar drinking beer and waiting for Brown to make a call from prison. The third member of their group was Tom Borris, a lawyer with the Orange County District Attorney's office, and the trio was posing as regular patrons of the tavern. When one of the customers came over to Borris and tried to sell him drugs, Newell looked the other way and Steinhart tried not to laugh.

"David gave a party in jail with candy after I called and told him that the killings had gone down," Steinhart says. "He was happy."

"If you could have seen the look on Brown's face when he saw us in court presenting him with the second set of charges on the murder-for-hire," Robinson says. "He squirmed like an amoeba."

"Brown changed my life," Steinhart says. "I prayed for him. I got him caught. I pulled his shorts. I knew he was scum, but I was willing to take his money."

"What's David doing now?" Newell says. "That's what I worry about. I don't think David will ever be done with his things. Potentially, Patti and Cinnamon and others are still in jeopardy."

Tony, looking serenely tough, is still reading the Bible, oblivious to the conversation in the room.

"God blessed me with a big mouth," Steinhart is saying, "so I could serve Him better. David knows that what he's done is wrong. But he keeps craving that money, that ego, keeps craving it. Both David and I knew that we were playing a game. The Lord planned all this to get me saved. If I'd gotten his money and gotten him out, I'da buried him in Australia. David is the kind of guy who's going to die proving that he's right."

He takes off on Jesus again, his legs pumping and arms akimbo, fully unwound now, his words coming almost too fast to decipher and his body language measuring 7.8 on the Richter scale. As a born-again Christian, he's frightening. What was he like as an all-out sinner?

"Some cops tried to set me up once on a deal as a burglar," he says. "They insulted me, man. I mean, they insulted me. Praise the Lord. I mean if they wanna set me up like they did with David, okay. All right. But not as a burglar. I'm a hit man. I'm a professional. They hurt my pride. They degraded me. Praise the Lord. I ain't nothin', man. Richard ain't nothin'. Nothin' but the worst things, the most evil. Jesus is all. He came into my cell and grabbed my shoulder and I knelt down and started to shake and cry. He says, 'Richard, now you're workin' for me.' Praise the Lord. Next day at a prayer meeting, they said who wants to volunteer for a prayer and I raised my arm. I didn't raise it. It just went up. I just started to pray. There are no drugs for this old addict. Now I pray when I've got pain. I'm not tough. God's tough. I've got a smile in my heart now."

Robinson and Newell indicate that they are busy men with crowded schedules and need to get back to work.

Steinhart stands and troops out, Pat and Tony right behind him with their Bibles. Newell follows them into the hall, where they chat for a few minutes about some other police business the biker is involved in. As Steinhart turns to go, the detective asks if he would like to attend a California Angels baseball game the next day in Anaheim. Steinhart's eyes dance and he says yes, that would be great. Newell hands him a couple of tickets and a parking sticker for the stadium, thereby ensuring, at least for the time being, that the wheels of justice will continue to churn in Orange County.

Later that afternoon in the lobby of the courthouse, Newell is preparing to leave for the day. He looks busy, determined and tired but has stopped long enough to talk once more about the people he works with as a detective. He is nothing if not patient. A man like Steinhart, he explains, can be helped, but ''a guy like David never can be. He doesn't recognize his part in anything. Richard cares for others. He likes to act tough and mean, but inside he does care. You can work with a guy like that. He can be saved. But not David.''

XXIII

The area around CYA smells of irrigated farmland and faint seaweed from the Pacific. Alongside the road into Ventura, peddlers sell California grapes, cantaloupe, watermelons, summer squash and sweet white corn. Small planes fly over the valley on the edge of town, looking like toys on the horizon. In lemon groves, green windmills are motionless in the summer air. On a perfect Sunday afternoon the sky is hot and the light is brilliant, landing on picnic tables at the compound and shimmering off Cinnamon's hair, turning it golden and honey and strawberry and golden red, with a few strands of purple. The young woman sits beside Brenda Sands, her mother, up from Orange County for another weekend visit, as she has done faithfully for the past five years. Brenda is dark-complected and pretty, with furtive eyes and a serious manner. She is petite, but one senses iron in her bones.

Since the trial ended a few weeks earlier, rumors have flown about the possibility of Cinnamon's being released soon. They are only rumors, but there is hope in her mother's face, an anticipation that wasn't there before. There is also relief. "I am so glad," she said after the verdict, "that he's locked up. So glad. I don't want him running around. I'm afraid he'll come after me.''

Cinnamon eats and talks and laughs in the sunshine, at ease with her mother. Around them on the grounds of CYA, which fans out in a horseshoe from the administration building, young women play softball on a diamond and young men lift weights behind a high-wire fence, their big silver radios giving the air a rhythmic beat. Pregnant inmates stroll by; the babies will be given to their parents or put up for adoption. At times during the day, when Cinnamon is not working at the in-house TWA office for six dollars an hour, she is free to walk the grounds with her new boyfriend. There is a lightness in her step, almost the tread of a happy young girl. At CYA, ''sprung'' means being in love. She's been sprung for a while and appears healthy and peaceful, as if her time inside the walls has been well spent.

Several tables away, Patti is eating pizza, brought in by visitors, and drinking soda. Her eyes jump from the ground to the sky to other inmates and over her shoulder to take in the guards. She cannot gaze directly at a man. With some regularity she glances over at Cinnamon and gives a small nod, but the two of them are not allowed to speak to each other during visiting hours. They send each other musical tapes through the prison mail and have formed a bond of solidarity that can live on very few words.

''My heart doesn't go out for many people,'' Patti says, ''but it does go out to Cinnamon.''

Patti wears the standard blue shirt of an inmate at the Ventura School, as CYA is called, and blue jeans. Her forehead is as prominent as her mother's, but the part of her that most closely resembles Ethel is her hands. They shake wildly, unstoppably. Sometimes, to escape the trembling, she sleeps sixteen hours a day. She still has nightmares in which Brown is beating her and she can't get away, still sweats heavily and refers to herself as ''a constant drip,'' still writes letters to him that she doesn't mail. In February of 1990, she wrote, ''All you care about is your

Perrier. When it comes time for you to die, I'm going to laugh. I hope you burn in hell because someday you're going to feel the pain I feel right now."

Patti takes college courses at the prison and has earned the title of "Honor Girl" for good behavior. Winning this designation knocks a few days off her sentence. Her peers at CYA have elected her the most likely to succeed on the outside, and when she leaves prison she wants to move to another state and become a counselor for children. She works in the CYA administration building for three cents an hour, taking inventory of the handcuffs and hand grenades stockpiled in case of an emergency (unsuccessful escape attempts are common and add a year to one's time). Patti bathes three times a day, scrubbing herself hard with a toothbrush. The previous winter she was sprung for a while but resisted the man's affections.

"I knew it was wrong," she says. "I'm a married woman."

For the first time since Linda died, Patti has begun to grieve the loss of her sister. Brown never let her do that, she says, and tried to talk her out of grieving, telling her that the murder had occurred for a planned and rational purpose, so there was no reason for a show of emotion. She attends group therapy sessions with six other young women who have taken part in murders. In the winter of 1990, Patti was finally able to say "dead" in one of these sessions, but she never wants to hear the word again. More than anyone in the Brown or Bailey family, she exudes pain. It flows out of her when she is sitting or talking. It's behind her language, her face, her movements. On March 19, 1990, the fifth anniversary of Linda's death, she requested some numbing drugs from a prison therapist because she knew the day "was going to be hellish." Despite the pain, she acknowledges that certain courses she's taken at CYA— "Coping With Abuse," "Values and Self-Image," "Coping With Anger" and "Sexual Abuse"—have helped. She believes that she is freer in prison than she ever was on the outside, and stronger.

"I'm putting David behind me," she says. "So what if

I get mad and angry sometimes? I can get over anything. I mean, I feel I am doing this now. No man's gonna run my life no more.''

After Brown's verdict, she finally did mail him a letter in which she asked him to tell her what allergies he might have passed on to Heather. She also asked for a divorce.

He quickly wrote back: ''I just received your letter and was very happy to hear from you. I just wish it wasn't so impersonal, blunt and cold. Your request for personal health info. is strange. Why allergies? What's it for? Did you write because I had my atty. check with you [only] to see if you're willing to write now? I've wanted to write you for a year and a half, but everyone said no. If you'd please answer my question, I'll be happy to answer yours, all of them. I promise I'm not being mean, I just don't know why you wrote right after I requested my atty. to check with you to see if you'd write. I don't know if you'd answer my letter if I just gave you your answers. I hope you're willing to write, God I hope so! I think it's important for us to know what all happened and why. For Krystal and Heather's futures too. I know I need to.

''First, Patti, I never ever wanted you killed. I know how it all looks. If you don't want me to explain, talk to the attys. and/or go over everything with the other people involved. At minimum, Pray to God for the truth to be felt in your heart. But I do swear I was blackmailed and forced to do what I did do, but I wouldn't pay so it might happen. My atty. (old atty.) did. Ask Rubright!

''Did you know my Dad had a stroke the first day of my trial? He's paralyzed now and stuck in a wheelchair. Boy am I depressed. Krystal tries to help take care of him.

''No Patti, I don't expect you to say you're sorry. I never would. The trial is over, you're getting out soon and I'm not mad at you—really, I swear. I was mad, but when Rubright got on the stand and explained how Newell and Robinson used you and made promises and bribed you—I know it wasn't your fault. I know what happened and why. You did what you felt you had to do. No, I'm not mad and I do understand. It wasn't your fault the way things went. As you said, God works in mysterious ways.

"I've talked with April S. and Donnell [two people unknown to Patti]. They made it clear that you have new boyfriends but won't say how serious your affairs are. So, if you've found someone you want and are happy, God bless and Good Luck. I will never interfere, you have my best wishes. You don't have to tell me, just let me know you want a divorce, that's all I need to know. But honestly, I hope not. I really hope not. Why do I hope not? Because you said a lot of things on the stand that I never heard before or knew about. You said you love me, and because you loved me so much, you wanted Linda dead. So, I just want to know the truth. Did Linda die because you wanted me and love me so much? Be honest now, the trial's over and my life is over so I deserve to know the truth. PLEASE. Was this love so great Linda died so we'd be together? For a little while or forever? I really don't know! Is it over now? Is it all gone? Only you know, so please tell me. These are all reasons why I can never be mad at you or hate you. I heard those things from you at the same time everyone else did. As you said, God works in mysterious ways, so did I find out about all this love you had for me after it's gone? That makes sense. I have prayed for a letter from you so much, but I was told how the D.A. had you wrapped around his finger so I knew better and was told not to write until now.

"Well, this is what it all boils down to, are we going to write now that the trial is over or say good-bye? Linda will have died for nothing if we don't take the chance now to communicate and understand everything that happened to this date. I know how I feel and Krystal feels, but not how you feel. Can you or will you tell me? Will we write each other now or say good-bye forever? Your choice! Do we stay married or get a divorce? If you have someone new now just write DIVORCE on a piece of paper and mail it to me. I'll send you my allergy info. and Good-bye. OK? I'll wish you every happiness—sincerely. You know where I'll be. If you'd like to write and understand everything like I want to do so badly, please let's write. I'd like to very, very much. If you don't care and have someone and are planning a new future, OK, I understand. I hope that all that love you mentioned to the whole world was honest and real enough that we can write and maybe understand everything that's happened, and then decide for sure what we all want for our future, and what's best for everyone. I truly hope you and Heather are well. You decide what you want to do, don't let your family decide for you. Please. You decide alone. Pray for Guidance that's real and true to all. Let God guide you, only God. Love & Care, David''

On Patti's wrist is a deep red scar from her latest and most serious suicide attempt in prison. She frequently touches it or rubs her bare arms, as if trying to remove something from her skin. When one of her visitors suggests that she was a victim of David Brown, she recoils.

"I'm no victim," she says. "Linda was the victim. I'm as guilty as anyone. Victims don't help kill other people, especially other victims. C'mon, I was seventeen. Cinnamon was only fourteen. She only knew about it for a month, but I knew about it for three years before it happened. I never felt like a victim, not ever since this happened.''

The young woman reaches for a can of soda and works the metal tabtop back and forth until she has removed it. She turns the thing over in her fingers and scratches it on the surface of the wooden picnic table, all the while talking about Brown. He told Patti that when he was a child members of his family molested him and beat him with a vacuum cleaner pipe.

"And he said a girl molested him," Patti says, digging into the table. "Anything's possible with his mom. Weird is a nice way to put it. If you get too close to her and start to itch, she feels that you're allergic to her. She's very paranoid and hypochondriac. So is Arthur. They both want attention. Arthur's sick. The mom's sick. David is sick. David's mom—the lights are on but no one's home. Whenever David wanted something from his parents, he'd just bribe them, give them money. Or he'd say that he felt sick and had high blood pressure and they'd give in."

Patti looks around at the other inmates and the guards who constantly walk between the tables. She has begun to cry and glances down, embarrassed, trying to stop the tears before they fall.

"I still think about him," she says. "I still wonder if he's eaten today and what he ate and what he's going to do this summer and if he's all right in prison. He hates being alone. The night she died was the first night he ever left by himself. Ever. He never took those drives alone. I should have known something was different that night. Once he left, you knew for sure it was supposed to go down. He always said he wanted it done but he didn't want to see it. He said, 'If you girls love me, you gotta do it.'"

Patti is no longer shaking quite so badly, the tears seeming to bring some inner calm. She scratches the face of the table with the metal tab, using it as if it were a pencil. "If I'da said something, none of this would have happened. I could have told a teacher at school or told Linda even before I moved in that David was doing funny things. The abuse... I can't talk about the abuse with anyone but a woman. I think Cinnamon was also abused."

She carves the wood. "If I talk about Linda in therapy and deal with her death, I'll start to forget about her. I don't want to do that, so I won't. I just don't want to forget her. I took my sister's life. I'm out here on this pretty day and she's not."

Nearby a young female inmate is working on the gray hair of an elderly woman visitor, cornrowing the locks. At another table an inmate combs a young girl's yellow hair, making it glisten in the sunshine. People smoke cigarettes and eat fast food brought in from Ventura. Babies cry and a young woman melts ice on her arm for relief. An American flag flies over the grounds and above the flag a sea gull drifts and floats, black against the sunlight, circling and diving, looking for something to eat. Atop the fences at CYA, coils of barbed wire catch the heat in their metal teeth and reflect it back toward the sun. Patti picks up a paper napkin and twists it until it is a mess of wrinkles, which she jams into the mouth of her soda can. She pulls a sheet of paper from her blue jeans and hands it across the table, explaining that it's a poem she found lying on the floor of the compound. She doesn't know who wrote it but says that it expresses her own feelings well:

> I know my name, I see my face
> Yet my soul seems out of place
> I don't know why I can't be found
> I try to speak, there is no sound
> I was lost and I want to cry
> The tears won't flow, I wonder why . . .

She refolds the paper, puts it back in her jeans and says that after her mother sold her to Brown for $5,000, he made a copy of the receipt he'd given to Ethel for the purchase, framed it and put it on the wall of Patti's bedroom in his home. She pauses, unable to continue with the story. She tries to speak again but chokes off the words. The afternoon is oddly silent.

"David did this to remind me that I was bought and paid for," she says. "He threw this up in my face all the time. I've got a lot of hate, but I don't want people to think that I'm a hateful, spiteful person. I hate him for what he did—not for what he did to me, but what he did to Linda. I wish he'd die. I'd be more peaceful if he did. I shouldn't have said that, but I did. Whenever I talk to someone here, I wonder if they know David or if he's sent that person up here to get me. I don't feel I can trust anyone. I don't want to trust anyone up here. If someone is nice to me, I say, 'Are you paid to care?' "

In the guard tower overlooking the tables, a man with a microphone announces that visiting hours are over this afternoon and it is time for the inmates to be locked up. Friends and relatives start to pack their food and leave. Cinnamon stands, waves to Patti and hugs her mother. Brenda walks toward the prison entrance. Patti lingers at the table, a guard hovering nearby as if to remind her that it is time to go, but she sits and takes another drink of soda and, when the guard has stepped away, digs the tabtop into the wood one more time. The California light is magnificent, and several huge white gulls have landed on the ground and are pecking at the grass. Patti looks down at the table where she has been carving what appears to be a word, picks up a napkin and furiously rubs at the thing, but it won't go away.

"I've destroyed state property," she says, giggling and covering the letters with her hand. "I might be punished."

She quickly stands and says good-bye, walking away from the table and disappearing among the crowd of inmates who are lining up to be strip-searched before being led back to their cells. The carving—"LINDA"—remains etched in the wood.